Apple Logo for Teachers

Apple Logo for Teachers

Earl Babbie

David Grady
Consulting Editor

Wadsworth Publishing Company ☐ Belmont, California ☐ A Division of Wadsworth, Inc.

Printed in the United States of America

2 3 4 5 6 7 8 9 10—88 87 86 85

ISBN 0-534-03392-X

Library of Congress Cataloging in Publication Data

Babbie, Earl
Apple Logo for Teachers.

Bibliography: p.
Includes index.
1. Computer graphics. 2. LOGO (Computer program language) 3. Apple computer—Programming. I. Title.
T385.B25 1984 001.64′24 84-5228
ISBN 0-534-03392-X

Education Editor:
Bob Podstepny

Production Editor:
Deborah M. Oren

Managing Designer:
MaryEllen Podgorski

Designer:
Fuhrman Allgood Design

Copy Editor:
Judith Hibbard

Technical Illustrator:
Lisa L. Sliter

Cover Photo:
Margarete Lyons

Brief Contents

Contents

Chapter 12 Outputs from Procedures 138

Chapter 13 Interactive Procedures 148

About the Author

Earl Babbie's nine textbooks in sociology and social research are respected and used around the world. Students particularly appreciate his ability to explain technical material by making it simple but not superficial. For good reason, *Survey Research Methods* and *The Practice of Social Research* have become preeminent in the field of social research methods.

In *Apple Logo for Teachers,* Babbie brings his explanatory abilities to bear on the topic of computers. Babbie began working with computers in 1959, and his specialization in research methods has taken him from the early computers to large main-frame machines to today's increasingly powerful microcomputers. Appropriately, Babbie used three separate computers in writing this book.

Consulting Editor David Grady has special expertise in education and computers. As editor of *Learning Magazine,* Grady was a leader in making the world of computers available to the classroom. His articles have been published in *Personal Computing* and *Computer Update*. He currently serves on the Advisory Board of the California Association for the Gifted and is the publications manager for Electronic Arts.

Preface

As a social scientist, I've worked with computers for about twenty-five years. I feel especially fortunate to have started so early in the evolution of computers, and they have always been a continuing source of challenge, fascination, and satisfaction for me. Given the exponential evolution of computers during those twenty-five years, moreover, I have found every year offering new and more exciting possibilities.

I have naturally wanted to share my love affair with computers, and this book is evidence. Over the years, however, I have observed a very interesting relationship between people's response to computers and their age.

Here's an illustration. About ten years ago, I began working with the University of Hawaii's time-sharing system. In essence, I sat at a typewriter-like computer terminal, typed instructions that were carried over phone lines to the university's central computer, and received the computer's response almost instantly. It completely transformed my experience of computers.

Almost immediately, I began telling all my colleagues about time-sharing. Dragging them by ones and twos into the computer room and seating them at the terminal, I would attempt to instruct them. Their responses were almost always the same. When I would say, "Now enter a C," my colleague would hesitate and then turn to me and ask, "This one?" "Yes," I'd urge a little impatiently. Cautiously, he or she would reach to the keyboard and press the letter C, sitting there apprehensively.

"You have to hit RETURN to enter it," I'd prompt, impatience increasing. "This key over here?" "Yes!" "Just hit it?" "YES!!" On it would go. I found my colleagues' reluctance to play with my new toy enormously frustrating, and I had made only one or two converts in five years.

Graduate students were a little better. When I invited them to the computer room, they came with little resistance. When I gave them explicit instructions, they generally complied. For the most part, however, I had the feeling they were merely submitting to my senior status. (After all, they might take a course from me or want to have me on their dissertation committee.) Few, if any, developed an independent interest in the computer.

Undergraduates were better than graduate students. When I taught a small seminar on the use of a computer system I had developed for analyzing social issues, about half the students in the class seemed genuinely interested in learning about the computer, although it was pretty rough at the start. Clearly, however, they were a bit less terrified of the computer than my colleagues and graduate students.

The real breakthrough in my sharing of computers with others came unexpectedly. As chairman of the Sociology Department, I received a call one day from a local elementary school to see if I'd be willing to meet with a delegation of fourth graders. The class had been broken up into small groups, and they were interviewing different professionals. I agreed to be their sociologist.

When the four young children arrived in my office at the university, I was all prepared to be a sociologist at the level of fourth graders. I invited them to sit down and began explaining sociology in my best Dick-and-Jane language. "Sociologists are interested in why people do the things they do. We mostly study the way people behave in groups."

Within a matter of minutes, I had crashed and burned. All four kids were fidgetting in their chairs, trying unsuccessfully to be polite. My attention was drawn especially to one little boy absentmindedly picking his nose and staring at the wall, obviously finding it more interesting than me. In desperation, I stopped midsentence to ask, "Hey, how would you like to see my computer?" They leaped from their chairs and ran to the door.

I led my now-very-much-alive little tribe across the hall and into the computer room. Before I could begin my lecture on how the terminal was connected by coaxial cables to the university computer, I found the kids shoving and pushing each other to gain control of the chair at the terminal. The boy who had minutes earlier been bored to death won the struggle and was soon leaning eagerly over the keyboard, his finger hovering over the keys, his eyes darting quickly from letter to letter.

As I began to instruct him in the complex log-on procedure, he shouted, "I'm going to type my name!"

"Don't do that. The computer won't understand. It'll just say you made a mistake."

My warning only provoked a staccato giggle from my little computer programmer. He proceeded to type his name. As soon as he hit RETURN on the keyboard, the terminal rattled its response: SYNTAX ERROR. Thus vindicated, I again began explaining that the computer was expecting a specific log-on code. Before I could finish, the little boy had entered his name again, producing shrieks of delight from all the other kids when the computer stubbornly insisted SYNTAX ERROR.

Soon he had given up his position at the controls, and each of the other kids took their turns entering their names, roaring ecstatically every time the computer protested. At last I had found a willing audience not the least intimidated by the computer. Whereas the adults would have been totally invalidated as human beings by committing a SYNTAX ERROR, the fourth graders were absolutely clear about who was in charge. They could command the computer to say SYNTAX ERROR any time they wanted.

Computers are here to stay. Computers already inhabit most corners of our lives, and they will continue to spread. While many adults are intimidated by computer technology, children are not. For them, computers are grand toys. With a little support, today's children will take command of the new technology and use it to improve the quality of life for us all.

Years after my encounter with that adventurous fourth-grade class, I found myself struggling to learn a new programming language called Pascal. I had been told it was the language of the future and had invested in five or six manuals, all purporting to teach me Pascal. No matter how much I read and experimented at the keyboard of my new microcomputer, I just couldn't get it. Finally, in desperation, I called my local computer store for advice and guidance. I reached the manager and explained my plight.

"Don't worry, our Pascal consultant is a real pro. I'm sure Eric can help you out."

"Great! can I speak to him?" Informed that Eric was out of the office, I asked when he was expected back.

"He doesn't get out of school until three. Why don't you call back around three-thirty." Two hours later, fifteen-year-old Eric patiently explained what I was doing wrong.

The ultimate purpose of this book is to make the computer experience available to children. More specifically, it is designed to enable teachers, parents, and others to teach the computer language Logo to children.

There are a number of good manuals already available as reference books on Logo, and this book is not intended to replace the existing manuals. In fact, I have not attempted to cover the more esoteric aspects of Logo. My purpose, instead, is to help you *learn* Logo and to prepare you to *teach* it. Rather than replacing the existing manuals, this book should prepare you to take full advantage of them.

My ultimate purpose in this book is to make computers available to children: as something that empowers rather than burdens them. If you are reading this book, then you share that intention. Since Logo supports children in mastering computers more than any other computer language, I am delighted to share Logo with you and to start our partnership on behalf of the children.

There are a number of people who have contributed immeasurably to this book. To begin, I want to acknowledge Jean Piaget, whose lifetime of research laid the philosophical foundation for Logo. Seymour Papert had the vision that computers could become tools of learning for children and made that vision real by creating Logo. While neither Piaget nor Papert had anything to do with the writing of this book, there couldn't have been such a book without their work.

Several people at Wadsworth Publishing Company were intimately involved in the creation of *Apple Logo for Teachers*. Steve Rutter, editor-in-chief, first suggested that I write the book, and Bob Podstepny, education editor, carried the project from start to finish. I'm especially grateful to Bob for his absolute commitment to the book through good times and bad.

Bob's efforts were joined by the dedication and good judgment of Debbie Fox, editorial associate; MaryEllen Podgorski, senior designer; and Debbie Oren, production editor. The most powerful thing I can say about the Wadsworth team is that we took this project from conception to bound books in less than a year.

Dave Grady has been a real partner by serving as consulting editor. He brought together expertise in computers and in education; his contributions have been invaluable.

Many reviewers around the country provided feedback on several drafts of the book, making it better at every turn. I appreciate their commitment to a book that would be of maximum value to both students and teachers. Special thanks to William Brown, Old Dominion University; Ricky Carter, Lesley College; Francis P. Collea, California State University, Fullerton; Suzanne Damarin, Ohio State University; Robert Goodson, Hyde Junior High School, Cupertino, California; Shirley Hill, California State University, Fresno; Leonard Kennedy, California State University, Sacramento; Mary Male, San Jose State University; Leah Rampy, University of Houston; Tim Riordon, Alpine Educational Computing Services, Eugene, Oregon; Ann Rule, St. Louis University; John C. Russell, University of Wyoming; Sally Standiford, University of Illinois; Pat Sturdivant, Houston Independent School District; David B. Thomas, University of Iowa; and Frank J. Watson, University of Vermont.

Finally, I want to thank my family—Sheila, Aaron, and Marion—for their direct contributions to the project and for putting up with my general absence during the past year. Happily, "absence makes the heart grow fonder" prevailed over "out of sight, out of mind."

Apple Logo for Teachers

Introduction

The subject of this book is Logo, a computer language that has attracted a great deal of attention among educators. Best known as a vehicle for young children learning to use the computer, Logo is a powerful tool for people of any age. Logo is known primarily for its computer graphics designs, but it also has a potent text-processing capability. The primary purpose of this book is to make the many powers of Logo available to those adults who wish to teach Logo to children.

The book has been written expressly for teachers-in-training, teachers-in-practice, and parents, although you are welcome here even if you don't fit into any of those categories. For the purpose of structuring the materials to be presented, I have acted as though you were a student in a college of education, learning Logo for the first time with an eye toward teaching Logo in the classroom later on. I've felt this approach would meet the needs of all readers, though there may be some parts of the book that are not directly relevant to your needs or interests.

While Logo is better used than talked about, I want to begin the book with a few comments on its history and its pedagogical roots. As you'll see, Logo is actually more than just another computer language. It was developed on the basis of a specific educational philosophy and makes more sense when you know that.

The Pedagogical Roots of Logo

The story of Logo is primarily the story of two men. The first is Jean Piaget, the Swiss developmental psychologist who dedicated his life to learning how children learn. Piaget is also known for his suggestions on structuring the educational process to support children as the builders of their own knowledge.

The second principal in the story of Logo is Seymour Papert, who worked with Piaget for five years in Geneva. Returning to the Massachusetts Institute of Technology (MIT) in the early sixties, Papert continued in his fascination with Piaget's work. In addition, however, Papert was particularly interested in the impact of computers on how and what children learn. Logo is the computer language Papert and his colleagues developed in accord with Piagetian principles.

In this short introduction, I'll review very briefly some aspects of Jean Piaget's great contribution to education. In doing that, I will also present some of Seymour Papert's commentary on Piaget—from the perspective of a computer culture—and give you some idea how Logo is intended to be a realization of the ideals of Piaget and Papert for education.

Children Are Natural Learners

Piaget and Papert agreed that learning is a natural and enjoyable human activity. Left totally to their own devices, people learn things. Papert called children "innately gifted learners," pointing to the great mass of knowledge children accumulate before they ever see the inside of a classroom. Among other things, they learn their native tongue, some elementary math and geometry, the fundamentals of logic and rhetoric, some artistic expression, and a wide range of social skills. All this knowledge is gained simply in the process of interacting with their environment. In a sense, learning is simply living, and living is learning.

Eventually, children discover that adults have created a separate part of life devoted to the learning process. At school, children discover a class of adults officially responsible for supervising the learning process. Piaget and Papert have suggested that all this separates children from knowledge. Knowledge becomes formalized and idealized, which is quite alien to the experience children have previously had in obtaining and holding it. Learning has become unnatural and difficult. It ceases to be alive. Moreover, education becomes something to do well or poorly in, a fundamental basis for social identity and self-esteem.

Logo addresses this general issue in several ways. First, students who have done poorly in conventional education often do great things with Logo. Logo has been used with exciting results in special education classes, for example. Even developmentally disabled children are often able to grasp the logic and techniques of Logo. Thus, Logo offers an alternative opportunity for success and esteem for children who have otherwise not done well in school.

Moreover, Logo tends to create a partnership between students and teachers in place of the traditional relationship, which places the teacher in a solidly dominant position over the student. In Logo, students are able to create things no one has ever created before, and teachers serve best as coaches—guiding and assisting rather than dictating.

Finally, where school often becomes a painful imposition on students, Logo is simply fun. Logo clearly revives the natural joy of learning that often gets lost in conventional education.

Concrete Learning

A fundamental principle for both Piaget and Papert is that children learn through concrete objects. Indeed, Papert began *Mindstorms,* his 1980 book about Logo, with a foreword entitled The Gears of My Childhood. Before he was two years old, Papert had developed a fascination with the various parts of automobiles, and his chief fascination was directed at the differential gear box. To his unending amazement, turning one gear caused the others to turn.

Though he wasn't to understand why or how the gears interacted until years later, the image of the gears turning each other was indelibly etched in his mind. Here was his most dramatic experience of cause and effect, of determinism. He concluded:

> **I believe that working with differentials did more for my mathematical development than anything I was taught in elementary school. Gears, serving as models, carried many otherwise abstract ideas into my head. I clearly remember two examples from school math. I saw multiplication tables as gears, and my first brush with equations in two variables (e.g., $3x + 4y = 10$) immediately evoked the differential. By the time I had made a mental gear model of the relation between *x* and *y*, figuring how many teeth each gear needed, the equation had become a comfortable friend.***

Papert referred to his gears as "objects to learn with," and suggested that learning depends heavily on such objects. One of the most potent objects for learning is a person's own body. Logo takes advantage of this by linking geometry, for example, to the child's knowledge of how his or her own body moves around.

Papert has taken a special interest in the objects—such as gears, arrows, or measuring spoons—that can be used for learning in different cultures. At the present time, clearly the most potent new object to learn with is the computer, and Papert has devoted much of his career to examining the ways in which computers can be brought into service for learning.

Simple to Complex

In his examination of how children learn, Piaget was particularly interested in how they build complex knowledge out of simple components. This developmental aspect of learning accounts for the term *genetic epistemology,* which is used to describe Piaget's work.

---

*Seymour Papert, *Mindstorms: Children, Computers, and Powerful Ideas,* (New York: Basic Books, 1980), p. vi.

Logo embodies this principle at its core. A few simple computer commands allow children to create simple designs on the video screen. Those deceptively simple commands and designs, modified only slightly, become more complex, however. Those modifications suggest others, and soon young children are creating truly sophisticated graphic designs.

From a somewhat different vantage point, this principle has different and perhaps more profound implications. Through Logo, children learn that complex problems can be broken down into sets of simple ones. Creating a picture of a person, for example, is a matter of creating a head, a body, arms, and so forth, and then putting them together. A house is an assembly of such objects as walls, doors, windows, and roofs. Logo, then, can be a potent force in training students to deal with complexity. In this regard, Papert speaks of breaking complex problems into *mind-size bites*.

The Creation of Logo

Papert's intention, as I have indicated, was to create a computer language that would reflect the insights of Piagetian psychology. It should give children real access to computers as concrete objects to learn with. It should allow them to divide large, complex problems into smaller mind-size problems. Finally, he felt it would need to be interactive—letting children talk to the computer and get immediate action and answers back.

Working with colleagues at MIT's Artificial Intelligence Laboratory and with the private research firm of Bolt, Beranek and Newman, Papert began the design of Logo. The name *Logo* is not an acronym for anything; it was coined from the Greek word for "word" or "thought."

In the attempt to create a concrete object to think with, Papert and colleagues developed a robot turtle who could serve as a partner in learning geometry. The turtle sat on a floor covered with butcher paper, and it had a pen that dragged along the paper.

A control box permitted children to issue orders to the turtle that it would obey. When the command FORWARD 50 was entered, the turtle would move fifty units along the floor, drawing a line on the paper. RIGHT 90 would cause the turtle to turn 90 degrees to the right. BACK 100 and it would back up one hundred units. The challenge was to think of instructions that would cause the turtle to draw geometrical designs, such as squares, triangles, or circles, on the floor. The children loved it, and so did the adults.

The main problem with the turtle, however, was logistical. Not every child could arrange to have a large room dedicated to an expensive robot turtle. As an alternative, Papert and associates designed a simulated turtle, which ultimately showed up as a triangle on a video screen. The fundamental system of giving the turtle directions, such as FORWARD 50 or LEFT 30, stayed the same, producing geometric paths on the video screen. This system was given the name *turtle graphics*.

In the years that have followed, Logo has been widely used in a variety of school settings—public and private, large classes and small ones. It has been used successfully with gifted children and in special education. While there are still no data available to document definitively the educational value of Logo, there is a growing body of anecdotal evidence to that effect.

Powerful Ideas

In *Mindstorms,* Papert speaks of how "one comes to appreciate how certain ideas can be used as tools to think with over a lifetime. One learns to enjoy and respect the power of powerful ideas. One learns that the most powerful idea of all is the idea of powerful ideas" (p. 76).

Logo offers a wealth of powerful ideas for children as well as for their teachers and their parents. Most of this book is organized around some of those powerful ideas. Frankly, I have a pretty romantic image of what your experience of this book might be. I'd like to have you grasp a particular Logo technique and be overwhelmed by its potential for children. Then I will present the next powerful idea, which will expand exponentially the power of what you already learned about Logo. The next powerful idea will take you to still another dimension, and so forth. I would like this book lead you into the most exciting educational experiences you have had in a long time. Writing the book was that exciting for me.

It's time now to stop *talking* about Logo and start *doing* it. So fire up your computer, turn to Chapter 1, and let the learning begin.

Chapter 1

Getting Started

This book will open up the world of Logo to you and support you in making it available to young people. While there are several versions of Logo, the focus of this book is specifically on *Apple Logo,* which is sold by Apple Computer, Inc. and works on the Apple II, Apple II Plus, and Apple IIe. Other versions of Logo have slightly different commands; some of these are discussed in Appendix F. Whichever Logo you are using, the fundamental logic is the same, and this book will train you in that logic.

In this chapter you will begin working with the computer. If possible, you should read this chapter and those that follow while at the computer so you can experiment with the operations being discussed. Although you can learn the fundamentals of Logo from a book, the real learning comes from hands-on experimentation.

Because this may be the first direct contact you've had with a computer, this chapter begins with a discussion of some of the concerns that people often have about working with computers. If you are already an old hand with computers, you can simply skim these first sections.

Computer Anxiety

Let's look at some of the fears you may have about working with computers—and find out what the truth is.

"I May Destroy the Computer"

Since the computer you are working with probably cost around two or three thousand dollars, it is only reasonable to worry about making a mistake that will damage the machine. Here's the bottom line: There is nothing you can type on the computer that will hurt it.

This is not to say that there is no way to hurt your computer. Don't use your computer to pound nails. Don't stand on it to look taller. Don't pour coffee into the computer. Don't take the cover off and start poking around inside with your Swiss Army knife. All these things can damage your computer, but nothing you might type on it can.

"I Might Erase or Damage Logo"

The Logo system is contained on the small floppy disk labeled Logo. You probably received two copies of the Logo disk when buying the program, which means you have a backup in case something awful happens to one of them. Most manufacturers, moreover, will replace a damaged disk for a modest fee.

It's very unlikely that you are going to do anything to hurt the Logo system contained on your disk, but it is possible to erase the program. If you are worried about that possibility, there is a way to protect Logo disks from accidental erasure.

Notice the square notch about an inch from the top edge of the disk on the right side as you look at it, as shown in the accompanying illustration. (The illustration was created in Logo, by the way.) This notch allows you to erase files and store new ones. If the disk didn't have the notch, you wouldn't be able to change any of its contents. The manufacturer of your disks also provided a method for covering the notch so your programs cannot be accidentally erased.

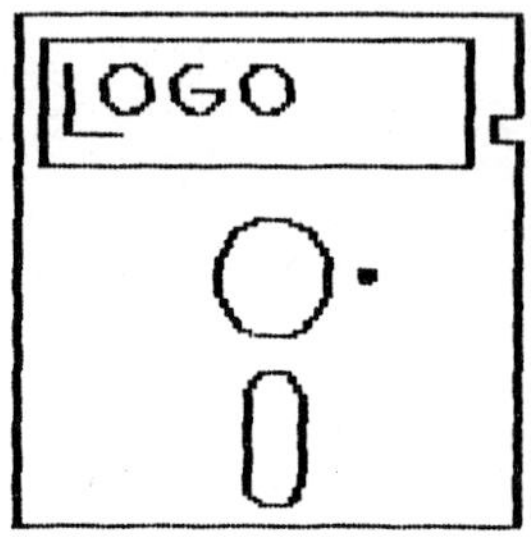

Floppy disk

If you have a box of blank disks, you will discover a sheet of metallic stickers. They vary in size, but a popular style is about three-fourths of an inch square. These stickers are designed to cover the notch. A disk with a covered notch is "write-protected," so its programs cannot be erased.

Place patch on disk

Fold patch over

To be safe, you should take a minute to write-protect your Logo disk. The accompanying sketches show how. If it's not convenient now, keep it in mind for later on.

We'll be dealing with disks throughout this book. Once you begin creating elaborate Logo productions, you'll want to save them for posterity. As discussed in Chapter 6 (and more fully in Appendix B), you can store your creations on floppy disks like the one your Logo system came on. You may be a little uneasy about handling disks at first, but you'll become more comfortable with them in time.

As with the computer itself, you should treat your disks with reasonable care. Don't punch holes in them. Don't grind out cigars on them. Don't put them on the radiator or store them near a powerful magnet. All these things can damage your disks, as can getting dirt into them. Treat the disks with reasonable respect, but you don't have to organize your life around them.

Here's an anecdote to set all this in perspective. One day, in the midst of writing this book, I spilled a glass of unpretentious white wine onto a box of floppy disks, including the ones containing the first draft of this book. For a moment I just sat there in disbelief, recalling my postponed plans to make backup copies as I watched the wine soaking into the disks. Not knowing what else to do, I cut open the cardboard containers, pulled out the magnetic tape disks contained inside, and pressed them between layers of Kleenex. Once dried, all the disks worked perfectly. While I'm not recommending that you bathe your disks in wine, I do want to avoid making you overly nervous about handling them.

Your computer is one of the best friends you have. Let's take a minute to look at some of its more admirable characteristics.

The Computer Is Infinitely Patient

Suppose you have turned the computer on, and it is sitting there waiting for instructions. You can't figure out what to do. You decide you'd better check your manual again, but you can't find it. It's not on the table where you thought you had left it. It's not on the kitchen counter. You can't find it in the car. As you search all over for your manual, the computer sits there waiting for instructions.

The computer really doesn't care. It will never say, "Come on. I don't have all day." Your computer does have all day. It will never make remarks about how you should always know where the manual is. While it has the capacity to remember how long you kept it waiting, it doesn't bother to remember nor will it tell anyone else. You can keep it waiting for instructions all day, and when you are finally ready to proceed it jumps off the mark instantly.

The Computer Is Infinitely Forgiving

Here is the biggest concern most people have the first time they sit down at a computer: "What if I make a mistake? Suppose I type something really dumb. I'll feel stupid." Whether you feel stupid is your own business. Your computer will never think you're stupid. If you make a mistake, your computer will point it out to you and wait for a new instruction. For example, once you start playing with Logo you might have a notion to type your name. Let's say you type ROBIN. If you do that, the computer will respond as follows:

```
I DON'T KNOW HOW TO ROBIN
```

This is one of the **error messages** of the Apple Logo system. If you have a different system, the message may be slightly different.

The message means exactly what it says. The computer doesn't know what it's supposed to do when you type ROBIN, so it says as much. It might be nicer if the computer said something like, "GEE, YOU'RE DOING REAL WELL, BUT THERE'S A SLIGHT PROBLEM WITH THE REQUEST YOU'VE MADE. IT'S PROBABLY MY FAULT FOR NOT KNOWING WHAT TO DO, BUT IF YOU TRY . . ." However, computers are designed to be as efficient as possible, so it will simply tell you it doesn't know any tricks called ROBIN.

But here's the special quality that your computer has that none of your other friends has: It doesn't ever hold your mistakes against you. It doesn't even remember that you made them.

Here's proof. Suppose you type ROBIN again. The computer will respond:

```
I DON'T KNOW HOW TO ROBIN
```

If you were to type ROBIN a thousand times in a row, the computer would respond the same way every time. It will never say, "Come on, what's the matter? Can't you read? Do you need to have a brick wall fall on you?" It just keeps asking for instructions.

To use the computer effectively—especially in the case of Logo—you'll need to alter the way you regard mistakes. We were all taught that making mistakes is bad. I can still remember getting school papers back marked with these two symbols:

Right .... wrong

It took me years to learn that *X*'s are not necessarily evil. Clearly mistakes were bad; students who made too many mistakes were held back a year.

In working with microcomputers, you will find mistakes are expected and valued *feedback mechanisms* that help you accomplish what you've set out to do. For example, it took me nine tries to create those symbols just the way I wanted them. I gave it a shot, looked at the result, modified my method, looked at the result, made another modification, and so on. Each round of mistakes brought me closer to the result I wanted, so I never felt wrong or stupid. This is an effective way to work with microcomputers.

The same is true of the error messages you receive whenever you ask the computer to do something it cannot do. In those cases, the computer will tell you the problem in your request, and that information should point you toward finding a solution. Error messages will be discussed throughout the book because they will be a powerful part of your learning.

Hardware

Enough talk—let's get down to work and have some fun with the computer. If possible, read the rest of this chapter sitting at your computer. After a description of the equipment, commonly known as **hardware,** we'll experiment with the Logo program. (Programs are referred to as **software.**)

Although it refers specifically to the Apple, the description applies generally to other microcomputer systems as well. You should consult the manuals that came with your computer if you need more information than is given here. In this book, we use boldfaced type for key terms or concepts, such as hardware. Here's what you need:

An Apple II, Apple II Plus, or Apple IIe with 64K or more of RAM (Random Access Memory). If you have less than 64K, the system simply will not load.

A disk drive with a controller card. The **disk drive** is a device that reads the information (software) contained on disks and writes information on them. It is connected to the computer by a flat cable and a controller card. The controller card is a plastic card containing a set of chips and other electronic devices that fits inside the Apple; the disk drive is connected to the card by the cable. (Each controller card can control up to two disk drives.) In addition to transmitting information between the disk drive and the computer, the cable also provides the electric current for running the disk drive. Thus, there is no separate power cord to plug in.

A video monitor (color or black and white). The **video monitor** is the visual display of communications between you and the computer. You can use a regular television set as your monitor, in which case you need a game adapter on the set. Or you can use a video monitor, which is like a television without a tuner. A video monitor connects by cable to an outlet at the rear right of the Apple. If you use a television set with a game adapter, you will need to plug it into a special outlet inside the case of the computer. (See your computer manuals if you have to assemble the equipment.) Unlike the disk drive, the monitor needs to be plugged into a separate AC outlet.

Now, let's return to the computer itself and start the system to see how it works.

Booting the System

Whereas you "turn on" a radio or an electric typewriter, turning on a computer is referred to as **booting the system**—from the phrase "pulling yourself up by your own bootstraps." When a computer system is first turned on, it must begin by teaching itself to be a computer. Fortunately, it is not necessary to know anything further about this as a philosophical or technical issue.

Here's how to boot the computer:

1. Turn on the monitor. Nothing will show at this point, but you want it on when the computer has something to say.
2. Slide the Logo disk in the opening at the front of the disk drive, with the disk's label facing up and near you. Slide the disk all the way into the disk drive. Then flip the disk drive gate closed.
3. Turn the Apple on, using the power switch located at the rear left of the machine.

Once you've turned the computer on, the following will appear near the top of the screen:

```
APPLE ][
```

This indicates that the computer is in the process of loading Logo from the disk into the computer's memory. While this is happening, a small red light on the disk drive will come on, indicating that the disk drive is in operation. Also, you will hear various sounds, known technically as *whirrs* and *zicks,* coming from the disk drive. The disk drive talks to itself while it is reading disks.

If these things do not happen when you boot the computer, then something is amiss. There is probably no need to worry. In all likelihood you have failed to connect all the parts of the hardware system; the disk drive may not be plugged into the controller card, for example. Recheck the manuals or ask someone who knows the system better than you do.

If you should accidentally open the gate of the disk drive while the drive is reading a disk, the worst that can happen is that the loading operation will abort (stop), and you can start over. Neither the disk nor the disk drive will be injured by this. In fact, if you close the gate quickly enough, it may simply pick up where it left off.

After the disk drive has whirred and zicked for around a minute, the drive will stop, and you will be presented with the following message on the screen:

```
PRESS THE RETURN KEY TO BEGIN

IF YOU HAVE YOUR OWN FILE DISKETTE,
INSERT IT NOW, THEN PRESS RETURN

(C) LOGO COMPUTER SYSTEMS INC. 1982
```

The computer is now ready to begin work. Before doing so, however, it is giving you a chance to substitute your own disk for the one containing the Logo program. Eventually, you will want to create some file disks for storing programs rather than filling up your system disks. Appendix B explains how to prepare disks for this purpose—called **initializing.** If you happen to have an initialized disk, you should remove the Logo disk at this time and replace it with your file disk. If you don't have a file disk now, just leave the Logo disk in the disk drive, and press RETURN (the key labeled RETURN).

Now you should be looking at the following:

```
WELCOME TO LOGO                                    A1.5
?
```

Congratulations—you now have a powerful computer system at your command. The ? on your screen—called a **prompt**—followed by the blinking **cursor** signals that the computer is waiting for your command. Let it wait. It isn't going anywhere.

Potential Problems

Throughout the remainder of this book, special attention will be paid to the problems or **bugs** that may crop up in your experiments with Logo. Let's look at some of the problems you might have confronted in booting the system. Skim these comments even if everything worked fine so you will have a fuller understanding of how the system works.

The computer's power-on light failed to light. This means the computer isn't getting power. Be sure the power cord is plugged into an electrical outlet and also plugged into the computer. Also, be sure that the on/off switch has been switched properly.

The disk drive doesn't do anything. Be sure the drive is plugged into the controller card and that the card is installed inside the computer. When you turn on the computer, the disk drive should begin whirring and zicking and the red indicator light near the gate of the disk drive should go on. Remember, you do not need to turn the disk drive on.

Nothing shows on the video screen. Make sure the video is plugged into an electrical outlet and turned on. Also, be sure the cable connecting the video and the computer is firmly attached at both ends.

The video display flickers erratically around the screen. Be sure the video cable connecting the computer with the video is firmly attached at both ends. Twisting the cable in the socket will sometimes clear up the problem. Also, you may need to adjust the horizontal and/or vertical hold knobs.

The disk drive keeps running on and on without stopping and without saying Logo is ready. With the drive running, open the gate and pull the disk out slightly, push it back in, and close the gate. If this doesn't work, turn the computer off, take the disk out, put it back in, and try again. Be sure that you are putting the disk into the drive properly: label side up with the label at the end of the drive near the gate.

The disk runs for a while and then stops, giving either no message or an obscure string of numbers on the screen. This could mean that your computer doesn't have the required 64K of memory. Or it could be caused by the presence of a special card (such as a modem card, used for telecommunications) in a slot of the computer. To check out the latter possibility, *turn off the computer* and then remove all the cards except the disk drive controller. Then try to boot Logo again. (Note: If you have never put cards in or taken them out before, you may want to get assistance from someone more experienced.)

If none of these remedies solves your problem, then you should consult your computer dealer.

Teaching Students to Boot the System

Although adults tend to be overly worried about hurting the computer, this is generally not a problem for children. In fact, those who are veterans of arcade video games may need some calming down in relation to the computer. Tell them that the computer is not as durable as arcade games.

You will want to work out procedures for booting the system that are appropriate to the age and experience of your students. With young children and those new to Logo, you may want to handle booting the system yourself. Let the students take over at the point where they can start entering Logo commands.

You will want to teach older and more experienced students to boot the system for themselves. If you do, you'll want to write-protect the disk as described earlier in the chapter so there will be no danger of them erasing the program. You will be surprised how quickly students learn to boot the system for themselves. This will not only make your life easier, but it will also put them more in control of their Logo work.

To review, here are the steps involved in booting the system that you will need to teach your students. You might want to put them on a poster mounted on the wall near the computer.

- ☐ Turn on the monitor.
- ☐ Place the Logo disk in the disk drive.
- ☐ Turn on the computer.
- ☐ When the computer asks for it, remove the Logo disk, replace it with a data disk, and press RETURN.

Now that you know how to get Logo loaded into the computer, the fun can begin. By the end of Chapter 2 you are going to be drawing graphic designs all over the screen.

Chapter 2

Elementary Turtle Graphics

At last we are ready to begin playing with Logo's graphics capability. To begin drawing designs, we'll need to find the Logo **turtle.** This is accomplished by entering SHOWTURTLE. Simply type it as one word and press the key labeled RETURN.

Turtle

Now the screen will show three things. First, a small triangle (the "turtle") is located near the center of the screen. You have finally met the turtle. In addition, you will see a question mark prompt and the cursor near the bottom left of the screen. The bottom four lines of the screen are reserved for your instructions to the computer. (We'll see how to get rid of them later.)

If you make a typing mistake, use the left-pointing arrow to erase typing mistakes. Then merely retype the material over the space erased by the left arrow.

A Powerful Idea

To create graphic designs on the screen, simply order the little turtle around and it will draw the designs. In the remainder of this chapter, you will learn and play with a few simple commands that make this possible.

Notice that the turtle has two important qualities: *location* and *direction*. At first, the turtle's direction is pointing straight up and its location is near the center of the screen. All the commands given to the turtle will change its direction and location. Let's begin.

How to Do It

FORWARD and RIGHT

To get started, let's have the turtle draw a line straight up from where it is now. Do this by typing:

```
FORWARD 50
```

and then press RETURN.

After you've typed and entered that instruction, you will notice that the turtle has moved ahead about an inch. (The turtle moves in units that are about 50 to the inch, although this varies somewhat among video monitors.)

Now let's see how to change the turtle's direction. Enter this command:

```
RIGHT 90
```

and press RETURN. (I'll stop reminding you to press RETURN each time. Use the RETURN key whenever you want the computer to act on what you've typed.)

Notice that the turtle has, logically, turned 90 degrees to the right. Now send it forward another 50 units. (Hint: FORWARD 50.)

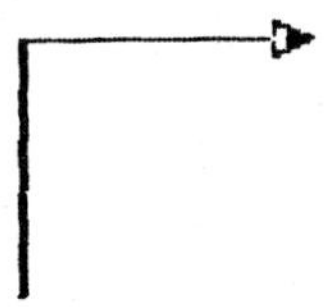

It has become traditional for books on Logo to begin with the creation of a square, so let's pay our dues and get on to other things. Enter the following and your initiation will be complete:

```
RIGHT 90
FORWARD 50
RIGHT 90
FORWARD 50
```

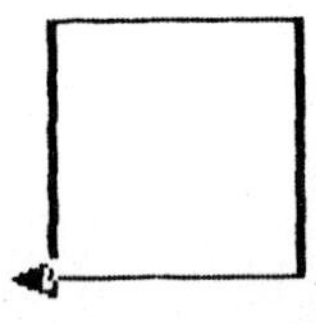

Congratulations—you have now created your first Logo design and you only needed to learn two commands. As you will discover, there are not all that many more to learn, but the possibilities for creation will begin growing exponentially. Now's a good time to note that as a general rule within this book, whenever a set of Logo commands is presented, the graphic results of those commands will appear in the margin directly across from the text, as in the previous example.

CLEARSCREEN

Now let's clear the screen. This is accomplished by simply entering CLEARSCREEN. Notice that when you clear the screen, the turtle bounces back to its original position in the center of the screen, pointing straight up. This turtle position is called HOME in Logo.

Cutting Corners

Now we're going to make Logo a lot easier. Just type the following commands, separated by spaces, and don't press RETURN until you've typed the whole set of commands.

```
CS FD 50 RT 90 FD 50 RT 90 FD 50 RT 90 FD 50
```

This latest instruction illustrates three more characteristics of Logo:

1. There are abbreviations for the turtle commands:

   FD = FORWARD
   RT = RIGHT
   CS = CLEARSCREEN

   (Why not try CS just to make sure it works the way it's supposed to?)
2. You can enter more than one instruction on a line. Just separate them with spaces.
3. You can enter commands that are longer than one line of the computer screen. The computer automatically carries your instruction onto the next line, inserting ! to draw your attention to what it did.

BACK (BK) and LEFT (LT)

Now let's try a couple of new commands: BACK (BK) and LEFT (LT). Try them out with the following:

```
BK 80 LT 60 FD 50 LT 60 BK 50
```

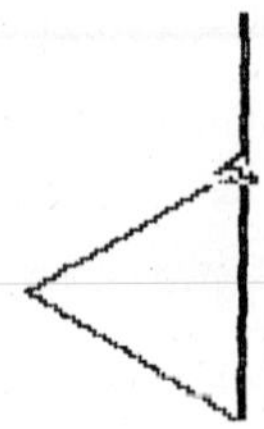

Notice that you have now drawn an upside-down pennant. Take a minute to trace the turtle's path through the instructions in your mind. If you have any trouble seeing how it drew the pennant, clear the screen and then reenter the instructions one at a time.

HIDETURTLE (HT) and SHOWTURTLE (ST)

By now, you may have felt that the turtle detracts somewhat from your designs. That's no problem for Logo, however. HIDETURTLE (HT) causes the turtle to vanish, whereas SHOWTURTLE (ST) brings it back again. The invisible turtle can still draw designs. Take a minute to experiment with these two commands. You can enter one after the other, making the turtle vanish and reappear again and again. Then demonstrate for yourself that you can draw designs with the turtle showing or hidden.

Illustrations

This section will present some illustrations of designs you can create, using the few Logo commands you have learned so far. There are two ways you can profit from the illustrations. First, read through the instructions step by step, tracing along the design as you do so. Second, enter the instruction into your own computer and see it work.

Triangles

Here are two triangles to accompany the square you already created:

```
CS RT 30 FD 50 RT 120 FD 50 RT 120 FD 50
```

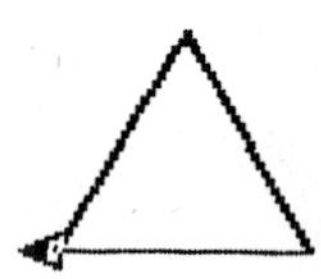

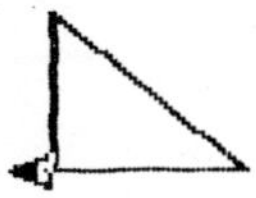

```
CS FD 30 RT 128 FD 50 RT 142 FD 40
```

You may remember from plane geometry that if you square the two short sides of a right-angle triangle and add the two squares, their sum will equal the square of the longest side. You can check this in the example above with sides of 30, 40, and 50. Notice also that the two angles—128 and 142—total 270 degrees. If you were to add RT 90 to the set of instructions, the turtle would be facing in its original direction: straight up. It would have turned a total of 360 degrees, having gone in a complete circle. This phenomenon is sometimes referred to as the *total turtle trip theorem*. Whenever the turtle turns a total of 360 degrees (or multiples of 360), it will be facing in the same direction as it began.

Stairs

Here's a way to get a set of stairs:

```
CS FD 10 RT 90 FD 10 LT 90 FD 10 RT 90 FD 10 LT 90 FD 10
```

Once you've tried this set of stairs, take a minute to experiment with it. What would happen if you changed the size of the steps (from 10)? Or, what if you changed the FDs to BKs?

Big T

As you'll see, we can use Logo to draw the letters of the alphabet. Here's an outlined T:

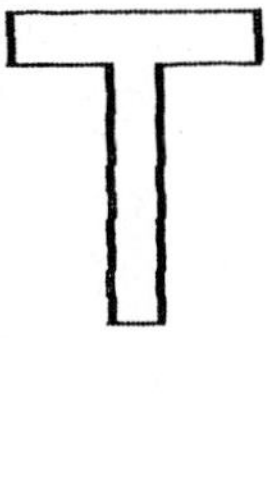

```
CS FD 50 RT 90 FD 20 LT 90 FD 10 LT 90 FD 50 LT 90 FD 10 LT 90 FD 20
      RT 90 FD 50 LT 90 FD 10 HT
```

(To make this book easier to read, the "overflow" of long lines is indented. You should type the whole thing as one continuous set of instructions, however, and let the computer break up the lines, as appropriate, on your screen.)

This should give you a basic understanding of how the elementary turtle commands operate. Now let's take a minute to look at some of the common problems people sometimes have. You may have already discovered one or more of these bugs.

Some Common Bugs

Misspelling commands. As a special, unheralded service, Logo will check your spelling for you. If you type FORWERD 100, Logo will respond:

```
I DON'T KNOW HOW TO FORWERD
```

This tells you that you are asking Logo to perform a trick it hasn't yet learned, in this case, a misspelling of FORWARD.

Omitting spaces. Logo requires that you separate commands such as FORWARD and RIGHT from their numerical specifications with a space. Thus, if you enter the command, FORWARD100, Logo will respond:

```
I DON'T KNOW HOW TO FORWARD100
```

As you can see, in this case, Logo has tried to do something called FORWARD100 and finds it doesn't know what that means. Later in the book you will learn how to teach Logo to act on the command FORWARD100 if you like—giving that command whatever meaning you want.

Here is a question for you: Do you suppose it causes a problem if you insert more than one space between the command and the numerical specification? Try it out for yourself and find out. That's the best way to learn Logo.

Omitting the numerical specification. As we've seen, some Logo commands (e.g., RIGHT, FORWARD) require numerical specifications, while others (e.g., CLEARSCREEN) don't. Suppose you simply entered the command LEFT. Here's what Logo will do with that:

```
NOT ENOUGH INPUTS TO LEFT
```

In this error message, Logo is reminding you that it cannot LEFT unless you specify how many degrees it should turn. Logo uses the term INPUT in reference to the information that must be supplied with some commands. While it is useful to remember which commands require inputs, Logo will remind you if you forget.

Exploring Further

The best way to learn Logo, as suggested earlier, is to play around with it. Try things. Ask yourself what would happen if you had issued a slightly different command. Then try it out. If it's convenient for you right now, why not take a break from your reading and simply mess around a bit? Here are some suggestions for directions you might want to pursue, but feel free to think up your own directions to pursue. (If you have trouble with any of the designs presented below, you can find the solutions at the end of the book.)

1. Experiment with common geometric shapes.

a

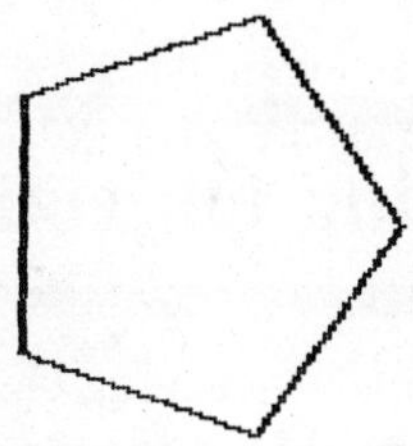

b

2. Try a boxy spiral.

3. Find the sets of commands needed to create letters and numbers in different type styles.

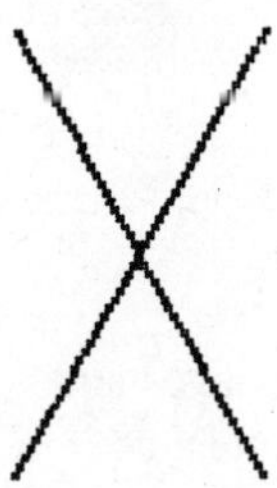

a

b

c

4. Or just mess around.

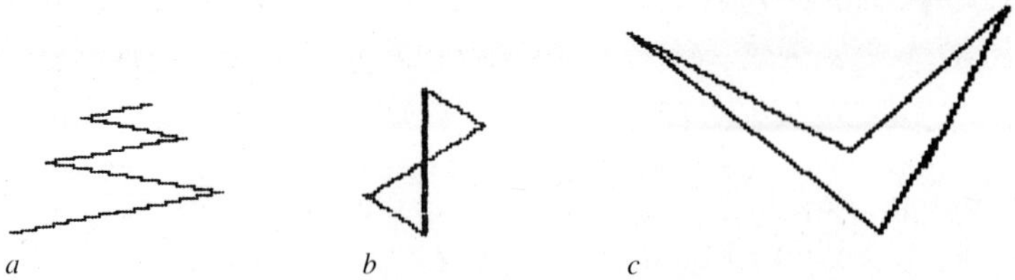

The point is not so much for you to recreate the designs presented above as it is for you to strike out on your own. You may want to begin with these designs, but you should then experiment with variations on them. See how far away from the illustrations you can get.

Teaching Objectives

When you start teaching children the materials contained in this chapter, you should focus your attention on the following objectives:

- ☐ Students will become familiar with the computer keyboard.
- ☐ Students will grasp the basic notion of drawing designs by moving the turtle around the screen.
- ☐ Students will think in terms of *direction* and *distance*.
- ☐ Students will learn and be able to use the fundamental Logo commands and abbreviations:

FD	FORWARD
BK	BACK
RT	RIGHT
LT	LEFT
CS	CLEARSCREEN
ST	SHOWTURTLE
HT	HIDETURTLE

- ☐ Students will become familiar with Logo's error messages and learn to regard errors as steps toward success rather than as failures.
- ☐ Students will go beyond the examples you present and experiment with designs of their own.

Teaching Techniques and Materials

This section contains suggestions for teaching the materials covered in this chapter. Clearly, you will need to decide what is appropriate in your particular teaching situation, but you should find more than enough ideas here to get organized.

Concrete Learning

As discussed in the Introduction, Piaget stressed the importance of learning through concrete objects and actions. You can take advantage of this in teaching the fundamentals of Logo. Here are some ideas created by other teachers of Logo.

- ☐ Young children may profit from creating little facsimile turtles out of walnuts, blocks of wood, lumps of clay, and so on. They will then be able to rehearse sets of Logo commands before submitting them to the computer.
- ☐ "Walking through" Logo commands is often a useful technique. Have one student give Logo commands and another follow them—pacing them out in the room. This capitalizes on the observation that students generally enjoy working together on Logo.
- ☐ It is always possible to draw Logo patterns on paper. Have students write out a command, draw the resulting turtle movement on paper, write another command, and so on. They can thus work out the blueprint of a design before they actually submit it to the computer.
- ☐ With older students who are able to use a ruler and protractor, you might set up a game in which one person announces a series of Logo commands and the rest of the students draw the designs on paper, seeing who comes closest to the desired design.

Anything you can devise to make Logo more concrete will be of assistance to your students. A good way to do this is to notice what concrete images come up for you when you play around with Logo. Maybe those images can be converted to solid objects, posters, drawings, or something like that. Anything that will make Logo more real will support your students.

Mind-size Bites

I have found that the more I learn about Logo and the more experienced I become, my biggest teaching problem is sometimes giving students too much at once. Following the guidance of Piaget and Papert, it is important that you present Logo in "mind-size bites"—treading the fine line between boring students by giving them too little and overwhelming them with too much at once.

There is, of course, no hard-and-fast rule for carving out mind-size bites. The proper portion will vary by age, by past computer experience, and from individual to individual within those categories. In fact, a given student will move quickly through some materials and slow down to a more deliberate pace elsewhere. The best advice is to watch and listen constantly for feedback from students. Learn to recognize the signs of confusion and of being overwhelmed on the one hand and boredom on the other. At the same time, watch for positive feedback, indications that you are right on the mark. Be especially attentive to questions such as "Is there any way to make it . . . ?" and comments such as "Hey, I'll bet you can make the turtle . . ."

Finally, treat your teaching "failures" the way you've been urged to regard errors in Logo: as tools to learn with. You probably will bore some students from time to time and overwhelm others. As long as you are conscious of these two outcomes, you will be able to keep improving your teaching ability.

Simple to Complex

It is important to let students begin at as simple a level as they want and move on to more complex materials at their own pace. Some students, for example, will have had little or no experience with typewriter keyboards or video games. They may need a little time to get grounded in basic skills that are second nature for other students.

When they begin giving Logo commands to the turtle, some students will want to take a lot of time with FORWARD. You may have noticed by now, for example, that if you send the turtle beyond the margins of the screen, it "wraps around" and reappears on the opposite side of the screen. Young children sometimes sit for what seems like a long time just moving the turtle in a given direction, watching it disappear on one side of the screen and reappear on the opposite side over and over. By the time they are done, however, they fully grasp the wraparound aspect of Logo.

Student Exercises

This section presents some exercises to use with students. Since the exercises represent a wide range of difficulty, select what is appropriate for particular students. Also, you should add to the examples given. And as your students get more familiar with Logo, they should be pressed into service writing exercises for each other.

Pencil and Paper Exercises

1. Draw the Logo designs that would be produced by these sets of commands.
   a. FD 50 LT 90 BK 25
   b. RT 45 FD 50 LT 45 BK 50
   c. LT 90 BK 50 FD 100
2. Which letters of the alphabet would be produced by these Logo commands?
   a. FD 50
   b. FD 50 LT 30 BK 60 RT 30 FD 50
   c. FD 50 RT 90 FD 20 BK 40
   d. FD 50 RT 90 FD 20 BK 20 LT 90 BK 20 RT 90 FD 10
   e. RT 45 FD 30 BK 60 FD 30 RT 90 FD 30 BK 60
3. What number can be drawn with a single Logo command?
4. For each pair of commands below, indicate whether they produce the same result.
   a. FD 50 LT 90
      LT 90 FD 50
   b. FD 100
      FD 25 FD 25 FD 25 FD 25
   c. RT 90 FD 50
      RT 45 RT 45 FD 25 FD 25
   d. FD 100
      FD 50 BK 25 FD 75

At the Computer

1. Answer the pencil and paper problems using the computer.
2. Recreate these designs on the computer, using Logo.

a

b

c

d

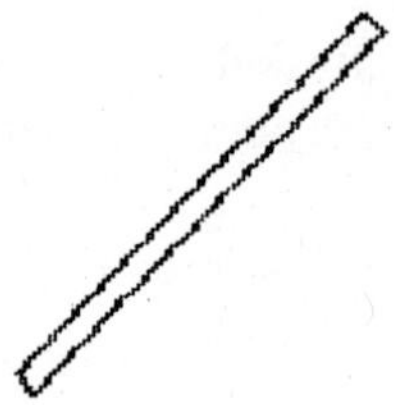

e

Lesson Plan Elements

The best way of consolidating your own understanding of Logo is to prepare a lesson plan for teaching it to children. This is a good idea even if you are a parent teaching only one child. Here are the elements you'll want to include in the lesson plan for this portion of Logo instruction.

- ☐ The use of the computer keyboard.
- ☐ The logic of turtle commands: drawing designs by specifying directions and distances for the turtle.
- ☐ The fundamental Logo commands:

CS	CLEARSCREEN
FD	FORWARD
BK	BACK
RT	RIGHT
LT	LEFT
ST	SHOWTURTLE
HT	HIDETURTLE

- ☐ Logo's error messages and how to use them.

Review of Logo Commands

ABBREVIATION	NAME	EXAMPLE	FUNCTION
FD	FORWARD	FD 50	Moves turtle foward.
BK	BACK	BK 90	Moves turtle backward.
RT	RIGHT	RT 45	Turns turtle to right.
LT	LEFT	LT 60	Turns turtle to left.
CS	CLEARSCREEN	CS	Erases the screen and sends the turtle HOME.
ST	SHOWTURTLE	ST	Displays the turtle.
HT	HIDETURTLE	HT	Causes turtle to disappear.

A Logo Challenge

Each chapter of this book ends with a problem that is more difficult than the rest of the chapter. The purpose of each activity is to give you an opportunity to stretch out a little. Don't worry if you can't solve a particular problem. You might come back to it later, after you've had more experience with Logo.

Here's your first challenge, if you choose to accept it.

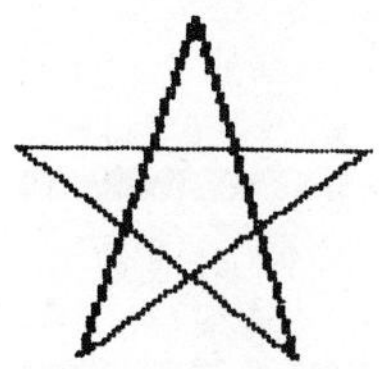

Chapter 3

Pen and Color Commands

By now, you should be comfortable with the basic Logo commands introduced so far: RIGHT, LEFT, FORWARD, BACK, and so on. Now a pattern will be established that will persist throughout the remainder of the book: the introduction of "powerful ideas."

In this chapter, you'll learn some new Logo commands that will let you do new things with the computer. As you master the new commands your overall ability to create computer designs will expand geometrically rather than arithmetically, because the new commands you learn will *combine* with the old ones rather than simply being added to them. This makes the new commands truly powerful ideas.

A Powerful Idea

If you have experimented a lot with the commands presented in Chapter 2, you will have discovered that you can do a lot with them. It's also possible that you have been frustrated at not being able to move around the screen *without* leaving a trail. Now your troubles are over. In this chapter you will learn how to lift the pen and put it down again. In fact, you will learn how to erase lines you don't like.

Here's something you probably did not think about at all. The designs you've been creating are probably a matter of white lines against a black background or some approximation of that.

As described in this chapter, it doesn't have to be that way. If you have a black-and-white monitor, you can switch to black-on-white and some interesting variations in between. If you have a color monitor, the sky's the limit.

How to Do It

PENUP (PU) and PENDOWN (PD)

Sometimes you may want to move the turtle around the screen without leaving a trail behind it. This is easily done. PENUP (PU) instructs the turtle to stop leaving a trail. To get back to drawing, simply enter PENDOWN (PD). Here's an example of how you might use this capability:

```
FD 10 PU FD 10 PD FD 10 PU FD 10 PD FD 10
```

Or consider this:

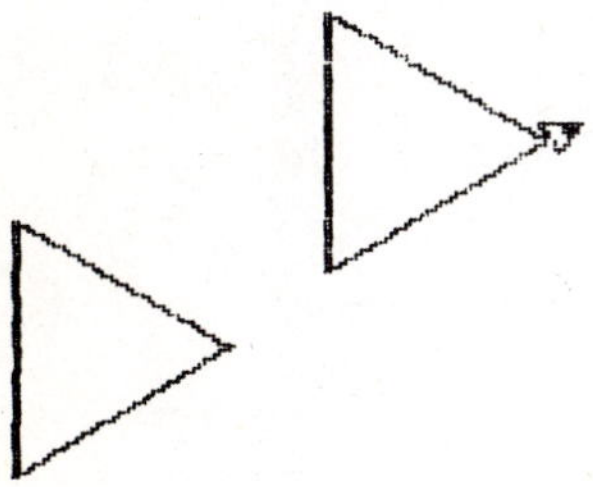

```
FD 50 RT 120 FD 50 RT 120 FD 50 RT 180 PU FD 80
PD FD 50 LT 120 FD 50 LT 120 FD 50 LT 120 FD 50
```

PENERASE (PE) and PENREVERSE

Sometimes you may want to erase something you have drawn on the screen. Suppose you went FORWARD 100 when you meant to go FORWARD 50. No problem. PENERASE (PE) does the job, as illustrated below:

```
FD 100
PE
BK 50
```

These are shown as separate instructions so that you can see what happens when you erase. You can enter them as a single line, but you'll have to keep your eyes open to see what happens.

Either PENUP or PENDOWN will cancel PENERASE. After either of these commands, turtle moves will leave a trail.

PENREVERSE produces some curious effects. Whenever the turtle moves across blank screen, it will leave a line. Whenever it comes upon previously drawn lines, however, it erases them. In other words, the turtle reverses whatever it crosses. Here's an illustration in two steps. The first step is:

```
RT 90 FD 30 PU FD 20 RT 180
```

Then, add this:

```
PENREVERSE FD 100
```

Notice what happens to the turtle's path in the second command. Moving from the turtle's position to the old line leaves a new trail. Once the turtle gets to the old line, it begins erasing. Finally, once it gets past the old line, it starts leaving a trail again. Simply put, under PENREVERSE the turtle reverses whatever it finds.

Colors

Logo has a capability of using different colors, both for the background of the screen and for the pen. If you are using a color monitor, this will add a whole new dimension to your graphics. The commands SETPC and SETBG set the colors for the pen and the background, respectively. The various colors are specified by the following numerical codes:

0 = Black
1 = White
2 = Green
3 = Violet
4 = Orange
5 = Blue

If you are using a black-and-white monitor, the color options are not completely irrelevant to you. For example, you can change the background to white and the pen to black. Try this, for example:

```
SETBG 1 SETPC 0
FD 50 RT 160 FD 50 RT 160 FD 50
```

If you have done this on your computer, you will see that the screen background has now shifted from black to white and the lines are being drawn in black. Actually, the computer screen now looks more like the diagrams presented in this book: black on white.

Now here's something to experiment with. First, enter SETBG 0 and draw a design on the screen. Then—without clearing the screen—change the background color to white with SETBG 1. Notice how both the background and the design change.

For even more fun, try this. Draw a design on the screen and then enter:

```
SETBG 1 SETBG 0 SETBG 1 SETBG 0 SETBG 1
```

As you can see, this produces a flashing appearance as the background and pen colors switch back and forth between black and white. (We'll have some fun with this effect later on.)

You may want to experiment with the other colors. You will definitely want to spend some time with colors if you have a color monitor. You should also experiment with them in black and white. On a black-and-white monitor, the various colors show up as different striped and checkered patterns. To get back to the standard format of white-on-black, enter:

```
SETBG 0 SETPC 1
```

You can also find out the current color assigned to the background and to the pen as follows:

PR BG
0
PR PC
1

The computer responds with the numeric codes of the colors currently assigned to the background and/or pen: 0 means the background is black and 1 means the pen color is white. As another general rule for this book, in interactive illustrations, such as this, the commands you would type appear in boldface, and the computer response is in regular type.

Illustrations

Here are a few examples of what you can do with your new knowledge of Logo.

Parallel Lines

Parallel lines, you'll recall from plane geometry, never meet this side of infinity, which is somewhere well beyond the bounds of your video screen. With these new commands, however, parallel lines fall well within your grasp. For example, enter:

```
LT 90 FD 50 PU RT 90 FD 10
RT 90 PD FD 50 LT 90 PU
FD 10 LT 90 PD FD 50
```

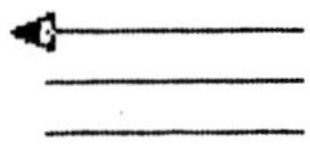

Boxes within Boxes

Because you are now able to lift the pen, you can create separate designs, even putting one inside another like this:

```
FD 10 RT 90 FD 10 RT 90 FD 10 RT 90 FD 10
PU LT 45 FD 15 RT 135 PD
FD 30 RT 90 FD 30 RT 90 FD 30 RT 90 FD 30
```

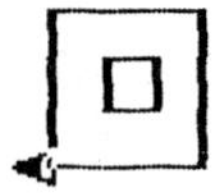

Corners

You never know when you are only going to want the corners of the box. Look what happens when you enter this line four times:

```
PU FD 20 PD FD 10 RT 90 FD 10
PU FD 20 PD FD 10 RT 90 FD 10
PU FD 20 PD FD 10 RT 90 FD 10
PU FD 20 PD FD 10 RT 90 FD 10
```

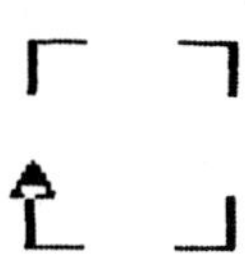

Sides

With a slight change, you can skip the corners and just have the sides.

```
FD 20 PU FD 10 RT 90 FD 10 PD
FD 20 PU FD 10 RT 90 FD 10 PD
FD 20 PU FD 10 RT 90 FD 10 PD
FD 20 PU FD 10 RT 90 FD 10 PD
```

Some Common Bugs

Forgetting to PU. From time to time, you will move the turtle from one place to another and discover you've left an unexpected trail, maybe from one design to another. As you will quickly realize, you have forgotten to lift the pen with PU. Usually you can correct your error easily. Let's say you entered FD 50 with the pen down instead of up. Just enter PE BK 50 PU FD 50 and you'll have things just the way you wanted them in the first place. Unless it's absolutely obvious to you why this is so, think your way through the several steps of the command and then try it on the computer.

Forgetting to PD. It's just as easy, of course, to forget to put the pen down again after a PU. I know I run the risk of insulting you by pointing this out, but I'll take the risk in memory of all those times I sat puzzled, wondering why the turtle wouldn't draw any of my designs. Eventually, I realized that I had lifted the pen without putting it back down again. So, any time nothing seems to work, enter PD just to be safe.

Forgetting to CS. When you create several different designs during a single Logo session, you need to clear the screen (CS) between designs. Otherwise, each new design will be drawn on top of the previous ones—and the turtle will start out from wherever the previous set of instructions left it, rather than from HOME.

Pen and background the same. Another way to fix Logo so nothing you do seems to matter is to set the background and pen at the same color. Try this, for example:

```
SETBG 0 SETPC 0 FD 100
```

As you'll see, the background is black, but when the turtle executes FORWARD 100 it leaves no trail. This is because the pen color is also set at black. If you happen to cross another line in this state, the turtle will operate like PENERASE (PE). Remember, you can check this possibility by entering PR PC PR BG to find out what the colors are.

Exploring Further

1. Draw a design on the screen and then write a set of commands that will display the design against each of the different background colors.
2. Demonstrate three ways of drawing a line and then erasing it, returning the turtle to its starting position.
3. Recalling the example of one box within another, experiment with placing other geometric shapes within each other—triangles, for example.
4. Place separate designs (not touching each other) around the screen.

Teaching Objectives

- ☐ Students will gain and demonstrate the ability to use the following commands and (where applicable) their abbreviations:

    PENUP (PU)
    PENDOWN (PD)
    PENERASE (PE)
    PENREVERSE
    SETBG
    SETPC
    PC
    BG

- ☐ Students will find ways to combine Logo commands and produce special effects other than just those you have illustrated.
- ☐ Students will find applications for the possibility of changing colors—whether they are using a color or a black-and-white monitor.

Teaching Techniques and Materials

Concrete Learning

It may be appropriate for young children to work with physical models of the turtle in grasping PD and PU. If they have made little turtles out of wood, clay, walnuts, or the like, have them practice lifting the turtles up from the paper. As one possibility, you could have them punch a hole through the turtle. This will be particularly easy with clay turtles, but you can drill a hole through a wooden model also. The hole should be the right size to accommodate a pen or pencil so the children can move the turtle around a piece of paper, physically lifting the pen up (PU) and putting it back down (PD).

Here's a more elaborate possibility. First, make a model turtle about four or five inches long with a hole in its center large enough for a piece of chalk. In addition to the chalk, cut the end off a kitchen sponge or create something else that can fit through the hole in the turtle and will erase the chalk. Now the students can simulate moving the turtle, lifting and lowering the pen, and even invoking PENERASE. (PENREVERSE is more difficult to simulate.)

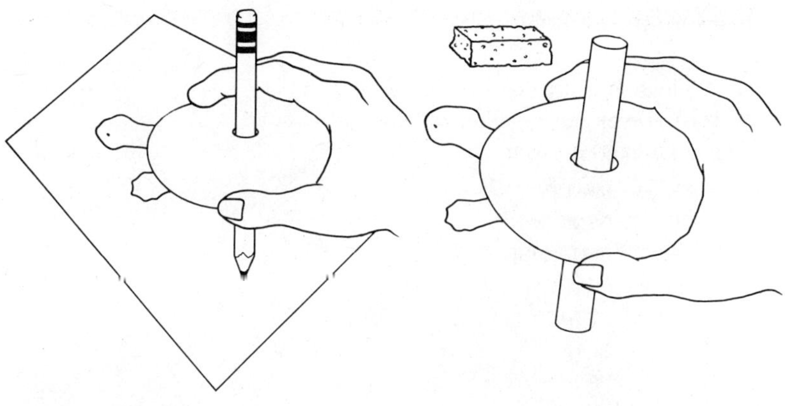

You will find that many students will grasp the operation of PU, PD, and PE easily. After all, these commands function very much like a pencil. Put it down to draw, lift it up to skip, and turn it around to erase.

Student Exercises

Pencil and Paper Exercises

1. Draw the designs that these Logo commands would produce:
   a. RT 45 FD 20 PU FD 20 PD FD 20
   b. BK 20 LT 90 FD 10 PU FD 10 PD FD 10 RT 90 FD 20
   c. PU FD 50 PD BK 50
2. Write out the Logo commands that will produce four unconnected squares on the screen.
3. Write out the Logo commands that will draw the roman numeral II.
4. What's wrong with these commands? Rewrite them so they would work as intended.
   a. PD 100
   b. PENARESE
   c. PU FD100 PD FD50

At the Computer

1. Check your answers to the pencil and paper exercises by entering the commands into the computer.
2. See how many roman numerals you can draw using Logo.
3. Create a set of dashes.

Lesson Plan Elements

Here are the elements you will want to include in your lesson plan for this portion of Logo.

☐ The logic of lifting and lowering the pen.
☐ The logic of erasing and reversing.
☐ The Logo commands:

PU	PENUP
PD	PENDOWN
PE	PENERASE
	PENREVERSE
	SETPC
	SETBG
	PR PC
	PR BG

☐ The use of background and pen colors.

Review of Logo Commands

ABBREVIATION	NAME	EXAMPLE	FUNCTION
PU	PENUP	PU	Lifts pen so it doesn't leave a trail.
PD	PENDOWN	PD	Lowers pen so it leaves a trail.
PE	PENERASE	PE	Instead of drawing lines, turtle erases lines it crosses.
(None)	PENREVERSE	PENREVERSE	Turtle changes whatever it passes over: black to white, white to black.
(None)	SETBG	SETBG 0	Sets color for the background of Logo designs.
(None)	SETPC	SETPC 1	Sets color for the pen.
(None)	PC	PR PC	Finds out the current color of the pen.
(None)	BG	PR BG	Finds out the current background color.

The pen and background color codes:

0 = Black	2 = Green	4 = Orange
1 = White	3 = Violet	5 = Blue

A Logo Challenge

Here is a Logo design that will become extremely easy when you've read the next chapter. Nonetheless, you already know enough to create the design now. See if you can figure out how.

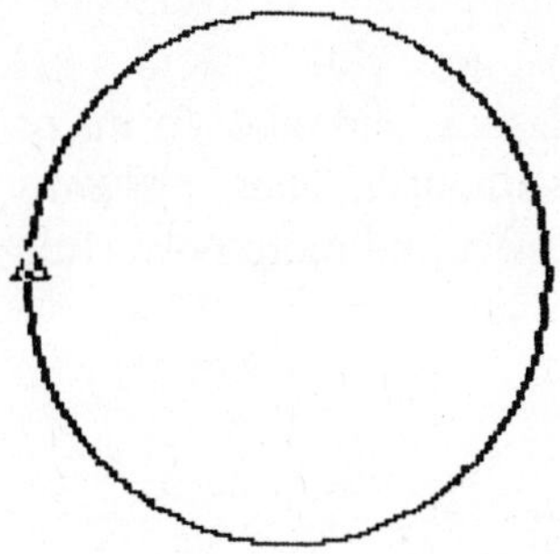

Chapter 4

REPEAT

As indicated at the beginning of Chapter 3, each chapter is organized around one or more powerful ideas. However, some Logo ideas are more powerful than others. In this chapter and in the two that follow, you are going to come face to face with three of the most powerful ideas of Logo. In this chapter, we'll look at a command called REPEAT.

A Powerful Idea

As the designs we've been creating have gotten more and more elaborate, you may have noticed that you often had to enter the same instruction repeatedly. In creating a box, for example, you entered FD 50 RT 90 four times in succession. Each instruction drew one side of the box and then turned at right angles to prepare for the next.

Fortunately, Logo has a command called—appropriately enough—REPEAT, which offers a welcome shortcut through such situations. REPEAT represents far more than a convenience, however. What makes it one of the most powerful ideas in Logo is that it opens possibilities for designs and other forms of computing that would be unthinkable without it. Thus, REPEAT will make your work with Logo both easier and more powerful. Here's how it works.

How to Do It

The basic format for using REPEAT is the following:

REPEAT *N* [*what you want repeated*]

where *N* = the *number of times* you want the instructions repeated. Notice that the instructions to be repeated must be placed within brackets: [and]. If you are using an Apple computer that doesn't show brackets on the keyboard, simply use the key marked SHIFT with the letters N and M, as follows:

SHIFT-N = [
SHIFT-M =]

Return of the Killer Box

Here's how to create a box using the REPEAT command:

REPEAT 4 [FD 50 RT 90]

In this example, the "what" you want repeated is FD 50 RT 90. You indicate that you want it repeated four times. That's all there is to it. Try it out and here's what will happen. This is a vast improvement over what you went through earlier.

Illustrations

Other Polygons

REPEAT provides an easy method for producing other polygons, such as triangles or pentagons. Here are a few examples.

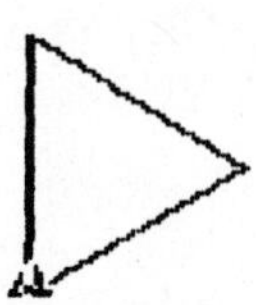

REPEAT 3 [FD 50 RT 120]

```
REPEAT 5 [FD 50 RT 72]
```

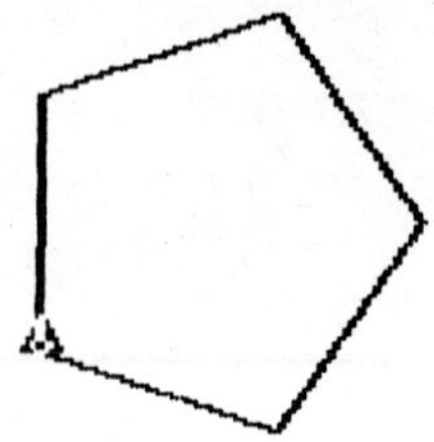

There is no practical limit to the number of sides of the polygons you can create: ten-sided, twenty-three-sided, and so on. As you move beyond triangles and squares, however, you will find yourself pondering the number of degrees to turn in each step. How would you know, for example, that RT 72 would produce a pentagon in the above illustration? Actually, the answer is simple.

Total Turtle Trip Theorem

As mentioned in Chapter 2, there is a geometric theorem called the *total turtle trip theorem* that says, in effect, the turtle must turn a total of 360 degrees (or multiples thereof) for it to return to the direction it was facing at the outset. You can demonstrate the theorem to yourself by entering any or all of the following:

```
RT 360
RT 180 RT 180
RT 120 RT 120 RT 120
```

If you enter RT 360, you probably won't even see the turtle wink, but it will turn around 360 degrees. You will notice something happening when you ask the turtle to turn 180 degrees twice. In increments of 120 degrees, it becomes even more apparent. But wait! We've slipped back into our old ways by entering RT 120 three separate times. (Congratulations if you thought to use REPEAT.) We could have accomplished the same thing with:

```
REPEAT 3 [RT 120]
```

Now, why don't you test the five increments of 72 degrees, as used in creating a pentagon.

```
REPEAT 5 [RT 72}
```

Success! The turtle ends up facing in its original direction.

The principle here, as you've perhaps figured out for yourself, is:

360 = (numbers of turns) × (degrees in each turn)

For example:

$360 = 1 \times 360$
$360 = 2 \times 180$
$360 = 3 \times 120$
$360 = 4 \times 90$
$360 = 5 \times 72$

The practical implication of this theorem is that you can determine the number of degrees to turn in each step of creating a polygon by dividing 360 by the number of sides. Thus, to create the pentagon, divide 360 by 5 to get 72 degrees per step.

When you combine turning 360 degrees in equal increments with moving FORWARD (or BACK) in equal steps, the result is a polygon. The distance moved in each step determines its overall size.

You are now equipped to create polygons with as many or as few sides as you want. Why don't you take a few minutes to experiment with this new range of possibilities. Here are some examples to prime your experimenting pump.

```
REPEAT 8 [FD 10 RT 45]
```

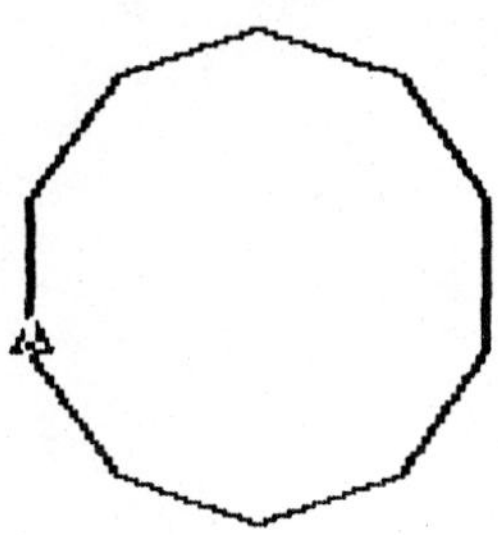

```
REPEAT 10 [FD 30 RT 36]
```

There's a little trick that makes this computation easier still. In Logo, you can divide two numbers through the use of a slash. For example:

```
360/6 = 60
360/5 = 72
```

So if you want to create an eleven-sided polygon, all you do is enter:

```
REPEAT 11 [FD 20 RT 360/11]
```

It doesn't matter that the result of 360 divided by 11 is 32.73; Apple Logo doesn't require whole numbers.

Take some time now to experiment with polygons.

What Is a Circle?

Every now and then, when students play around with polygons like this, one of them will have a powerful insight: "Hey, a circle is just a polygon with lots of small sides!" You may have had this insight in your own experimentation.

In theory, a circle is a polygon with an infinite number of infinitesimally small sides. In Logo practice, you can create a workable circle with fewer, somewhat longer sides. Try this:

```
REPEAT 360 [FD 1 RT 1]
```

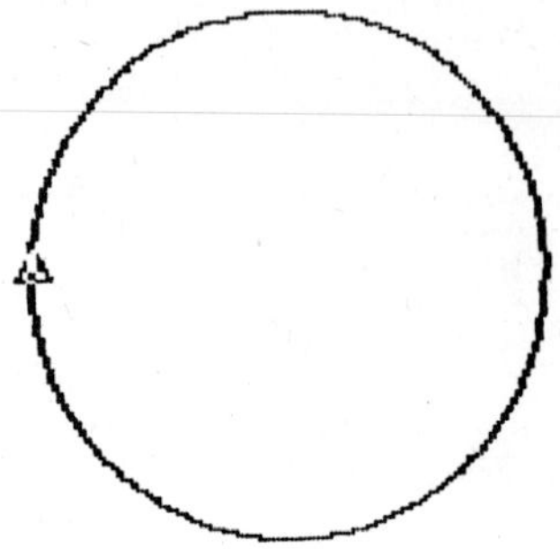

Actually, you can create a perfectly workable circle even more easily than that. Here's another version:

```
REPEAT 36 [FD 10 RT 10]
```

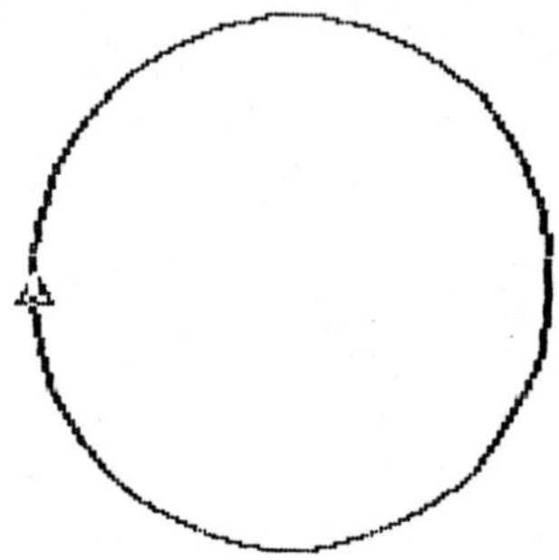

Take some time to experiment with circles. Find the smallest number of sides that will produce something that looks like a circle.

Stairs

Of course, REPEAT's utility is not limited to the creation of polygons. It works anywhere you want to perform the same operations again and again. You may recall how we created a set of stairs earlier in the book. Here's an easier way.

```
REPEAT 7 [FD 10 RT 90 FD 10 LT 90]
```

Experiment with more, smaller steps; then try fewer, larger ones.

CTRL-G

Here's an essential companion for REPEAT. Let's suppose you happened to enter REPEAT 10000 [FD 50 RT 1]. You might want to try it, but read the rest of this section first. Probably you would regret the instruction—which causes the turtle to run on and on and on.

CTRL-G stops any Logo command in midstream. To see how it works, enter the command mentioned above, watch it for a while, then hold down the CTRL ("CONTROL") key and press G. The turtle will stop racing around the screen and Logo will report: STOPPED!

Some Common Bugs

Omitting the number of REPEAT*s*. If you enter this command:

REPEAT [FD 50 RT 90]

Logo will protest as follows:

NOT ENOUGH INPUTS TO REPEAT

This error message is merely a reminder to tell Logo how many times to repeat the instructions.

Missing one or both of the brackets. If you forget to use brackets to enclose the instructions you want repeated, Logo *may* protest. (In some circumstances the closing bracket can be omitted, but this is not good practice.)

Incorrect instructions. REPEAT gives you an opportunity to make the same old mistakes in a new context. As you've already learned, simply entering FD without the numerical input will cause Logo to protest: NOT ENOUGH INPUTS TO FORWARD. REPEAT 10 [FD] produces the same result. (It only says it once, however, not ten times.)

Exploring Further

1. If 360 degrees will take the turtle in a full circle, how would you go about drawing arcs like these?

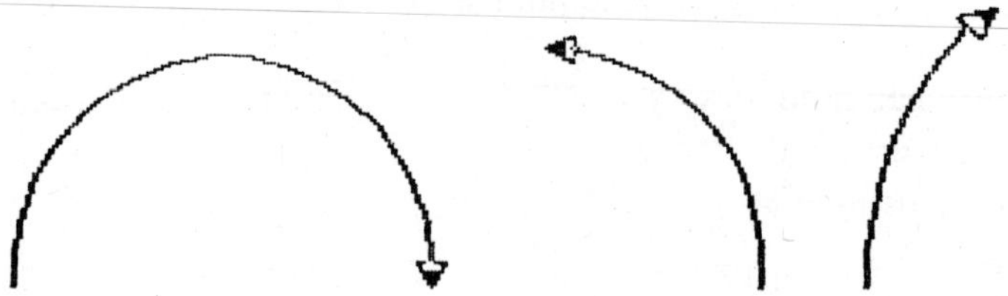

2. Suppose you created a design on the screen and then entered this:

   ```
   REPEAT 100 [SETBG 1 SETBG 0]
   ```

   Take a minute to figure out what would happen. Then try it. Then try variations on the theme.
3. You've seen that REPEAT 5 [FD 30 RT 72] produces a pentagon; what do you suppose would happen if you doubled the 72 while still REPEATing five times? Try it and then try other variations.
4. Recall that we REPEATed seven times to create stairs earlier. What do you suppose would happen if you entered the same instruction, REPEATing 100 or 200 times? (Try it and find out for yourself.)

Teaching Objectives

- ☐ Students will learn the logic and mechanics of using REPEAT.
- ☐ Students will begin using REPEAT as a labor-saving device.
- ☐ More important, students will find ways of using REPEAT as a really *powerful idea*—something that opens up new possibilities that were not available previously.
- ☐ Students will learn how to use CTRL-G to save themselves from boredom.
- ☐ Students will understand the total turtle trip theorem and be able to use it in creating polygons of various forms.

Teaching Techniques and Materials

Concrete Learning

The key here is for students to grasp the notion of a set of instructions as a unit that can be repeated again and again. Here's a way of demonstrating this concretely.

On a standard sheet of paper, draw a simulation of the following Logo command:

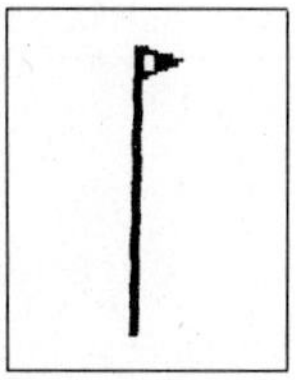

FD 50 RT 90

This sheet of paper now represents the unit that we need to REPEAT in order to make a box. You can illustrate this concretely by making three photocopies of the sheet. Now you have four identical units, each composed of FD 50 RT 90. Place them on the table or floor, one at a time. Lay down one; then, noticing which way the turtle was facing, lay down the next one, and so on. Here's what it looks like:

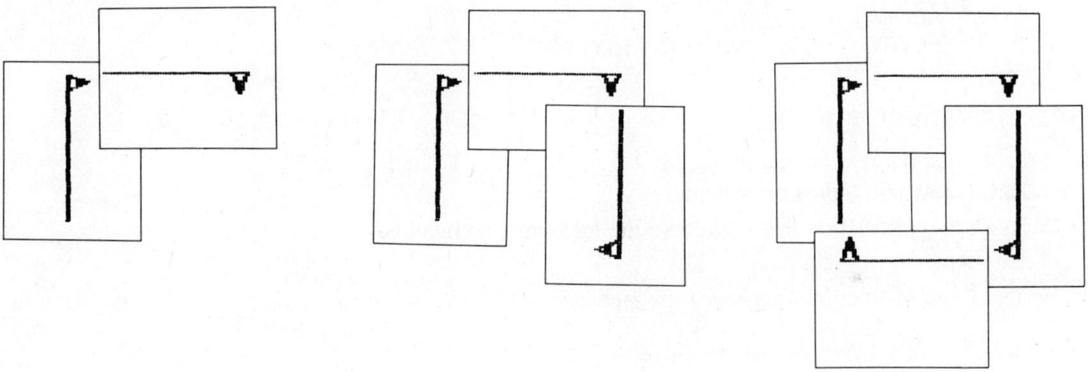

This should give your students a concrete grasp of REPEAT, so they will be able to take full advantage of it in their work with Logo. (Note: you can create the same effect with overhead transparencies.)

Mind-size Bites—Simple to Complex

REPEAT, for all its power, is a model of mind-size simplicity. Make sure that students grasp the basic format for REPEAT commands first. Use the simplest of instructions inside the brackets at the outset. With young children, you may want to begin by rotating the turtle without moving FORWARD or BACK. Then add new elements inside the brackets, one at a time.

Student Exercises

Pencil and Paper Exercises

1. Using REPEAT, write the instruction that would produce a triangle.
2. What design would be produced by this instruction?

   REPEAT 100 [FD 50 RT 90]

3. Complete this Logo instruction so as to draw a square-looking letter U.

   REPEAT ______ [______ 30 ______ 90]

4. What's wrong with these Logo instructions?
   a. REPEAT [FD 50 RT 60]
   b. REAPET 4 [FD 50 LT 20]
   c. REPEAT 36 (FD 10 RT 10)
   d. PU FD 50 RT 90 PD REPEAT 15 [RT 10 LT 5]

At the Computer

1. Write a Logo instruction that will cause the turtle to turn around and around without going anywhere.
2. Write a Logo instruction that will cause the turtle to take hundreds of tiny steps in a straight line.
3. Write a Logo instruction to produce this pattern:

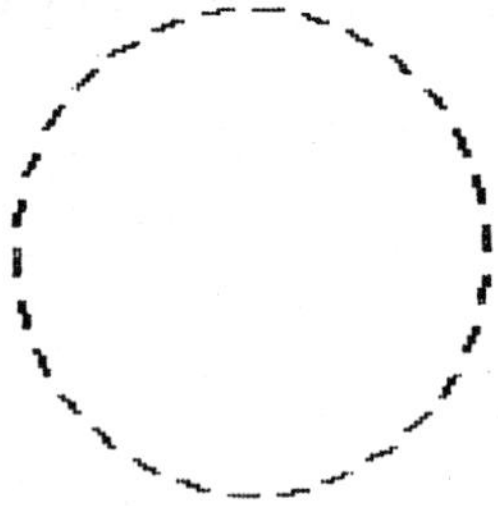

4. Enter this instruction:

   ```
   REPEAT 17 [FD 5 RT 20]
   ```

   Notice that the figure doesn't "close." Experiment with the instruction and modify it so that it produces a neat, seventeen-sided polygon.

5. Enter this instruction:

   ```
   RT 20 REPEAT 1000 [FD 1000]
   ```

   Now . . . do something to make it stop.

Lesson Plan Elements

- ☐ The technique for using REPEAT.
- ☐ Using CTRL-G to stop operations.
- ☐ REPEAT as a powerful new tool rather than just a convenient shortcut.
- ☐ Total turtle trip theorem, especially in regard to the creation of polygons.

Review of Logo Commands

NAME	EXAMPLE	FUNCTION
REPEAT	REPEAT 4 [FD 50 RT 90]	Causes Logo to repeat the operations contained in the brackets as many times as are specified.
CTRL-G	CTRL-G	Interrupts Logo in the middle of whatever it is doing at the time.

A Logo Challenge

All it takes is a one-line instruction to produce this:

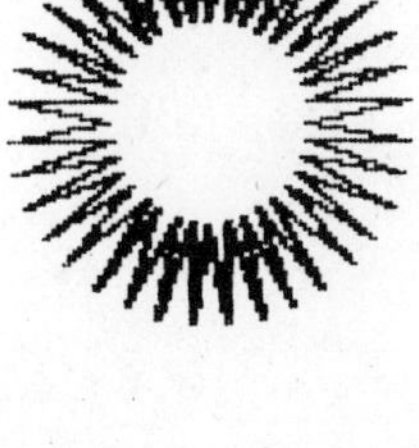

Chapter 5

Nesting REPEATS

If you've had a chance to play around with REPEAT, you have undoubtedly seen what a powerful idea it is. This chapter we will show that we've only scratched the surface of what REPEAT means. In particular, it will demonstrate what happens if you REPEAT a REPEAT.

A Powerful Idea

Certain powerful ideas have unexpected consequences. They can create a discontinuity in the way things are going. REPEATing a REPEAT—known as **nesting** one REPEAT inside another—is one of those ideas.

As you begin experimenting with nesting, notice how this new technique opens up a new world of design possibilities.

How to Do It

You already know how to use this technique, though you may not know that you do. Look at the following design for a minute and see if you can figure out how to create it. Then read on and discover how it was accomplished.

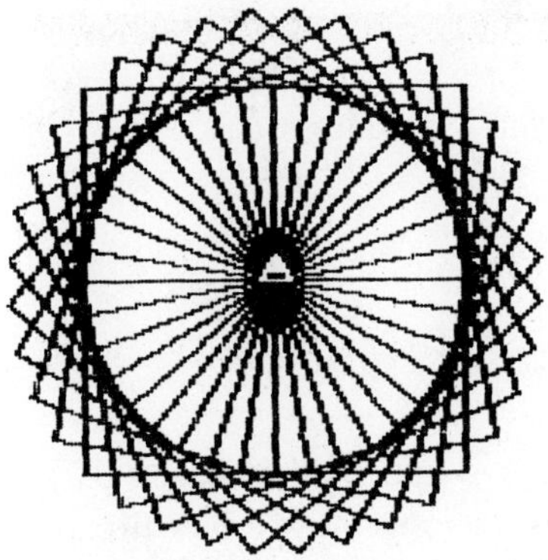

If you couldn't figure out the answer to this puzzle, don't feel bad. It wasn't easy. If you saw through to the answer, congratulations!

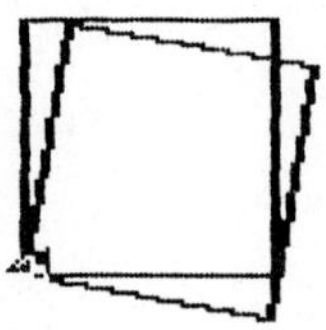

Creating the design *is* easy, however. It's based on our old friend, the box. In fact, this fancy design is nothing but thirty-six boxes. Start by drawing a box. Rotate the turtle 10 degrees to the RIGHT and draw another box.

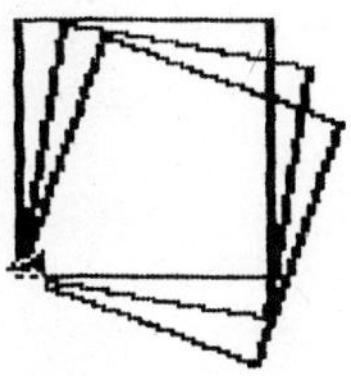

Rotate 10 degrees and draw another box.

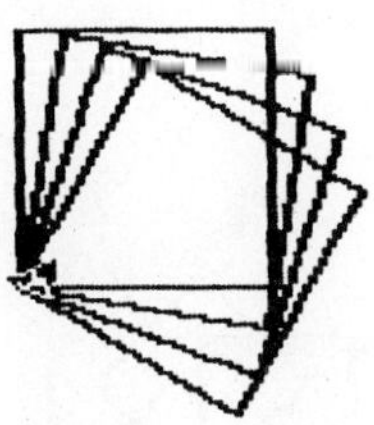

Do it again.

And on it goes. The full design takes thirty-six repetitions of the cycle of (1) drawing a box and (2) rotating it 10 degrees to the RIGHT. Take a minute to see if you can figure out the way this is accomplished.

Here's the instruction that was used to create the design:

```
REPEAT 36 [REPEAT 4 [FD 50 RT 90] RT 10]
```

This is the way it works, step by step. First, the boldfaced part of the instruction shown below tells Logo to draw a box fifty units on a side.

REPEAT 36 [**REPEAT 4 [FD 50 RT 90]** RT 10]

After it draws a box, returning the turtle to its starting point, Logo will next turn 10 degrees to the right.

REPEAT 36 [REPEAT 4 [FD 50 RT 90] **RT 10**]

Finally, we have asked Logo to perform that pair of operations 36 times.

REPEAT 36 [REPEAT 4 [FD 50 RT 90] RT 10]

Since it turns 10 degrees each of the thirty-six times, the whole instruction will bring the turtle back to its starting point again.

Illustrations

Having Fun with Boxes

Here are just a few of the things you can do by repeating boxes, making little changes between boxes.

```
REPEAT 8 [REPEAT 4 [FD 30 RT 90] LT 45] HT
```

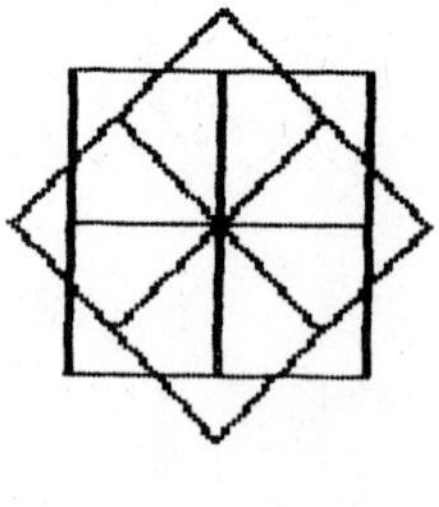

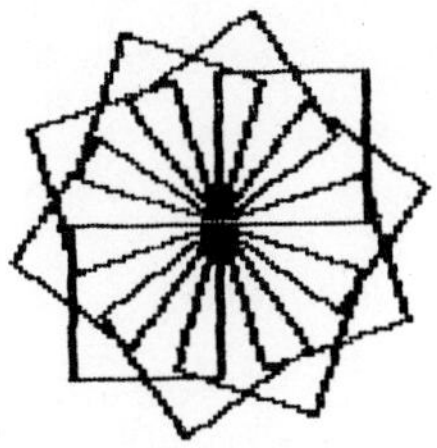

REPEAT 10 [REPEAT 4 [FD 30 RT 90] LT 36] HT

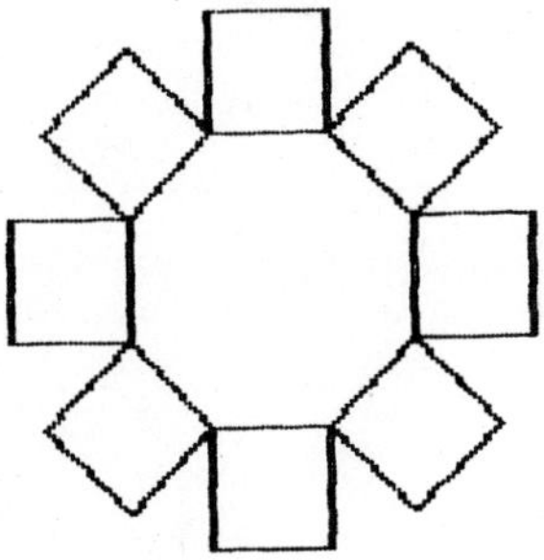

REPEAT 8 [REPEAT 4 [FD 25 RT 90] FD 25 LT 45] HT

Triangular Designs

You can do just about as much with triangles as you can with boxes. Here are a few examples:

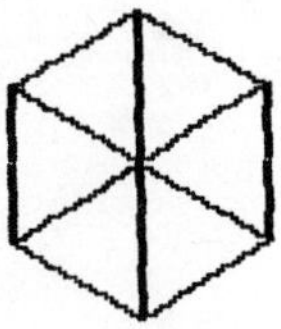

REPEAT 6 [REPEAT 3 [FD 30 RT 120] LT 60] HT

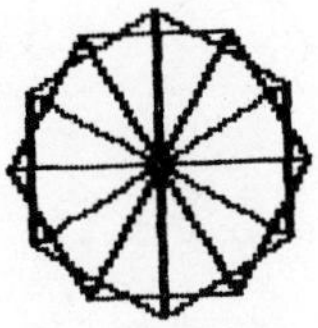

REPEAT 12 [REPEAT 3 [FD 30 RT 120] LT 30] HT

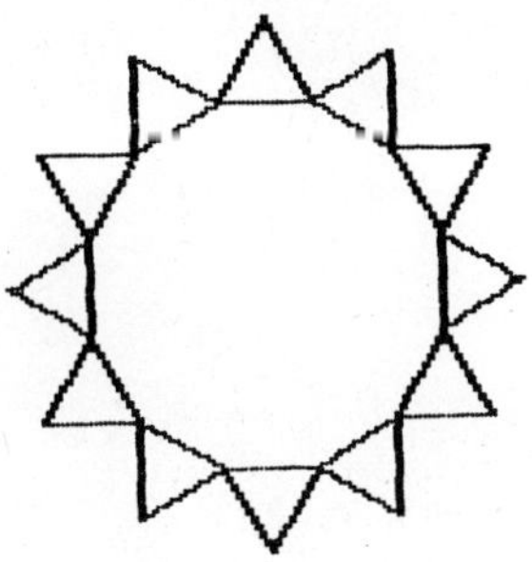

REPEAT 12 [REPEAT 3 [FD 20 RT 120] FD 20 LT 30] HT

These are just a few of the designs achieved by nesting REPEATs. While it would be possible for you to create designs like these manually, you'd need the attention span of a rock. Fortunately, the computer has that.

Some Common Bugs

Omitting the number of REPEAT*s*. As pointed out in Chapter 4, this is a common mistake in using REPEAT. Of course, you double your chances of this bug when you use two REPEATs, as well as creating a more complex instruction.

Omitting brackets. It's easy to make this error when you nest one REPEAT within another. What's wrong with this instruction, for example?

```
REPEAT 10 [RT 45 REPEAT 4 [FD 20 RT 20]
```

As you may have noticed, there must be another closing bracket at the end of the line: RT 20]]. The second closing bracket combines with the opening bracket that follows REPEAT 10, completing the specification of what is to be done ten times.

Exploring Further

As you experiment with the nesting of REPEATs, you should feel free to proceed both deductively and inductively—both from the top down and from the bottom up. Sometimes you may want to map out carefully the consequences of Logo instructions before trying them at the computer. At other times, you should be willing to wing it. Try an instruction, see how it turns out, modify it, and try again.

1. Study each of the following designs; see if you can figure out how each was created, and then create your own variations.

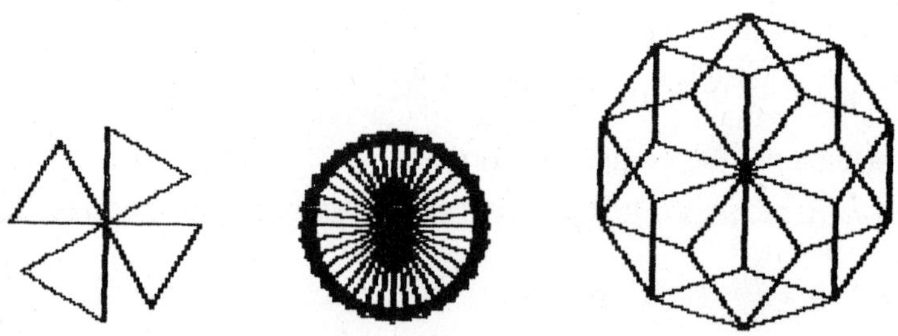

a *b* *c*

2. Here is a famous optical illusion diagram. Sometimes it looks like one block piled on top of two below it, sometimes like two on top and one below. You can create this with one Logo instruction containing nested REPEATs. Try it.

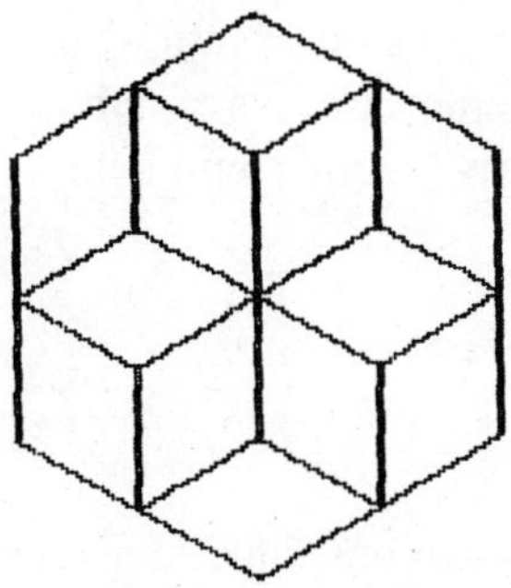

3. Try adding PU and PD to your designs, creating designs like this.

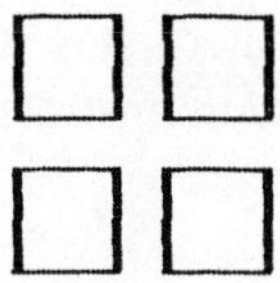

Teaching Objectives

- ☐ Students will learn the mechanics of nesting REPEATs.
- ☐ Students will be able to explain the logic of nesting REPEATs.
- ☐ Students will create more imaginative and elaborate designs than before.

Teaching Techniques and Materials

Mind-size Bites—Simple to Complex

The key to students' grasping this technique lies in their ability to see it as a set of elements. Remind them of the basic logic of REPEAT, as discussed in Chapter 4. Recall that a box is simply a set of four smaller elements, each composed of a line (e.g., FORWARD) and a turn (e.g., RIGHT). Now students need to see that the REPEAT unit that creates a box can also be an element in a more complex instruction.

This approach follows directly from Piaget's observations of how children learn. First they learn simple, mind-size units. Then they learn to put those simple units together into something more complex.

Concrete Learning

The working of nested REPEATs can be demonstrated concretely, as follows. On several sheets of tracing paper or plastic sheets, draw identical boxes. Then have the students place the sheets on top of each other, rotating each box by some standard degree. This way they can see how designs are created, step by step. Overhead transparencies can also be used to demonstrate this.

This technique is especially useful if you have relatively few computers for the students to work with. Have them plan out several designs with pencil and paper, writing out the instructions they feel will produce them. Then have students try out the instructions on the computer, making whatever adjustments are required to produce the desired designs.

Paper and pencil exercises like this have both positive and negative side effects. On the positive side, they encourage students to grasp the abstract principles of Logo and give them experience in top-down programming. On the negative side, however, there is a danger that students will come to regard their "mistakes" as something bad. It is important, therefore, that you not make them feel inadequate when their computer work does not result in the desired designs the first time. Instead, they should regard debugging as a natural and legitimate step in computer programming.

As a general rule, if students consistently get it right the first time, it's possible that they are not being adventurous enough to take full advantage of Logo's potential. With a little encouragement from you, they will learn to delight in the unexpectedly bizarre results they sometimes produce. Many times such "mistakes" become the serendipitous beginnings of something new and wonderful.

Student Exercises

Pencil and Paper Exercises

1. Complete the instruction that will create the accompanying design:

   REPEAT 2 [REPEAT ______ [FD 30 RT 120] LT ______]

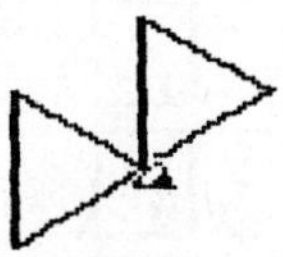

2. Complete the instruction that will create the accompanying design:

   REPEAT ______ [REPEAT 3 [FD 30 RT 120] ______ 60]

3. Complete the instruction that will create the accompanying design:

   REPEAT 3 [REPEAT 4 [FD 30 RT ______] RT ______]

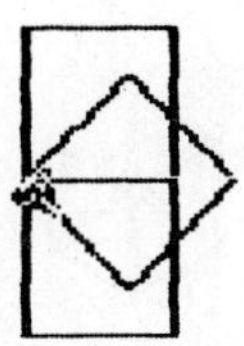

4. Write an instruction containing a nested REPEAT and draw the design you think it will produce.
5. What's wrong with these Logo instructions?
   a. REPEAT [REPEAT 4 [FD 20 RT 90] RT 60]
   b. REPEAT 4 REPEAT 5 [FD 30 RT 72] RT 30

6. Match instructions a, b, and c with designs x, y, and z.
   a. REPEAT 4 [REPEAT 4 [FD 20 RT 90] FD 10]
   b. REPEAT 5 [REPEAT 3 [FD 20 RT 120] RT 30]
   c. REPEAT 3 [REPEAT 4 [FD 20 RT 90] RT 120]

x

y

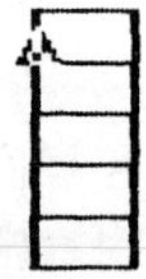
z

At the Computer

1. Write a Logo instruction to create this design:

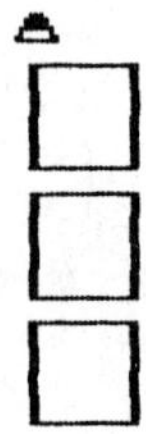

2. Write a Logo instruction to create this design:

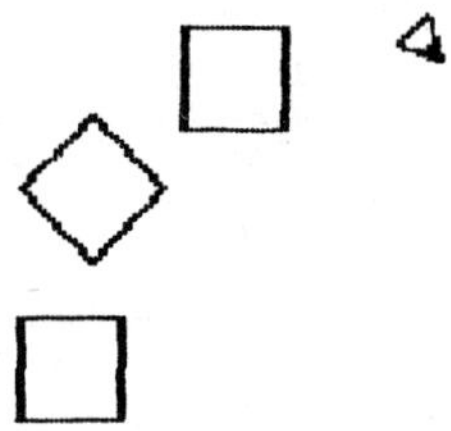

3. Write two different Logo instructions, each of which will create this design:

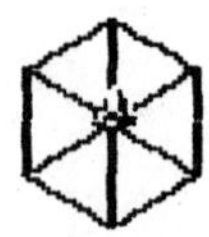

4. Correct the following instruction so it will produce this design:
   REPEAT 6 [REPEAT 3 [FD 20 RT 90] RT 60]

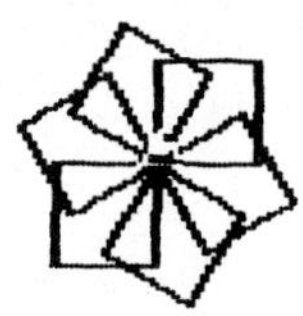

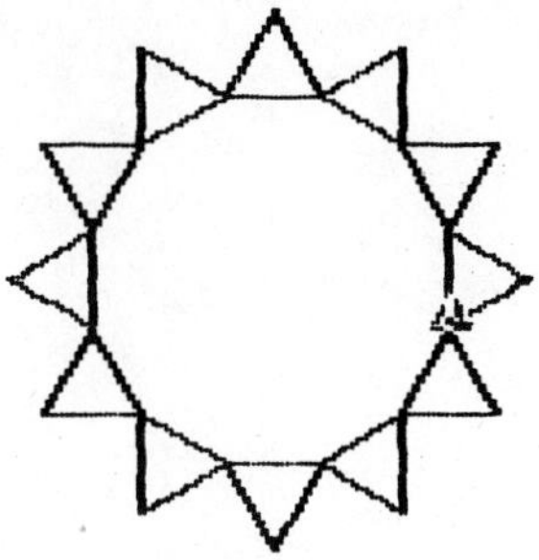

5. Correct the following instruction so it will produce this design:

```
REPEAT 12 [REPEAT 3 [FD 20 RT 100] LT 30]
```

Lesson Plan Elements

- ☐ The logic of treating REPEAT units as elements to be included in more complex instructions.
- ☐ The technique of using nested REPEATs.
- ☐ The ability to debug Logo instructions to make them produce desired designs.
- ☐ Opportunities to be more adventurous in creating elaborate designs.

A Logo Challenge

Nesting REPEATs will allow you to create this design. See if you can do it.

Chapter 6

Procedures

The problem with what you've learned so far is the impermanence of the designs you make. Any time you want to repeat an old design you have to reenter the old command, and some of your designs may be getting fairly long and complex. Moreover, if a particular command doesn't yield the result you want you have to reenter the whole thing, making the appropriate changes. All this is about to change dramatically.

A Powerful Idea

In this chapter you will learn how to create **procedures:** permanent, reusable sets of Logo instructions. From now on, you will be able to create sets of instructions, save them, and run them again and again, whenever you want. In essence, a procedure works like this: First, you assign a name to some set of procedures; then, every time you enter the name of the procedure the computer will perform all the operations you have specified.

Like REPEAT and nesting REPEATs, however, this new technique represents much more than simple convenience. The ability to write procedures opens up a new range of possibilities not previously available to you. You are going to create more imaginative designs than before. Moreover, you are going to be able to debug your Logo instructions far more easily than before—so you'll be able to get things exactly the way you want them.

The ability to create procedures is even more powerful than a simple convenience. In a real sense, you are going to begin creating *your own computer language*. By now, you probably feel at home with commands like FORWARD and RIGHT. In this chapter you are going to learn how to create procedures that work the same way as the standard Logo commands, except that you can make them as elaborate as you want.

How to Do It

Creating Procedures

Here's the general format for creating procedures:

TO <name>
<instructions>
END

Begin by typing the word TO followed by the name you want to assign to the procedure. You can use just about any name you want as long as it doesn't include spaces (use periods or dashes if you want to separate words). Be sure to enter the actual *name* of the procedure and the *instructions* for it where these words are shown in lowercase within angle brackets; don't type the brackets.

The word TO followed by a name tells the computer that you want to create a procedure. In response, the computer changes its prompt character from ? to >. Now you can begin entering Logo instructions. You can enter one line or several. Enter them just the way you have been doing so far. You can enter single commands on separate lines or string them together on the same line. The only difference is that the computer doesn't act on any of the instructions. Every time you press RETURN, the computer simply responds with another > prompt.

Once you are through entering instructions, enter the word END on a separate line and press RETURN. This tells the computer you are done. It will respond by telling you the procedure has been defined. You will then be given the familiar ? prompt.

To illustrate, let's create a procedure called BOX that will draw a square. *Boldfaced type is used here to show the commands you type in, but these will not appear that way on your screen.* Proceed as follows:

```
?TO BOX
>REPEAT 4 [FD 50 RT 90]
>END
```

Once you've typed END, the computer will respond with:

```
BOX DEFINED
?
```

Now you have created a procedure called BOX, which the computer recognizes. Notice that the ? prompt has returned, indicating that the computer will again follow instructions as soon as they are given. You've just created your first procedure!

To run the procedure, just type BOX and press RETURN. The computer draws a square. Type CS to clear the screen and then type BOX again. The computer will draw this square every time you type BOX. All you need to do is enter the name of a procedure, and the computer will proceed to execute each of the instructions in that procedure one by one, in order.

Editing Procedures

If you make a mistake while typing a line of instructions, you can simply backspace and correct it. Once you've completed the line, however, you can't go back to it *at that point*. Once you've finished creating the entire procedure, however, you can reenter it in the **edit mode** and make all the changes you want. You can correct errors, make alterations, expand the procedure, and so on.

If you decide you want to change the size of the square produced by BOX, you can enter the edit mode as follows:

```
EDIT "BOX
```

This is the format always used in editing procedures. *The quotation mark just before the procedure name is essential.* If you omit the quotation mark, Logo will draw the square and then say BOX DIDN'T OUTPUT TO EDIT. This will be explained later; for now, just know that it won't destroy the world if you forget the quotation mark. You won't get into the editing mode either, so remember to use it.

Once you have entered the edit mode, your screen will look something like this:

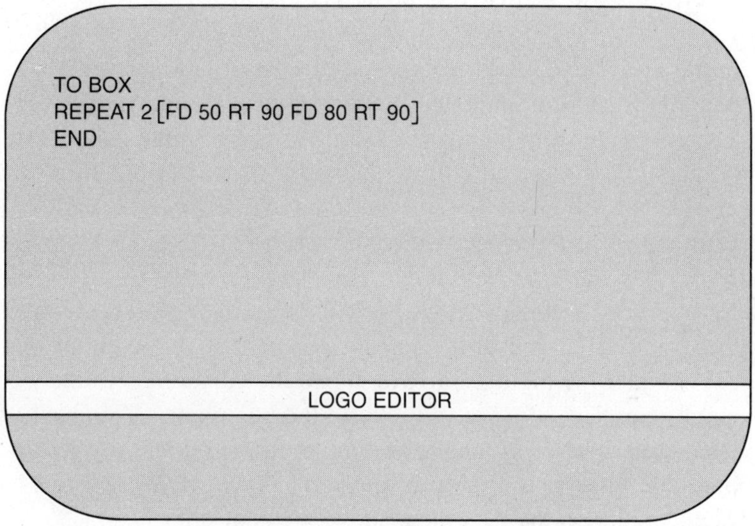

Notice that your cursor is flashing on top of the T in the upper-left corner of the screen. The editing process consists of two things: moving the cursor and making changes.

Making changes is pretty straightforward, and you've already been working with that part of the process. First, *to add new material,* you simply type it in. For example, type XXX on your computer now. (Do *not* hit RETURN.) Here's what will appear on your screen.

```
XXXTO BOX
REPEAT 4 [FD 50 RT 90]
END
```

As you can see, anything you type shows up wherever the cursor is located at the moment. The character on which the cursor is superimposed, as well as all characters to the right of the cursor on that line, move to the right when you enter new material.

To erase unwanted materials, simply pass the cursor across it, using the left arrow. Do that now to get rid of the XXX just entered. Here are some other methods for erasing materials:

- ☐ CTRL-D erases the character on which the cursor is flashing.
- ☐ CTRL-K erases the character on which the cursor is flashing and everything to the right of it on the current line.

In this section you will be exposed to a lot of editing commands. Don't be intimidated by the number of commands. There is no need to memorize them. As you become experienced with editing you will undoubtedly remember the commands that you use a lot, and the reference diagram on the following page will remind you of the rest.

Now let's learn how to move the cursor around. Starting from the upper-left corner of the screen, you can move the cursor anywhere using the right arrow. When the cursor gets to the end of one line, it moves directly to the beginning of the next. Using the right arrow, move the cursor to the middle of the second line. From here, you can move up, down, right, or left. The diagram on the next page shows ways of doing that.

Take a few minutes to move the cursor around the procedure. Try each of the commands shown in the diagram. Notice that when you attempt an impossible move (such as pressing CTRL-N when you are already on the last line), the computer merely beeps and doesn't move.

Now you will see how to use some of these editing commands to change BOX. Enter ESC < to get to the beginning of the procedure, and you will see how to do the editing, step by step.

Begin by making the square larger.

Up
ESC <
CTRL-P

Left CTRL-A CTRL-B CTRL-F CTRL-E **Right**

CTRL-N
ESC >
Down

ESC <	Moves cursor to beginning of procedure
ESC >	Moves cursor to end of procedure
CTRL-P	Moves cursor up to the **P**revious line
CTRL-N	Moves cursor down to the **N**ext line
CTRL-A	Moves cursor to left end (beginning) of line
CTRL-E	Moves cursor to right **E**nd of line
CTRL-B	Moves cursor **B**ack one character to the left
CTRL-F	Moves cursor **F**orward one character to the right

Logo procedure editing reference diagram

☐ CTRL-N gets you to the second line of the procedure.

☐ Use the right arrow or CTRL-F to reach the space between 50 and RT.

☐ Use the left arrow to erase the 50, and then type 75. This will make the square half again as big as it was. (If you prefer some other size, enter another number.)

After completing these changes, check to see if the procedure still works. Enter CTRL-C to indicate that you are finished editing. The computer will respond:

```
BOX DEFINED
?
```

Type BOX and enter it to see how the procedure works. You should now see a somewhat larger square on the screen. To get back to editing, type EDIT "BOX.

Suppose you want to have the square drawn in the lower-left corner of the screen. To do that, you have to move the turtle before it draws the square. The instructions to accomplish that should appear between the first and second lines of the procedure. (The first line is the name.)

In order to create some space for the new instructions, move the cursor to the beginning of the second line of the procedure. Now enter CTRL-O. Your screen should look like this:

```
TO BOX
REPEAT 4 [FD 75 RT 90]
END
```

Take a minute now to consider how you can move the turtle down and to the left, before it begins drawing the square. Here's one way:

```
TO BOX
PU LT 90 FD 100 RT 90 BK 50 PD
REPEAT 4 [FD 75 RT 90]
END
```

You can enter either this solution, as indicated by italic type, or one of your own. Be sure to use PU and PD to lift the pen and to lower it afterward. Once you've entered the new line, you are ready to try out the program to see how the changes worked. To leave the editing mode, just enter CTRL-C again. (If you want to leave the editing mode without saving any of the changes you've made, enter CTRL-G.)

Try out the new version of BOX to see if it accomplished what you intended. Now, try some more editing on BOX. Edit BOX so as to place it in the upper right-hand corner of the screen. Or make it twice as large, or half as large. Then, you can create some other procedures.

Illustrations

Some Old Favorites

To begin, you can create procedures for some of the designs you've worked out in earlier chapters.

```
TO RECTANGLE
REPEAT 2 [FD 50 RT 90 FD 80 RT 90]
END
```

```
TO TRIANGLE
REPEAT 3 [FD 50 RT 120]
END

TO PENTAGON
REPEAT 5 [FD 50 RT 72]
END

TO CIRCLE
REPEAT 36 [FD 10 RT 10]
END

TO STAR
REPEAT 5 [FD 50 RT 144]
END
```

Create the procedures by entering them as shown above. Then run them by simply typing their names.

Getting Fancier

One of the nice things about procedures is that you can create and fine-tune much more elaborate designs than would have been practical otherwise. Here's an example:

```
TO FIGURE1
REPEAT 6 [REPEAT 4 [FD 30 RT 90] RT 60]
PU FD 50 RT 95 PD
REPEAT 36 [FD 9 RT 10]
RT 85 PU FD 51 PD
REPEAT 36 [PU FD 60 PD FD 10 PU BK 70 RT 10]
HT
END
```

Notice that FIGURE1 is run together without a space. You must not have spaces in procedure names, although you can use periods to separate parts of procedure names if you want. Thus, for example, this procedure could be called FIGURE.1.

By going through this procedure line by line, you will see how it works, as well as how such procedures are typically created.

I began with a general idea of the design I wanted to produce: one of the designs that can be produced by rotating a box, adding a circle around it, and then adding a ring of rays beyond that. I started by naming the procedure and creating the rotated-box design.

```
TO FIGURE1
REPEAT 6 [REPEAT 4 [FD 30 RT 90] RT 60]
```

Initially, I had the box bigger than this one (fifty units on a side, rather than thirty). When it began to look as though the whole design wouldn't fit on the screen, I reduced the size of the box.

At the completion of the rotated-box design, the turtle was in the center of the design, facing straight up. The next command lifted the pen (PU) and moved it 50 units FORWARD. It took a little experimentation to see how far I had to move the turtle to get outside the rotated-box design.

```
PU FD 50 RT 95 PD
```

Since I wanted to create a circle next, and the turtle was facing straight up, I had to rotate it to the side (in this case, to the RIGHT). At first, I rotated it 90 degrees. Since my circle was created by moving FORWARD, then RIGHT, then FORWARD, and so on, my first attempt produced a circle that was off-center. Think about it for a minute, and you may be able to see why that is so. Or you can edit the procedure and see for yourself what happens. With a little more experimenting, I found that RT 95 did the trick.

```
REPEAT 36 [FD 9 RT 10]
```

This command draws the desired circle. Notice that it moves FORWARD 9 units for each turn of RIGHT 10 degrees. I had to experiment with the units to get a circle that encircled the rotated-box design by the same distance on all sides.

```
RT 85 PU FD 51 PD
```

This command moved the turtle back into the center of the design. Notice that I have turned 85 degrees to the RIGHT, including the 95-degree turn that started the circle. Also, I

Saving Your Procedures

Once you've created procedures, you will want to save them for later use. You can accomplish this by storing all your creations on disk. Here are some simple instructions for saving the procedures you've already created; Appendix B gives detailed instructions on managing your disk files.

Be sure your disk is in the disk drive, and then enter this:

```
SAVE "CHAP6
```

This command will make a permanent disk copy of all the procedures you've created, using the name CHAP6. If you want to get back to these procedures later on, all you'll need to do is enter LOAD "CHAP6. (You can, of course, use other names, but notice that you need to add the quotation mark as shown.)

It's important to realize that the SAVE command saves everything currently in the computer, not just a particular procedure. If you add some more procedures and want to save them, you can execute another SAVE using a new name (which will resave the old material as well as the new) or you can erase the existing disk file and then save the new version. This second method is more efficient (it doesn't fill up your disk as fast) and is done as follows:

```
ERASEFILE "CHAP6
SAVE "CHAP6
```

found—through experimentation—that it took 51 units FORWARD to bring the turtle home again.

```
REPEAT 36 [PU FD 60 PD FD 10 PU BK 70 RT 10]
```

From the center of the design, this command causes the turtle to (1) lift the pen, (2) move FORWARD 60 units, which takes it beyond the perimeter of the design so far, (3) lower the pen, (4) draw a ten-unit line, (5) lift the pen and return to the center of the design, (6) turn RIGHT 10 degrees, and (7) do all that thirty-five more times. All this took a bit of experimentation, in conjunction with the other instructions in the procedure.

```
HT
END
```

Finally, I hid the turtle so the design would look better. END signals the computer that the procedure is complete. My purpose in providing these autobiographical notes on the creation of procedures is to give you a sense of the process. I am not suggesting that you should always operate the way I did in this instance; this is just one of the possibilities.

Some Common Bugs

Choosing a reserved name. If you attempt to create a procedure and name it with one of the names already used in Logo (for example, FORWARD), the computer will draw your attention to that, as follows:

```
TO FORWARD
FORWARD IS A PRIMITIVE
```

Primitive is the term used in reference to those names that are a part of the Logo program.

Reusing an already-defined name. If you try to redefine a procedure name, the computer will respond, quite appropriately:

```
TO BOX
BOX IS ALREADY DEFINED
```

This will keep you from inadvertently erasing a procedure you have spent hours creating.

Omitting the quotation marks when EDIT*ing.* To EDIT a procedure, you must type a quotation mark (") immediately prior to the procedure's name—for example, "BOX. If you fail to do this, the computer will run the procedure and then print an error message. If you enter EDIT BOX, the computer will draw a box and print an error message like this one.

```
BOX DIDN'T OUTPUT TO EDIT
```

This message will make more sense in Chapter 12, which deals with outputs. For now, just know that you need to use the quotation mark in specifying a procedure for EDITing.

Forgetting to END. Sometimes you'll start creating a procedure and forget to enter END. Typically, you'll enter several commands that won't result in anything, since the computer is still storing everything you type as parts of the procedure. Once you discover what you've done, END the procedure as you're supposed to, then EDIT and erase the unwanted lines.

Exploring Further

1. Create a procedure that will draw a seven-sided polygon.
2. Create a single procedure that will place geometric designs (such as squares, stars, or triangles) around the screen.
3. Write a procedure to draw a disc as shown here.

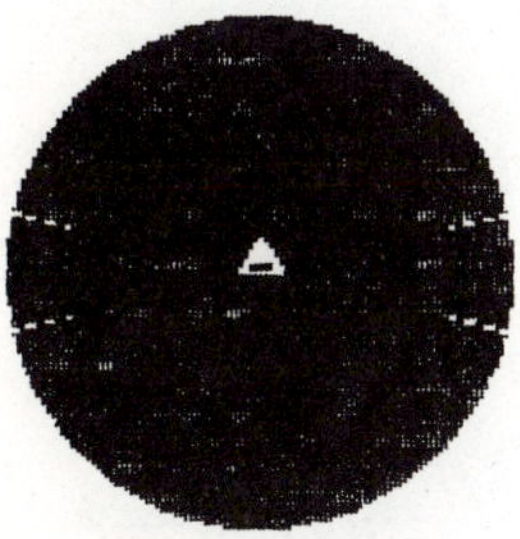

4. Now try to create this variation on (3) above.

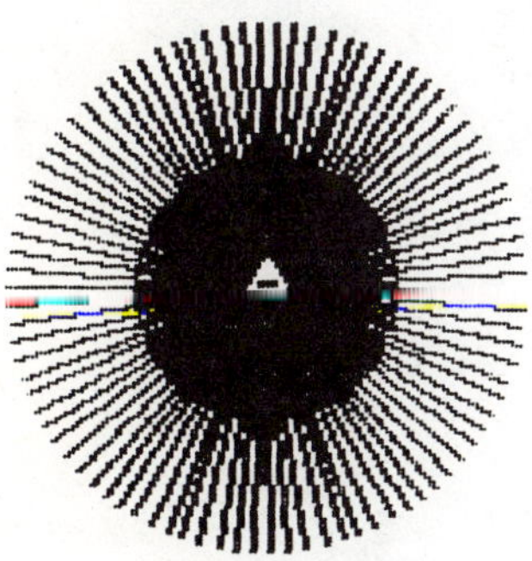

Teaching Objectives

- ☐ Students will understand and be able to explain the logic and the power of creating procedures.
- ☐ Students will be able to create and run procedures.
- ☐ Students will be able to edit procedures.
- ☐ Students will be able to save their procedures on disk.

Teaching Techniques and Materials

Mind-size Bites

In presenting the materials of this chapter, don't push students into terribly complex procedures. You can let them go as far as they want on their own, but Chapter 7 will simplify matters in a way that will allow them to make very complex designs with little or no effort.

The key idea at this point is to have students understand the fundamental logic of procedures: creating a set of instructions and giving it a name that, henceforth, will cause the computer to carry out the set of instructions whenever the name of the procedure is entered as a command. In a sense, procedures are a way of reducing a complex set of instructions to a mind-size bite.

Simple to Complex

Encourage students to create simple procedures and then elaborate on them. It's best to get students to create something that works first; then they can change it, add to it, make it more imaginative.

Encourage students to see their procedures as collections of discrete operations. Each line of the procedure has specific purposes. If students have become adept at entering several commands to create a complex design, they should transfer the same process over to the construction of procedures.

Student Exercises

Pencil and Paper Exercises

1. Write a procedure to create a box.
2. Write a procedure to create a triangle.
3. Correct the error in this procedure:

```
TO PROC
REPEAT 4 [FD 50 RT 90]
REPEAT 5 [FD 60 RT 144]
```

4. Correct the error in this procedure:

```
STAR
REPEAT 5 [FD 60 RT 144]
END
```

5. Correct the error in this procedure:

```
TO PROC
PU LT 90 FD 50
REPEAT 3 [FD 50 RT 120]
END
```

6. Complete this procedure:

```
_____ PROC
LT 45 FD 50 RT 45
REPEAT 4 [BK 50 RT 90]

______
```

7. Complete this procedure:

```
TO PROC
__________ [FD 50 RT 90]
END
```

At the Computer

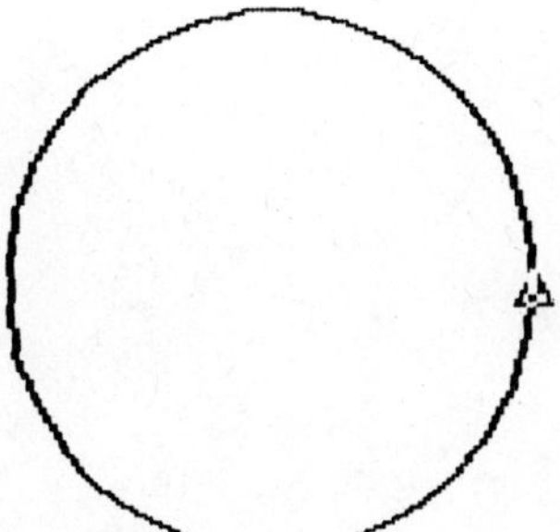

1. Create the procedure listed below. Then EDIT it so that it creates the design shown.

```
TO CIRCLE
REPEAT 36 [FD 10 LT 5]
END
```

2. Create the procedure listed below. Then EDIT it so that it creates the design shown.

```
TO RECTANGLE
REPEAT 2 [FD 50 LT 90 FD 100 RT 90]
END
```

3. Create the procedure listed below. Then EDIT it so that it creates the design shown.

```
TO PENTAGON
REPEAT 4 [FD 50 LT 60]
END
```

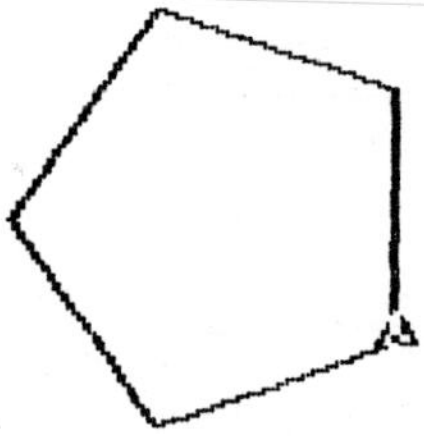

4. Create the procedure listed below. Then EDIT it so that it creates the design shown.

```
TO WAVY
LT 90 PU FD 100 RT 90 PD
REPEAT 3 [REPEAT 36 [FD 3 RT 10] REPEAT 36 [FD 3 LT 10]]
END
```

5. Think back now to some of the designs you created earlier and write procedures for them.

Lesson Plan Elements

- ☐ The logic of procedures.
- ☐ The mechanics of creating procedures.
- ☐ The fundamentals of editing procedures.
- ☐ Saving procedures on disk.

Review of Logo Commands

NAME	EXAMPLE	FUNCTION
TO	TO BOX	Initiates the creation of a procedure named BOX.
END	END	Signals the completion of a procedure definition.
EDIT	EDIT "BOX	Initiates the edit mode, so changes to the procedure named BOX can be made.
CTRL-C	CTRL-C	Terminates the edit mode.

Also see Logo procedure editing reference diagram on page 66.

A Logo Challenge

Chapter 7

Nesting Procedures

Your life is about to get much easier as Logo becomes even more powerful. This chapter will look at the nesting of procedures, which is similar to the nesting of REPEATs described in Chapter 5.

A Powerful Idea

In Chapter 6 you saw that procedures are sets of Logo instructions held by the computer and acted on one after another whenever the procedure's name is entered. Just about any instruction you can give to the computer for immediate action can also be included as part of a procedure, to be held for deferred action. But consider this: If you can enter the name of a procedure and have it acted on, why can't you put one procedure inside another? You can! And your computer work will never be the same afterward.

Following a pattern that must be getting familiar to you, this new development in Logo will be more than a convenience. As you are going to see, it is especially empowering in the realm of problem solving.

How to Do It

Actually, there is nothing new for you to learn in this chapter. You already know how to create procedures. Now you know that you can put one procedure inside another. In the remainder of the chapter you are going to explore some of the implications of that capability.

Here's a simple example to get started. Create a simple procedure that moves the turtle FORWARD 50 and turns it RIGHT 90.

```
TO SIDE
FD 50 RT 90
END
```

Now create a box, using the simple procedure you've just created. Here's how to do it:

```
TO BOX
REPEAT 4 [SIDE]
END
```

This new procedure simply REPEATs SIDE four times, with this familiar result.

Now create a new procedure that uses BOX as a component. Here is a variation on some of the designs you created earlier.

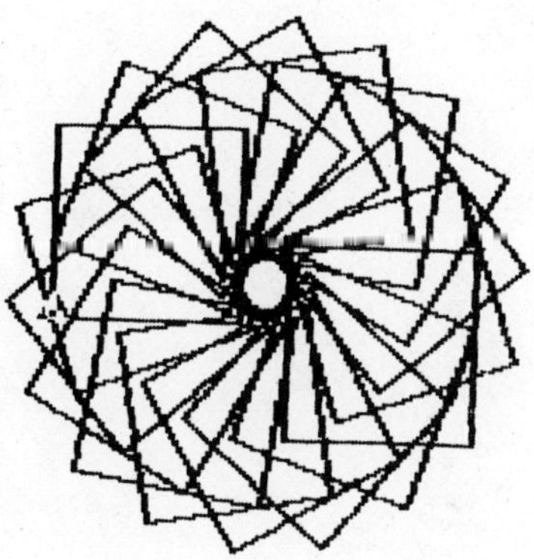

```
TO DESIGN
REPEAT 18 [BOX FD 20 RT 20]
END
```

(Note: This won't work unless you've created BOX.)

Procedures, Superprocedures, and Subprocedures

You could go on and on. You could use DESIGN in another procedure. Then you could call up that procedure in still another procedure. There is no limit to this except the computer's memory.

In Logo, the term **superprocedure** refers to a procedure that includes other procedures. A **subprocedure,** on the other hand, is a procedure that is included within some other procedure. Obviously, a given procedure can be both a superprocedure and a subprocedure; such designations always exist in relation to other procedures. Nonetheless, the two terms are useful in thinking about the relationships among procedures in the construction of complex designs.

Problem Solving

Now a little purpose will be put into the exploration of Logo so you can begin to see its real educational power. Perhaps more than anything else Logo offers children powerful tools for problem solving. There are two fundamental principles:

1. A big problem can be broken into many small problems.
2. We can learn through correcting our errors.

Illustrations

To explore the Logo approach to problem solving together, we'll need a problem to solve. Let's set ourselves the task of building a house on the video screen, with a door, windows, a roof, and a chimney. You should start by getting a picture of a house in your mind. Of course, it won't be the same as the picture I have in my mind, but they should be similar enough that we'll feel we are working on the same project.

In the next few pages, I will go with you through the process of building the house. You'll get the most value from this exercise if you try to stay a step or two ahead of me as we go along. When it's time to put a roof on the house, see if you can figure it out. Then, whether you were successful or not, see how I handled it. Maybe you'll like your solution better than mine, which is fine.

Let's begin. First, we want to construct the main frame of the house. Here's a procedure that might do the job:

```
TO FRAME
REPEAT 2 [FD 50 RT 90 FD 80 RT 90]
END
```

Notice that I've constructed a rectangle instead of a square: [FD 50 RT 90 FD 80 RT 90] creates two sides of the rectangle, and I've had the computer do it twice. Why don't you create a FRAME procedure for yourself and run it?

Once you've run FRAME, you'll see it's definitely a rectangle, but it has some problems in being the basis for the house we are building. First, it's a little small. Also, it would be nicer to move it lower and more to the left of the screen. You have already learned everything it takes to make those changes. You can change the size of the frame by increasing the FD commands in the program, and you can move it by shifting the beginning point.

I have revised FRAME to move the starting point and to make the rectangle bigger. (Changes and additions to the previous command are indicated by italics.)

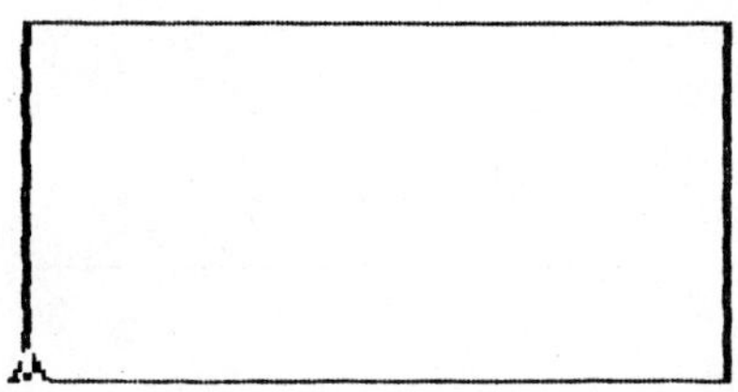

TO FRAME
PU LT 90 FD 100 RT 90 BK 50 PD
REPEAT 2 [FD *75* RT 90 FD *150* RT 90]
END

Let's put a couple of windows in our house. To do that, we create a window-making procedure. Enter this:

```
TO WINDOW
```

Whoops! Notice that Logo answers, WINDOW IS A PRIMITIVE. This indicates that WINDOW already means something to Logo, so we have to pick another name. Let's call it WNDW and try this as our first attempt at a window:

```
TO WNDW
REPEAT 2 [FD 10 RT 90 FD 5 RT 90]
END
```

Now clear the screen (CS) and try WNDW. Well, that's about the smallest window I've ever seen. Let's edit it as follows:

```
TO WNDW
REPEAT 2 [FD 30 RT 90 FD 15 RT 90]
END
```

That looks more like the size we need, so let's add some crosspieces to make it look more like a window. Take a minute to figure out what you'd do before looking at my solution. You might find it useful to draw the design out on paper. Just be sure to keep track of which way your turtle is pointing.

Here's one solution:

```
TO WNDW
REPEAT 2 [FD 30 RT 90 FD 15 RT 90]
FD 15 RT 90 FD 15 LT 90 FD 15 LT 90 FD 8 LT 90 FD 30
END
```

Now let's put the window inside the frame of the house. In fact, let's create a **superprocedure,** HOUSE, to hold all the parts. As a first try, let's start the HOUSE this way:

```
TO HOUSE
CS
FRAME
WNDW
END
```

Except for having the window on the floor at the corner of the house, we're off and running. That can be corrected easily enough by moving the turtle between FRAME and WNDW. In the meantime, we might as well add a second window. Here's how I did it:

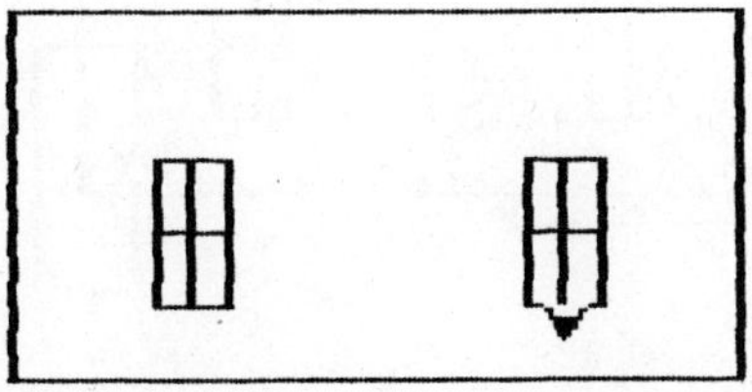

```
TO HOUSE
CS
FRAME
FD 15 RT 90 PU FD 30 LT 90 PD
WNDW
LT 90 PU FD 70 LT 90 PD
WNDW
END
```

It certainly looks workable. We may want to rearrange the windows later on, but let's leave them like this for now. Next, let's create a door. Here's a first attempt:

```
TO DOOR
REPEAT 2 [FD 50 RT 90 FD 20 RT 90]
END
```

Getting a little fancy, let's create a doorknob for the door. While we could create it as part of DOOR, we might as well make it a separate procedure. That way, we can use it in other projects later if we want. Here's a reasonable doorknob:

```
TO KNOB
REPEAT 36 [FD 1 BK 1 RT 10]
END
```

Next, we'll place the doorknob on the door, as follows:

```
TO DOOR
REPEAT 2 [FD 50 RT 90 FD 20 RT 90]
FD 25 RT 90 PU FD 16 PD
KNOB
END
```

Now we're ready to place the door in the house. To do that, we need to remember where we left the turtle after the second window and move it to where we want the lower-left corner of the door. Here's one way:

```
TO HOUSE
CS
FRAME
FD 15 RT 90 PU FD 30 LT 90 PD
WNDW
LT 90 PU FD 70 LT 90 PD
WNDW
PU BK 15 LT 90 FD 45 RT 90 PD
DOOR
END
```

Unfortunately, the door has been placed over on the edge of the house. If you watched the turtle carefully, moreover, you would have seen that it drew the door upside down—which explains why the doorknob is on the left side of the door rather than on the right.

Obviously, we have lost track of where the turtle was located and which way it was pointing when it completed the second window. There are any number of ways of remedying this problem. Here's a method that uses another useful Logo command. When Logo comes to the command STOP in a procedure, it does just that. This allows you to examine the result of a procedure at some stage prior to completion.

Let's stop HOUSE as soon as it completes the second window:

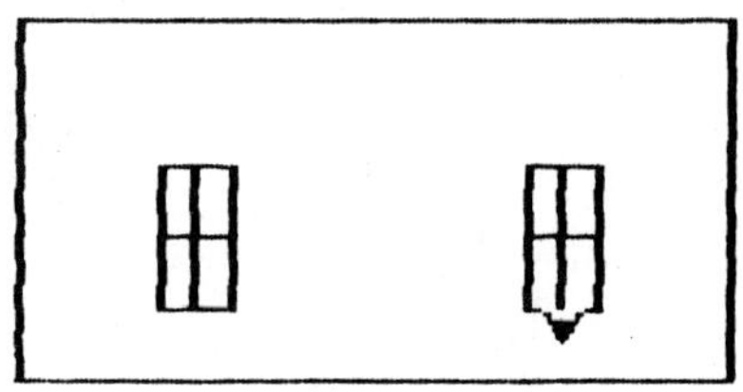

```
TO HOUSE
CS
FRAME
FD 15 RT 90 PU FD 30 LT 90 PD
WNDW
LT 90 PU FD 70 LT 90 PD
WNDW
STOP
PU BK 15 LT 90 FD 45 RT 90 PD
DOOR
END
```

If you run HOUSE now, you'll see that the turtle is facing down, at the bottom of the right window. Thus, instead of BK 30 LT 90, we want to move the door with FD 30 RT 90. Let's make those changes and drop the STOP command. Notice that I've also added HT (HIDETURTLE) at the end of the procedure, so the turtle is no longer superimposed on the doorknob. Here's what your procedure should look like now:

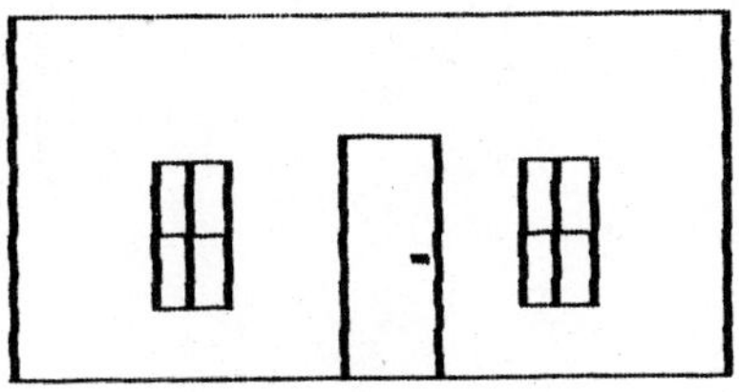

```
TO HOUSE
CS
FRAME
FD 15 RT 90 PU FD 30 LT 90 PD
WNDW
LT 90 PU FD 70 LT 90 PD
WNDW
PU FD 15 RT 90 FD 45 RT 90 PD
DOOR
HT
END
```

Now, let's complete our house with a roof. Here's one way of drawing one kind of roof. I suggest that you do the following: (1) Create the procedure just as I've done, (2) go through it in your mind, getting a picture of what the result should look like, and (3) enter ROOF to see if it looks the way you imagined.

```
TO ROOF
PU BK 50 LT 90 FD 100
PD BK 170 RT 80 FD 50
LT 80 FD 152 LT 80 FD 50
END
```

Finally, let's create a chimney for the roof.

```
TO CHIM
REPEAT 2 [FD 20 RT 90 FD 10 RT 90]
REPEAT 5 [FD 2 RT 90 FD 10 LT 90 FD 2 LT 90 FD 10 RT 90]
END
```

Now all that's left in the project is to put the chimney on the roof and then put the roof on the house. Here's how to put the chimney on the roof:

```
TO ROOF
PU BK 50 LT 90 FD 100
PD BK 170 RT 80 FD 50
LT 80 FD 152 LT 80 FD 50
BK 50 RT 80 BK 50 RT 90 BK 5
CHIM
END
```

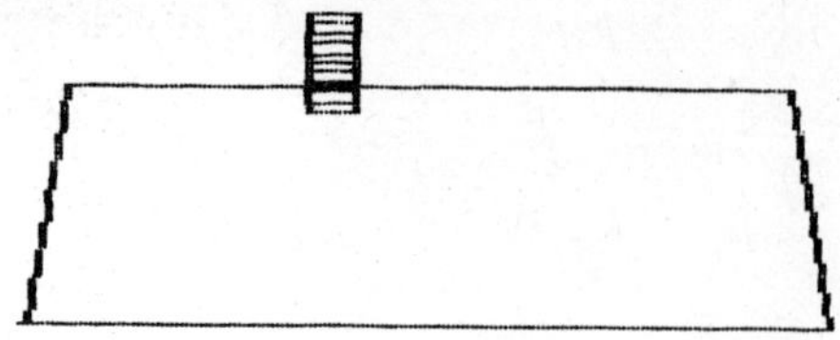

Now, let's lift the roof up on the house. The main trick here is placement. We began the roof by moving the turtle to the lower-left area of the screen, so the roof would fit on the screen. Either we can change those initial instructions of ROOF, or we can experiment with placement in HOUSE. Try your hand at placing the roof on the house. Then compare what you've done with the solution shown below.

```
TO HOUSE
CS
FRAME
FD 15 RT 90 PU FD 30 LT 90 PD
WNDW
LT 90 PU FD 70 LT 90 PD
WNDW
PU FD 15 RT 90 FD 45 RT 90 PD
DOOR
LT 90 PU FD 100 LT 90 BK 5 RT 90 PD
ROOF
HT
END
```

This extended example should bring home two essential pedagogical aspects of Logo. First, large and complex problems can be broken down into small, simple parts. Second, making mistakes to correct is a powerful tool for producing desired results. Both of these are generally true of computer programming, but they are far more apparent and accessible in Logo than in other languages.

Some Common Bugs

Inappropriate placement. As you have seen, when you put pieces together to form a whole, it's easy to put pieces in the wrong places—like the first placement of the window and the door in the HOUSE example.

Forgetting direction of turtle. Often, when you are having trouble putting pieces together, your problem may be a function of the direction the turtle was facing at the end of the previous operation.

Inappropriate sizes of pieces. You have also seen that it can take a little experimentation before the various pieces of a whole design are sized appropriately for one another.

Failure to lift pen. Whenever you are moving the turtle around the screen a lot to place the pieces of a design, it's easy to forget to lift the pen; hence, you leave an unseemly streak across the design.

Exploring Further

1. Make the HOUSE fancier. Add a front walk, more windows, and so on.
2. Sketch a picture you would like to create in Logo. Identify the component parts of the picture (such as FRAME, DOOR, or ROOF). Write procedures for each of the parts. Put them all together to create the whole picture. You might create a sailboat, a person, or a street map of your block.
3. Create a set of procedures so that one is put inside a second, which is inside a third . . .
4. Use nested procedures to create abstract designs by rotating simple geometric figures.

Teaching Objectives

- ☐ Students will be able to nest one or more procedures inside another.
- ☐ Students will be able to break complex designs into their component parts.
- ☐ Students will be able to put the component parts of a design together to form a whole.
- ☐ Students will be able to use STOP in debugging their designs.

Teaching Techniques and Materials

Mind-size Bites

The use of nested procedures exemplifies the Piagetian principle of mind-size bites. Students should be encouraged to create simple procedures that capture manageable chunks of the designs they want to create. Whereas you have created some rather complex instructions in previous chapters (nested repeats and the like), your students should now be encouraged to write simple procedures. They can create lots of them.

Any time they are having difficulty with a design, encourage them to see if they can break their task into smaller components. Have them get accustomed to looking for the mind-size bites.

Simple to Complex

As seen in this chapter, the Piagetian principle of moving from the simple to the complex is also a matter of moving from the complex to the simple. Encourage your students to move freely in both directions.

On the one hand, you should have them experiment with simple designs. How many complex patterns can they create—through nested procedures—from a simple box, a rectangle, or a triangle? This is an instance of bottom-up programming.

At the same time, the special power of the techniques covered in this chapter shows up in top-down programming. Beginning with a complex idea, they will learn to identify its simpler parts; then they can assemble the parts into the complex design they originally envisioned.

Both of these approaches are legitimate and valuable for your students. As students begin experimenting with Logo, notice which of these approaches individual students seem inclined toward. Acknowledge them for their approach and then draw their attention to the other possibility. Thus, when you find students who carefully plan out complex designs, breaking them into their component parts, encourage them to experiment with designs just to see what happens. And those who are experimenting without any plans should be encouraged to try their hands at planning. Don't try to change anyone; just be sure students know both approaches are available and valuable.

Student Exercises

Pencil and Paper Exercises

1. For each of the designs shown below:
   - ☐ Draw each of the component parts.
   - ☐ Write a procedure to create each of the parts.
   - ☐ Write a superprocedure to combine the parts.

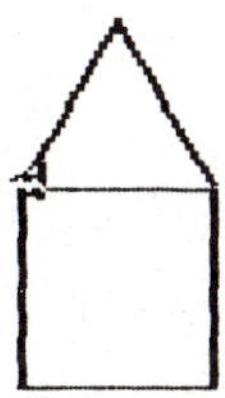

a

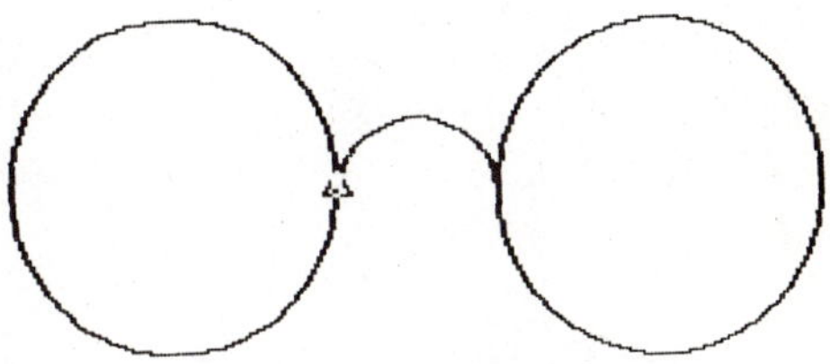

b

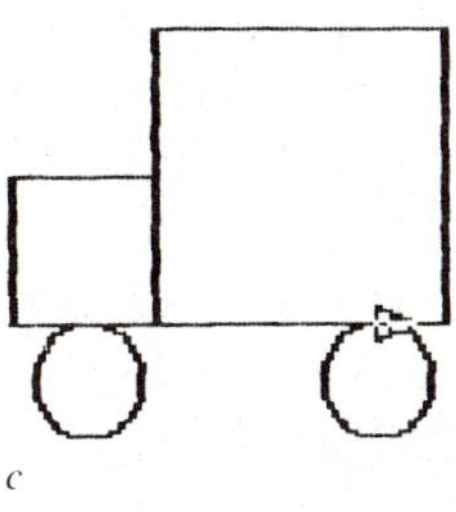

c

d

2. Draw a picture you would like to create in Logo. Then:
   a. Draw each of the component parts.
   b. Write a procedure to create each of the parts.
   c. Write a superprocedure to combine the parts.
3. Write a procedure to draw a simple geometric design, such as a square or a triangle. Then write a superprocedure that uses the first procedure to create a complex design.

At the Computer

1. Test out the procedures you created in the previous section and debug them.
2. Create three different designs based on a square, using nested procedures.
3. Change these procedures so that they will create the design shown.

```
TO FIVE
REPEAT 5 [FD 30 RT 72]
END

TO FIVES
REPEAT 3 [FIVE RT 108]
END
```

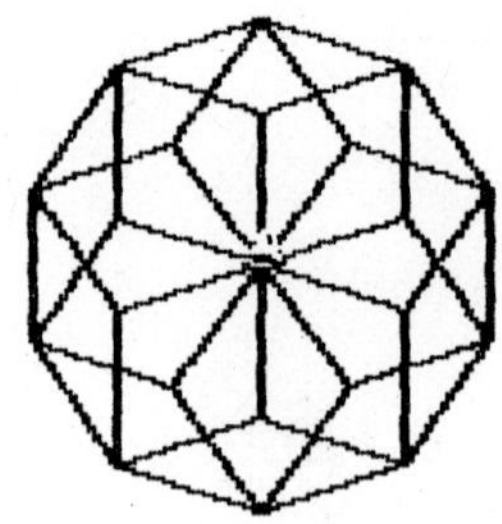

4. Correct these procedures so that they will create the design shown.

```
TO FIVE                  TO DESIGN
REPEAT 5 [FD 30 RT 72]   FIVE
END                      RT 90
                         STAR
TO STAR                  END
REPEAT 5 [FD 45 RT 144]
END
```

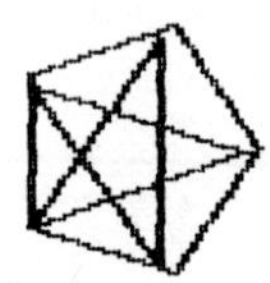

Lesson Plan Elements

☐ The logic of nested procedures.
☐ The mechanics of nesting procedures.
☐ Breaking complex designs into simple components.
☐ Putting the pieces together.
☐ The use of STOP.

Review of Logo Commands

NAME	FUNCTION
STOP	Causes procedure to stop its operations upon reaching this command.

A Logo Challenge

Here is a design you can create by nesting procedures within one another.

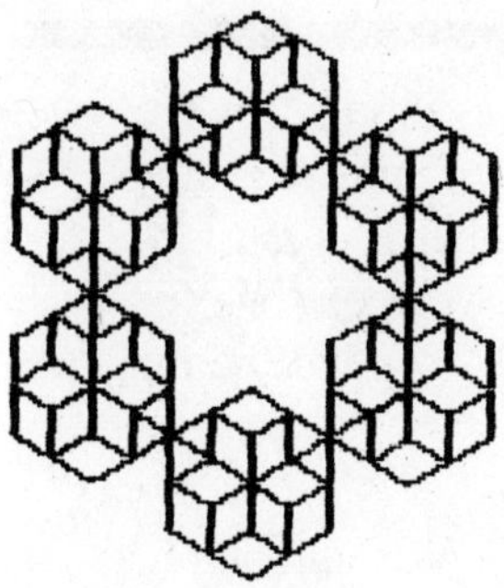

Chapter 8

Words and Numbers

A Powerful Idea

So far, you have been dealing with Logo as though it were an electronic sheet of paper on which to draw fantastic designs. This image is a useful one, but not altogether accurate. In actuality, Logo is more like *two* sheets to work on: one for graphics, the other for text. In this chapter, you will be introduced to the text screen.

Here you will learn about the printing of words and numbers. Not only can you have the computer print back what you type in, but you can also use a lot of the techniques learned in connection with graphics: REPEAT, for example. Later chapters, moreover, will examine a number of additional techniques that apply specifically to text materials.

How to Do It

CTRL-L, CTRL-T, and CTRL-S

To begin with, there is the matter of the two screens. These three commands will give you more control over the display on your screen. Notice that you currently see a graphic design in the top portion of the screen, with the bottom four lines devoted to showing your instructions.

CTRL-L dedicates the entire screen to graphics. Enter it now to see what happens. If you prefer, you can achieve the same effect by entering FULLSCREEN.

CTRL-T has just the opposite effect, dedicating the entire screen to the instructions you've given the computer. Try it out. TEXTSCREEN will also get this effect for you.

Finally, CTRL-S gets you back to the standard format: graphics and text. You can also achieve this by entering SPLITSCREEN. Take a minute to move back and forth through the various formats. There is no limit to the number of changes you can make, and you can even change formats while the turtle is drawing designs.

To move on to the main topic of this chapter, enter TEXTSCREEN and notice that the screen is now filled with the various commands you have been entering.

PRINT (PR)

You are about to see what the computer can do in the domain of words and numbers instead of graphics.

The most elementary instruction we can give the computer in this domain is to PRINT something. Try entering this:

```
? PRINT 23
23
?
```

Notice that the computer follows your instruction and prints 23. As you will see, this is only the beginning of its printing capabilities. Before moving on, you should note that Logo understands the abbreviation PR for PRINT. Thus, PR 23 will produce the same result as PRINT 23. Why don't you try it?

The computer can also follow commands to print alphabetical materials. There are two ways of handling this. If you want the computer to print only one word or string of characters, the following instruction will accomplish that:

```
?PR "EARL
EARL
?
```

Notice that this format requires a quotation mark immediately preceding the word you want printed. There must be *no* space between the quotation mark and the word and *no* closing quotation mark.

If you want to print something that contains spaces, this can be accomplished through the use of brackets. Try this:

```
?PR [HEY, THIS IS GETTING TO BE FUN!]
HEY, THIS IS GETTING TO BE FUN!
?
```

TYPE

Sometimes you want to print several entries on the same line. Here's what happens if you try to do that with PRINT:

```
?PRINT "HELLO PRINT "THERE
HELLO
THERE
?
```

As you can see, the computer prints the two words on different lines: PR adds a carriage return to the end of whatever we ask it to PRINT, moving the cursor to the left end of the next line.

The command TYPE works exactly like PRINT except that it does not add a carriage return. Here's an example:

```
?TYPE "HELLO TYPE "THERE
HELLOTHERE?
```

Now the two words are on the same line—but they are squeezed together with no space in between. As you will see, there are several ways of handling this problem. You have already seen how to handle the problem using brackets. Here's another solution.

CHAR 32

In Chapter 18 you will see that the computer has a numerical code for each of the characters it prints. The code for A, for example is 65. B is 66. There is even a code for space: 32.

TYPE CHAR 32 will cause the computer to skip a space. Here's an example:

```
TYPE "HELLO TYPE CHAR 32 PRINT "THERE
HELLO THERE
?
```

This may seem like a very complicated way of accomplishing not very much. In subsequent chapters, however, you will see the incredible possibilities it opens up.

Illustrations

Although Logo's text processing is separate from its graphics, some of the things you've learned in connection with graphics also apply to text processing. Here are some examples.

REPEAT

The REPEAT technique that you learned to use in graphics can also be used with text materials. Here's an example:

```
?REPEAT 10 [PR [YOU CAN SAY THAT AGAIN.]]
YOU CAN SAY THAT AGAIN.
YOU CAN SAY THAT AGAIN.
YOU CAN SAY THAT AGAIN.
YOU CAN SAY THAT AGAIN.
YOU CAN SAY THAT AGAIN.
YOU CAN SAY THAT AGAIN.
YOU CAN SAY THAT AGAIN.
YOU CAN SAY THAT AGAIN.
YOU CAN SAY THAT AGAIN.
YOU CAN SAY THAT AGAIN.
?
```

Or try this:

```
REPEAT 1000 [TYPE "LOGO]
```

Here is an abbreviation of what you'll get.

```
LOGOLOGOLOGOLOGOLOGOLOGOLOGOLOGOLOGOLOG!
OLOGOLOGOLOGOLOGOLOGOLOGOLOGOLOGOLOGOLO!
GOLOGOLOGOLOGOLOGOLOGOLOGOLOGOLOGOLOGOL!
OGOLOGOLOGOLOGOLOGOLOGOLOGOLOGOLOGOLOGO!
LOGOLOGOLOGOLOGOLOGOLOGOLOGOLOGOLOGOLOG!
OLOGOLOGOLOGOLOGOLOGOLOGOLOGOLOGOLOGOLO!
GOLOGOLOGOLOGOLOGOLOGOLOGOLOGOLOGOLOGOL!
OGOLOGOLOGOLOGOLOGOLOGOLOGOLOGOLOGOLOGO!
```

Nested REPEATS

Here is an example of what you can do with nested REPEATs in the text-processing mode. Enter this:

```
REPEAT 10 [REPEAT 2 [TYPE "HIP TYPE CHAR 32] PR "HOORAY!]
```

and your result should look like this:

```
HIP HIP HOORAY!
HIP HIP HOORAY!
HIP HIP HOORAY!
HIP HIP HOORAY!
HIP HIP HOORAY!
HIP HIP HOORAY!
HIP HIP HOORAY!
HIP HIP HOORAY!
HIP HIP HOORAY!
HIP HIP HOORAY!
```

Procedures

You can learn to write text-processing procedures, just as you learned to write graphics procedures. Here's an example to illustrate this possibility. Run it and see what happens.

```
TO GREET
REPEAT 40 [TYPE "HOW]
REPEAT 40 [TYPE "ARE]
REPEAT 40 [TYPE "YOU?]
END
```

Procedures and Superprocedures

By the same token, you can create procedures and then pull them together in a superprocedure. Here's the previous example done differently:

```
TO HOW
REPEAT 40 [TYPE "HOW]
END

TO ARE
REPEAT 40 [TYPE "ARE]
END

TO YOU
REPEAT 40 [TYPE "YOU?]
END

TO GREET
HOW
ARE
YOU
END
```

Just enter GREET to initiate the process.

Some Common Bugs

Omitting quotation mark or brackets. When you want to PRINT or TYPE a single word, you must precede it with a quotation mark ("). Or you can include alphabetical data between brackets. If you enter:

```
PRINT ABC
```

the computer will respond:

```
I DON'T KNOW HOW TO ABC
```

Adding space between quotation mark and word. You'll get the same error message if you put a space between the quotation mark and the word:

```
?PRINT " ABC
I DON'T KNOW HOW TO ABC
?
```

Omitting space preceding quotation mark. Whenever you want to PRINT or TYPE something, don't forget to put a space before and after the command PRINT or TYPE. If you omit the space, the computer will attempt to read the expression as one long word. For example:

```
?PRINT"HELLO
I DON'T KNOW HOW TO PRINT"HELLO
?
```

Exploring Further

1. Experiment with nested REPEATs for printing text materials.
2. Write several procedures that contain paragraphs of a form letter. Then write some superprocedures that will print out different versions of the letter.
3. Write twenty or so lines of poetry (?) as separate procedures (labeled A, B, C, and so on) and then write haphazard poetry with commands like these:

   ```
   Q G E C
   D H R A
   ```

4. Write a graphics procedure that draws a box. Call it GBOX. Then create the following text procedure:

   ```
   TO TBOX
   PR [THIS IS A BOX]
   END
   ```

   Then enter this command:

   ```
   REPEAT 10 [TBOX GBOX]
   ```

Teaching Objectives

- ☐ Students will be able to show ways in which Logo is relevant to words and numbers as well as to graphic designs.
- ☐ Students will grasp and be able to explain the notion of two screens: graphics and text.
- ☐ Students will be able to use PRINT (PR) and TYPE.
- ☐ Students will be able to use CHAR 32.

Teaching Techniques and Materials

Mind-size Bites—Simple to Complex

It is essential in making the shift from graphics to text that, at first, students have an opportunity simply to accommodate to that shift. Be careful not to give too much to them initially, because they will have to shift gears and begin thinking text rather than graphics. To begin, you may want to have them experiment with moving back and forth between the two screens.

Then have them learn the mechanics of PRINT and TYPE. Once they have fully grasped these commands you can suggest that they experiment with REPEATs, procedures, and the other commands explored in this chapter.

Student Exercises

Pencil and Paper Exercises

1. What's wrong with this command?

   ```
   PR HELLO
   ```

2. What's wrong with this command?

   ```
   PR "HOW ARE YOU DOING TODAY?
   ```

3. Complete this command so it will produce the result shown:

   TYPE "HAPPY __________ TYPE "BIRTHDAY

   HAPPY BIRTHDAY

4. Write an instruction that will produce the following result.

   OBOY!OBOY!OBOY!OBOY!OBOY!OBOY!OBOY!OBOY!
   !OBOY!OBOY!OBOY!OBOY!OBOY!OBOY!OBOY!OBO!
   Y!OBOY!OBOY!OBOY!OBOY!OBOY!OBOY!OBOY!OB!
   OY!OBOY!OBOY!OBOY!OBOY!OBOY!OBOY!OBOY!O!
   BOY!OBOY!OBOY!OBOY!OBOY!OBOY!OBOY!OBOY!!

5. Write a text-processing procedure.
6. Write several paragraphs as separate procedures. Then write a superprocedure to print them out.

At the Computer

1. Write a command that will cause the computer to print your full name.
2. Write a command that will cause the computer to print your full name one hundred times on one hundred different lines.
3. Write one instruction with several parts that will cause the computer to write:

   HELLO,
   HOW
   ARE
   YOU?

4. Write a procedure with five TYPE commands that will result in the following:

   HELLO

5. Write a procedure that uses both text and graphics. You might want to write an explanation of some aspect of Logo, for example.

Lesson Plan Elements

- ☐ Two screens: text and graphics.
- ☐ FULLSCREEN CTRL-L | TEXTSCREEN CTRL-T | SPLITSCREEN CTRL-S
- ☐ PRINT (PR) TYPE
- ☐ CHAR 32
- ☐ REPEAT and procedures.

Review of Logo Commands

ABBREVIATION	NAME	EXAMPLE	FUNCTION
CTRL-S	SPLITSCREEN	SPLITSCREEN	Causes most of the video screen to be dedicated to graphics, with the bottom four lines used for text.
CTRL-L	FULLSCREEN	FULLSCREEN	Dedicates the entire screen to graphics.
CTRL-T	TEXTSCREEN	TEXTSCREEN	Dedicates the entire screen to text.
PR	PRINT	PR 23 PR "HELLO PR [ONE TWO]	Prints alphabetical and numerical data and moves to the next line.
	TYPE	TYPE "HELLO TYPE 23 TYPE [ONE TWO]	Same as PRINT *except* it does not move to the next line.
	CHAR 32	TYPE CHAR 32	Inserts a space between alphabetical data.

A Logo Challenge

Write a procedure to produce the following result:

```
ROSES ARE RED,
  VIOLETS ARE BLUE.
LOGO IS DYNAMITE,
  AND SO ARE YOU.
```

Chapter 9

Elementary Calculations

A Powerful Idea

Chapter 8 explained that there are two screens in Logo: one for graphics, the other for text. Although you saw that Logo can print numbers, most of your attention was drawn to alphabetical characters rather than numbers. This chapter will focus on numbers.

At the same time, you'll see that Logo is hardly limited to printing the numbers you enter. In fact, you have a powerful calculator at your fingertips. Now you'll see how it works.

How to Do It

Here are some simple examples to familiarize you with the basic symbols and syntax involved in Logo as a calculator:

```
?PR 3 + 5
8
?PR 5 - 3
2
?PR 3 * 5
15
?PR 5 / 3
1.66667
?
```

Notice that the asterisk (*) is used for multiplication and the slash (/) is used for division.

It is important to recognize the logic of these instructions. If you simply enter 3 + 5, the computer will do the calculation you request. It will respond with an error message, however:

```
I DON'T KNOW WHAT TO DO WITH 8
```

The computer has calculated 5 + 3 as 8, but you haven't told it what to do with the result. The most apparent choice, though not the only one, is to have the result PRINTed or TYPEd. That's why the opening examples all began with PR.

Surely you have not missed the irony involved in the computer giving you what you want in the process of telling you that you haven't told it what to do. If you want, you can simply enter the calculations you want performed without PR or TYPE and get your answers—delivered by an error message. There are arguments on both sides as to how you should proceed in this situation. On the one hand, you should be encouraged to use Logo with elegance, and failing to specify PR in this instance seems somehow clumsy. On the other hand, you might profit a great deal in your interactions with computers if you thumb your nose at what it expects and routinely accept the error message without feeling you've been bad or wrong. Decide what serves you best.

More than one operation can be performed on a single line, as in the following:

```
?PR 123 + 456 + 789 + 123456789
123458157
?PR 2 * 3 * 4 * 5 * 6
720
?
```

As your calculations grow more complex, you will need to be more conscious of their logical structures. Consider the following, for example:

```
4 + 4 / 8
```

There are two possible answers, depending on the order in which you perform the operations. If you *add* first, your answer is 1; it's 4.5 if you *divide* first. Enter the equation into your computer to find out which way *it* performs the operations.

In ambiguous cases such as the one just discussed, the computer performs all multiplications and divisions first; then it performs additions and subtractions. Thus, you should have gotten 4.5 if you solved the problem on your computer.

It is often smart to use parentheses in posing complex problems. The computer will perform all the operations posed within a set of parentheses before using the result of those operations outside the parentheses. As an illustration, enter the following:

```
PR (4 + 4) / 8
```

Consider these two questions at this point. First, do you suppose it is necessary to put spaces between the numbers and operators in requests such as those you have been experimenting with—in other words, would 3+4+5 work as well as 3 + 4 + 5? Try to find out for yourself.

Second, is it necessary to put a space between PR and the rest of your command—would PR3+5 work as well as PR 3+5? Again, the best way to find out is to try it.

Scientific Notation

If you play around with this aspect of Logo long enough, you are certain to create some very large or very small numbers eventually. When you do that, the computer will seem to get a little weird. Here's an example:

```
?PR 99999 * 99999
9.99979E9
```

Right away, you probably have a hunch that the answer here is not just a shade under 10. It's probably quite a lot more than that. A clue to what's going on is found at the right end of the answer: E9. In the computer culture, this is known as **scientific**

notation and it means "move the decimal point 9 places to the right." In other words, the computer's answer is 9999790000.

One purpose of this method of reporting large numbers is to warn you that the answer is approximate. If you think about it a moment, 99999 * 99999 is going to end in 1, certainly not in 0000. Since there is a limit to the precision of the computer's calculations in dealing in such large numbers, the scientific notation warns us that the result is not necessarily precise.

A similar convention operates with very small numbers. Suppose you divide 1 by 10,000:

```
?PR 1 / 10000
1.N4
?
```

As you may have anticipated, this says that the decimal point should be moved four places to the left, producing 0.0001 as the answer. The E notation means the decimal point should be moved to the right, and the N notation means it should be moved to the left.

Advanced Math

Unless you have had a lot of training in mathematics, you might feel somewhat threatened by a section entitled Advanced Math. You can skip this section if you want, but try it and you might find this the most painless experience of math you've ever had. Your computer is prepared to perform all sorts of complex calculations for you.

Square roots, for example, are a breeze. Try these:

```
PR SQRT(16)
PR SQRT(25)
PR SQRT(12345.6789)
```

You might be surprised by the last answer, which is something you are unlikely ever to have learned with pencil and paper.

Logo will also select **random numbers** for you. The following instruction is all it takes.

```
RANDOM 1000
```

This instruction will select at random a number anywhere from 0 through 999. Notice that if you keep entering that instruction, you'll get a different answer each time. This feature may be useful when you set about creating designs later. As a preview of things to come, you might want to enter REPEAT 100 [PR RANDOM 1000].

Illustrations

Placing Circles

As you've seen earlier, Logo draws circles by moving around the circumference with no reference to the center point. This can be a problem in some situations. Suppose you want to draw a set of concentric circles. You might proceed in two steps. First, create a procedure to draw three circles as follows:

```
TO CIRCLES
REPEAT 36 [FD 5 RT 10]
REPEAT 36 [FD 10 RT 10]
REPEAT 36 [FD 15 RT 10]
END
```

Here's what it would create.

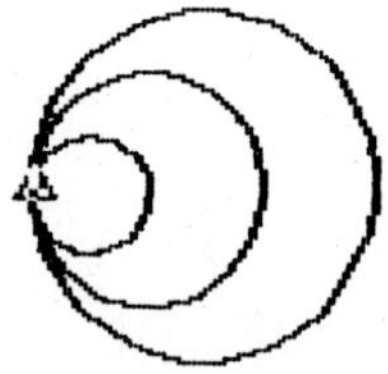

The problem is that the circles are not arranged around a common center. To create concentric circles, you need to find out how to draw a circle of a specified radius around a specified center point.

Begin with the relationship between the radius and the circumference of a circle: the length of the circumference is pi times twice the length of the radius. So, for example, if you want a circle with a radius of 15 the circumference would be:

```
2 * 15 * 3.1416
```

For the circle to be drawn as a 36-sided polygon, each side should be 1/36 of the circumference or (2 * 15 * 3.1416)/36 units long. (3.1416 is an approximation of pi.) To carry out such calculations and measurements by hand would be quite a chore. But see how easy it is with Logo:

```
TO CIRCLE
REPEAT 36 [FD (2 * 15 * 3.1416) / 36 RT 10]
END
```

To draw the circle around the turtle's original location, simply add these two lines, which move the turtle to the circumference of the circle and back to the center after the circle is drawn.

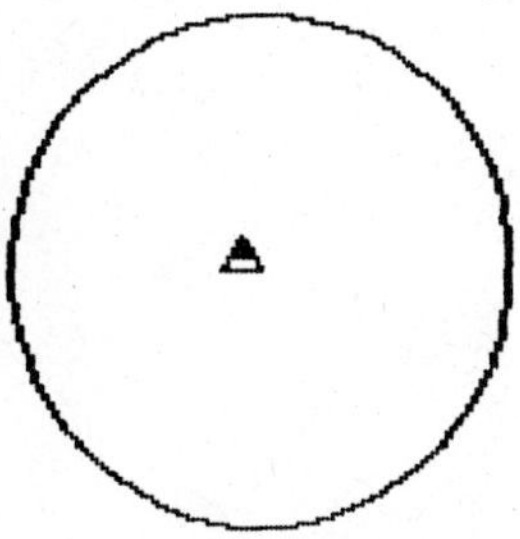

```
TO CIRCLE
PU FD 15 RT 90 PD
REPEAT 36 [FD (2 * 15 * 3.1416) / 36 RT 10]
PU RT 90 FD 15 RT 180 PD
END
```

Now you can add instructions to the procedure to create two more circles.

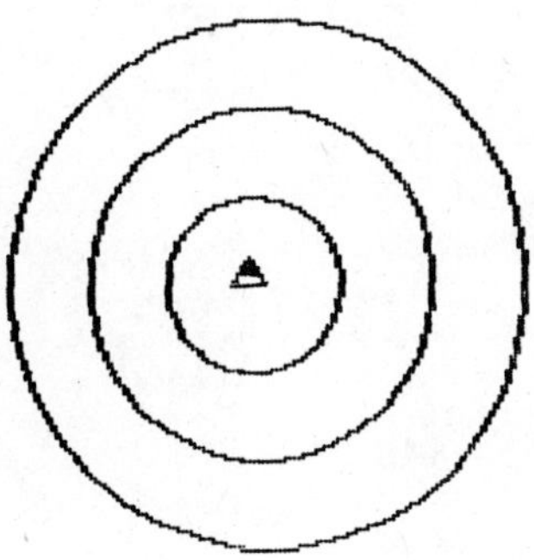

```
TO CIRCLES
PU FD 15 RT 90 PD
REPEAT 36 [FD (2 * 15 * 3.1416) / 36 RT 10]
PU RT 90 FD 15 RT 180 PD
PU FD 30 RT 90 PD
REPEAT 36 [FD (2 * 30 * 3.1416) / 36 RT 10]
PU RT 90 FD 30 RT 180 PD
PU FD 45 RT 90 PD
REPEAT 36 [FD (2 * 45 * 3.1416) / 36 RT 10]
PU RT 90 FD 45 RT 180 PD
END
```

Random Movements

Any time you get tired of making up designs for the computer to run, you can turn that task over to the computer itself. Try this, for example:

```
REPEAT 100 [FD RANDOM 100 RT RANDOM 360]
```

Enter that instruction and the result will probably look something like this figure.

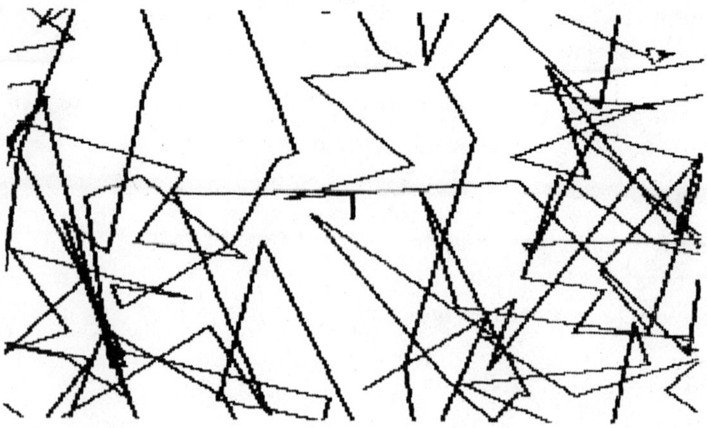

Of course, yours will not look exactly like this, because the computer is selecting distances to move FD and angles to turn RIGHT at random. To demonstrate this fully, create the instruction as a procedure and then repeat the procedure several times.

```
TO RANDY
REPEAT 100 [FD RANDOM 100 RT RANDOM 360]
END

REPEAT 25 [CS RANDY]
```

Some Common Bugs

Trying to divide by zero. You can't do this. If you try it, the computer will draw your attention to that fact.

```
?PR 1 / 0
CAN'T DIVIDE BY ZERO
?
```

That's pretty much to the point.

Using incomplete equations. Logo handles different incomplete calculation requests in various ways. Here are some examples.

```
?PR 3 + 4 +
7
?PR 4 - 3 -
NOT ENOUGH INPUTS TO -
?PR 5 * 3 *
15
?PR / 3
NOT ENOUGH INPUTS TO /
?
```

Forgetting parentheses. In complex equations, Logo may perform operations in a different order than you intended if you have used parentheses improperly. Suppose you wanted to calculate the average of three numbers: 10, 20, and 30. The answer is obviously 20, but look at this interaction with Logo:

```
?PR 10 + 20 + 30 / 3
40.
?
```

Clearly, the computer has first divided 30 by 3 and then added the resulting 10 to the other two numbers. Here's the correct format.

```
?PR (10 + 20 + 30) / 3
20.
?
```

Exploring Further

1. Use REPEAT to make variations on the CIRCLE procedure created earlier in the chapter. Try these first.

   ```
   REPEAT 4 [CIRCLE]
   REPEAT 18 [LT 20 CIRCLE]
   ```

2. Modify CIRCLE so it will draw arcs in reference to a particular point.
3. Experiment with this:

   ```
   REPEAT 100 [FD RANDOM 100 RT 90]
   ```

Teaching Objectives

☐ Students will be able to use the fundamental mathematical functions + − * / and they will:

Use notations correctly.

Use parentheses so that operations will be performed in the right order.

Print out the results.

☐ Students will be able to select RANDOM numbers.

Teaching Techniques and Materials

Concrete Learning

If you want to teach the concept of RANDOMness, you might want to relate the Logo function to other random operations such as flipping a coin or rolling dice. As one example, you could have students flip a coin one hundred times, counting the number of heads and tails. Then replicate the process in Logo as follows:

```
REPEAT 100 [TYPE RANDOM 2]
```

Notice that RANDOM 2 produces 0s and 1s. You can call the 1s "heads" and the 0s "tails" (or the other way around, if you want). The point is to show that both methods select about half heads and half tails.

In a more elegant demonstration, you can write a procedure to simulate rolling a pair of dice. Here's the statement that rolls one die:

```
1 + RANDOM 6
```

Remember that the instruction RANDOM 6 selects from among the numbers 0 through 5. Adding 1 changes this range to the numbers 1 through 6. Here's the procedure that simulates the roll of two dice:

```
TO DICE
TYPE (1 + RANDOM 6) + (1 + RANDOM 6)
END
```

Enter this procedure and run it a few times to see that it works. Then you'll be ready to run an experiment with your students. First, have them organize to roll a pair of dice one hundred times. If there are ten students, have each student roll the dice ten times and record the results. If there are twenty students, they can each roll the dice five times, or they can form teams of two and roll the dice ten times per team: other variations can be used. Ultimately, you want a record of the number of 2s, 3s, 4s, and so on.

You can simulate the process using Logo as follows:

```
REPEAT 100 [DICE TYPE CHAR 32]
```

These exercises should help students understand RANDOMness in a concrete form.

Mind-size Bites

It's important to introduce Logo's mathematical capabilities in mind-size bites. Show students how to add, subtract, multiply, and divide *pairs* of numbers first. Then you can expand to include several numbers in a single equation.

As your calculations get more complex, you can use parentheses to achieve the goal of mind-size bites. Encourage students to break complex calculations into smaller components, enclosing the components within parentheses.

Student Exercises

Pencil and Paper Exercises

1. What will be the computer's answer to this problem?

```
PR 5 + 5 / 10
```

2. What will be the computer's answer to this problem?

```
PR 2 + 4 * 2 + 6
```

3. What will be the computer's answer to this problem?

```
PR (2 + 3) * (4 + 5)
```

4. Write a Logo instruction that will calculate the mean (average) of these numbers: 4, 5, 6, and 7.

At the Computer

1. Solve the following mathematical problems using Logo:
   a. 2 × 3 × 4
   b. 100 ÷ 25
   c. 10 × 10 ÷ 20
2. Using a single Logo instruction, multiply 5 times 6, subtract 7, add 2, and then take the square root of the result.
3. Add parentheses to the instruction shown below so that it will yield 7 as the answer.

```
PR 8 + 6 / 2
```

4. Use Logo to select ten random numbers among the numbers 1 through 100.

Lesson Plan Elements

- ☐ The fundamental mathematical operations: + − * /
- ☐ SQRT
- ☐ RANDOM

Review of Logo Commands

NAME	EXAMPLE	FUNCTION
+	2 + 5	Addition.
−	7 − 2	Subtraction.
*	3 * 3	Multiplication.
/	49 / 7	Division.
SQRT	SQRT(4)	Finding the square root.
RANDOM	RANDOM 10	Selecting random numbers, in this case among the numbers 0 through 9.

A Logo Challenge

Write a procedure that will print out the following multiplication table.

$3 \times 1 = 3$
$3 \times 2 = 6$
$3 \times 3 = 9$
$3 \times 4 = 12$
$3 \times 5 = 15$
$3 \times 6 = 18$
$3 \times 7 = 21$
$3 \times 8 = 24$
$3 \times 9 = 27$
$3 \times 10 = 30$
$3 \times 11 = 33$
$3 \times 12 = 36$

Chapter 10

Variables

A Powerful Idea

Thus far in exploring Logo, you have used both numerical and alphabetical values to make the computer perform a variety of tricks. Thus, you have learned to say FD 100, with the 100 specifying how far the turtle should move; REPEAT 4 tells the turtle to perform a particular operation four times. Similarly, PR [HOW ARE YOU] specifies exactly what you want printed.

In this chapter, you will discover that it is possible to manipulate numerical and alphabetical values as **variables.** You are going to create variables, giving them names and assigning values to them; thus, when you subsequently use the names, the computer will know the values you want it to use. In part, this is merely a convenience. Often you will want to use the same complex number or set of numbers again and again. It's much easier to use a short variable name each time rather than entering everything that name stands for. Yet like so many other features of Logo examined in the book, this one turns out to be very powerful indeed. The ability to create variables opens up many other possibilities, which are examined in this chapter.

How to Do It

Creating PI

In Chapter 9, you saw some uses you could make of the value of pi in creating circles and arcs. If you experimented with those possibilities, you may have become a little tired of entering the value of pi each time you wanted to use it. And unless you are generally familiar with pi, you may have had to look up its value each time. Here's a simple solution to that problem:

```
?MAKE "PI 3.1416
?PR :PI
3.1416
?
```

In the first line a variable, PI, was created and assigned the value of 3.1416. There are three elements in this operation: (1) The word MAKE informs the computer that you are about to assign a value to a variable; (2) the variable is then named, with that name preceded by a quotation mark; and (3) the name of the variable is followed by the value being assigned to it. All three of these elements are necessary.

The second line asked the computer to PRINT the value assigned to the variable. Notice that the name of the variable is now preceded by a colon (:) instead of the quotation mark. It is important to remember this critical shift. The name of a variable must be preceded by the quotation mark when it is being created, and must be preceded by a colon whenever the value is retrieved subsequently.

Once you have created this variable, you can use it in all the ways as the numerical value. Here are some legitimate uses of PI. Try them to see what happens.

```
PR 3 * : PI
PR SQRT(: PI)
FD PI RT 10 * :PI
```

Now if you want to calculate the circumference of a circle (two times the radius times pi) with a radius of 7.4, you merely enter:

```
PR 2 * 7.4 * :PI
```

The computer responds with the circumference: 46.4955.

Moving a step further, if you want to use the circumference of a circle in other calculations, you could define the circumference as follows:

```
MAKE "CIRCUM 7.4 * 2 * :PI
```

Now, the variable :CIRCUM has been assigned the value 46.4955, and it can be used in further calculations.

Numerical Strings

You can also create variables and assign them a string of values instead of only one. Here's an example of how to do that:

```
?MAKE "NUMS [74 19 123 456 0]
?PR :NUMS
74 19 123 456 0
?
```

Notice that brackets are used here to enclose the set of numbers being assigned to the variable. Don't forget: you precede a variable name with a quotation mark when assigning its values and with a colon when retrieving its values.

FIRST and LAST

Often, you will be especially interested in the first or last items in a string such as the one just created. The uses for this will become more evident soon. For now, you can learn how to retrieve those values. What could be simpler than this:

```
?PR FIRST :NUMS
74
?PR LAST :NUMS
0
?
```

Among other things, this allows the use of specific numbers in the string for calculations. Here's an example:

```
?PR :PI * FIRST :NUMS
232.478
?PR :PI * LAST :NUMS
0
?
```

The first instruction above tells the computer to retrieve the FIRST number in :NUMS, multiply it times PI, and then PRINT the result. The second instruction asks for the same operation, using the LAST number in :NUMS.

ITEM

Sometimes you want other values in the string. Let's say you want to see the second number in :NUMS. Here's how you could retrieve it.

```
?PR ITEM 2 :NUMS
19
?
```

As you will see later in the chapter, this can be a very powerful command.

Alphabetical Variables

Variables can be assigned letters and words as easily as numbers. Consider these possibilities:

```
?MAKE "NAME "EARL
?PR :NAME
EARL
?
```

```
?MAKE "NAME [EARL]
?PR :NAME
EARL
?
```

There are two ways to assign a single-word value to a variable name. In both cases, the name of the variable is preceded by a quotation mark—for example: "NAME. In the first example, another quotation mark is used to indicate the value (EARL) being assigned to the variable. As an alternative, the value can be specified within a set of brackets, as illustrated in the second example.

As in the case of numerical data, a list of words can be assigned to a variable name, using brackets to indicate the list of values:

```
?MAKE "PHRASE [THE QUICK RED FOX]
?PR :PHRASE
THE QUICK RED FOX
?
```

The commands FIRST, LAST, and ITEM work with alphabetical variables as well as with numerical ones. You can experiment with them now if you like, but these capabilities will be examined more fully in Chapters 17 and 18.

File Management for Variables

When you create a variable and assign it a value—for example, MAKE "NUM [5 10 15 20 25]—you have written it into the workspace. When you give a command using an assigned variable—such as PRINT [ITEM 2 :NUM] * 2—or run a procedure that calls for such variables, Logo searches through the workspace, looking for the variable name. When you SAVE the workspace, the variables are saved right alongside the procedures.

Here are some commands that will get you a listing of the names and values of variables in your workspace:

- ☐ PONS gets a listing of all variables in the workspace.
- ☐ ERN "HSE erases the name and value that were assigned to the variable HSE.
- ☐ ERN [HSE NM] erases both of the variables specified.

For the most comprehensive listing, simply entering POALL will produce a detailed listing of all procedures and variables in the workspace.

Illustrations

Here's a look at some of the ways you can employ the techniques just introduced and some extensions on what you have already seen.

Making Variables from Other Variables

In the discussion of PI and CIRCUM, you saw that it is possible to use one variable in defining another. Here's another example.

```
?MAKE "X [1 2 3 4 5 6 7 8 9]
?MAKE "Y FIRST :X
?PR :Y
1
?
```

Incrementing ITEM

Changing the values of variables is a commonly used and powerful technique in computer programming, and it can be used to great advantage in Logo. In particular, it is often useful to increase the value of some variable in a regular manner. Here's a simple illustration of how to change the value of a variable:

```
?MAKE "X 1
?PR :X
1
?MAKE "X :X + 1
?PR :X
2
?
```

The first three lines in this illustration should be familiar to you now. The first assigns the value of 1 to the variable, the second line requests the PRINTing of the value, and the third line is the computer's response. The fourth line is the critical one. It tells the computer to MAKE "X and specify as its new value *the old value plus one,* or :X + 1. Once this has been accomplished, the value of :X is 2.

Using REPEAT

Incrementing of values of a variable is often accomplished through the use of REPEAT. Here's a simple procedure and the result it will produce:

```
?TO NUMBER
>MAKE "X 1
>REPEAT 20 [PR :X MAKE "X :X + 1]
>END
NUMBER DEFINED
?NUMBER
1
2
3
4
5
6
7
8
9
10
11
12
13
14
15
16
17
18
19
20
?
```

Take a few minutes to study this procedure and understand how it works. Once you feel you understand it, answer this question: What is the value of :X now? When you have an answer, check it by entering PR :X.

Walking Through a List of Values

Here's a practical use of the techniques just developed. Recall the earlier string of values for :NUMS—[74 19 123 456 0]. Assume you want to multiply each of these values times PI. Here are two commands that will get the job done, either entered directly, as shown here, or as a procedure.

```
?MAKE "IT 1
?REPEAT 5 [PR :PI * ITEM :IT :NUMS MAKE "IT :IT + 1]
232.478
59.6902
386.416
1432.56
0.
```

Some Common Bugs

Forgetting the quotation mark. When you create a variable name and assign it a value, you must precede the name with a quotation mark. If you fail to do that, the computer will attempt to perform the name as though it were a procedure, probably with this result:

```
?MAKE PI
I DON'T KNOW HOW TO PI
```

Forgetting the colon. When you retrieve the value of a variable, you must precede the name with a colon. Failing to do this has the same effect as just described.

```
?PR PI
I DON'T KNOW HOW TO PI
```

Mixing up the quotation mark and the colon. The switch from quote to colon, which differentiates the creation of a variable from its use, will probably be the source of a few errors in your use of Logo. Either you will try to create a variable using the colon or you'll try to use a variable with the quotation mark. These two errors generate different error messages, however, as shown here:

```
?MAKE :NAME 5
NAME HAS NO VALUE
?
```

(If :NAME *does* have a value, the computer does nothing.)

```
?PR "NAME
NAME
?
```

Forgetting brackets in assigning strings. When you assign a string of values to a variable, you must enclose those values inside a set of brackets. Examine this interaction:

```
?MAKE "NUMS 1 2 3 4 5
I DON'T KNOW WHAT TO DO WITH 2
?PR :NUMS
1
```

As you can see, the computer has created the variable requested, but it only assigned the value 1 to it. When it arrived at the second value, it regarded it as part of a new instruction and didn't know what was wanted.

Trying to operate on a string. While you can perform calculations with the individual values of a string, you cannot calculate with the whole thing at once. Here's an example of what this means:

```
?MAKE "NUMS [1 2 3]
?PR SQRT(:NUMS)
SQRT DOESN'T LIKE [1 2 3] AS INPUT
?
```

To solve this problem, you need to select individual values (with FIRST, LAST, or ITEM) and perform the calculations on each value separately.

Using too large an ITEM. :NUMS, as just defined, has three values: 1, 2, and 3. If you asked for the *fourth* value, the computer would respond as follows:

```
?PR ITEM 4 :NUMS
TOO FEW ITEMS IN [1 2 3]
?
```

Exploring Further

1. Create a variable named :RAND and have the computer assign it a random number as its value.
2. Write a procedure, using variables, that simulates the roll of a set of dice and reports like this:

   YOU HAVE ROLLED A 6 AND A 3 FOR A TOTAL OF 9

3. Write a procedure that creates a variable containing three names and then lists them on separate lines.
4. Create a procedure using variables to produce the following:

   1
   2
   4
   8
   16
   32
   64

5. Write a procedure that selects five random numbers and prints their square roots.

Teaching Objectives

- ☐ Students will learn how to create numeric and alphabetical variables using MAKE.
- ☐ Students will learn how to use FIRST, LAST, and ITEM.
- ☐ Students will learn to use ERN, ERNS, PONS, and POALL.
- ☐ The more advanced students will learn to increment an index by using REPEAT.

Teaching Techniques and Materials

Concrete Learning

Students who have had no algebra may have some initial trouble understanding the basic logic of names representing numbers and text. Here's a way you might introduce them to that notion.

Write the letter A on one side of an index card and the number 1 on the other side. On another card, write the letter B on one side and the number 2 on the other side. Mark eight more cards in a similar fashion, using the letters C through J and the numbers 3 through 10.

Now spread the cards out on a table with the letters facing up. Tell the students that each card has a number on the bottom. Separate two cards from the rest and ask students to guess what the sum of the two hidden numbers are. After they've guessed, turn the cards over so they can see the numbers and calculate the sum.

Turn the first two cards over again so their letters are facing up. Repeat the process with two different cards. Then try it with two cards they have seen previously. The point is for them to begin remembering the numerical values associated with the letters. Eventually someone will recognize the pattern associating the numbers and letters.

Once they get comfortable with this use of letters to represent numbers, tell them that they can assign names to numbers in Logo, showing them the instructions required to assign and retrieve values and pointing out that the names of variables can be longer than single letters. It might be useful to have the students create some index cards of their own to remind them of the Logo syntax. For example, one such card might have `:NUM` on one side and `MAKE "NUM 23` on the other side. Filling out cards like these will give them practice with the notations for assigning and retrieving values. Also, they can probably think up games of their own that will use the cards.

Once students have become comfortable with assigning numerical values to variable names, show them how alphabetical values can be assigned. Start with single words, and then move to multiple-word assignments. Again, it might be useful to create cards, as described.

Mind-size Bites—Simple to Complex

Begin with the simplest of variable assignments. Then combine those simple examples to form something more complex. Here's an example of a useful progression:

```
?MAKE "X 10
?PR :X
10
?MAKE "Y 5
?PR :Y
5
?PR :X + :Y
15
?MAKE "Z :X + :Y
?PR :Z
15
?
```

Once students are comfortable with this, introduce them to the use of variables in connection with REPEAT. Then show them how to increment the values of a given variable, causing the REPEATed instruction to operate on a different number each time.

Student Exercises

Pencil and Paper Exercises

1. Complete these instructions:
   a. MAKE _______NUM 10
   b. ___________ "NAMES [SAM MARY JANE]
   c. PR _______NAMES

2. What's wrong with these instructions?
   a. PR "X + "Y
   b. MAKE "NAMES "JOE PAT JAN
   c. MAKE :X 23
3. Write an instruction to assign your first and last names to the variable :NAME. Then write the instruction using the variable that will cause the computer to print only your first name. Then write the instruction that will cause it to print your last name.
4. Assume you had entered this instruction:

   MAKE "COLORS [RED BLUE GREEN YELLOW PURPLE]

   What would the computer do in response to these instructions?
   a. PR FIRST :COLORS
   b. PR LAST :COLORS
   c. PR ITEM 3 :COLORS
   d. TYPE ITEM 2 :COLORS TYPE ITEM 4 :COLORS
5. What would the computer respond if you entered these instructions?

   ```
   MAKE "NUMS [2 4 6]
   PR (FIRST :NUMS) * (ITEM 2 :NUMS)
   ```

At the Computer

1. Create a variable named HOUSE that contains a list of five parts of a house.
2. Write a procedure—*without* using REPEAT—that will print a list of the five parts of HOUSE.
3. Now write a procedure—using REPEAT—to print the list of parts of HOUSE.
4. List all the variables in your workspace.
5. Erase :HOUSE and list your variables again to verify that it's gone.

Lesson Plan Elements

- ☐ MAKE
- ☐ FIRST LAST ITEM
- ☐ Incrementing an index.
- ☐ PONS ERN POALL

Review of Logo Commands

NAME	EXAMPLE	FUNCTION
MAKE	MAKE "NUM 5 MAKE "NUMS [1 2 3 4 5] MAKE "NAME "HARRY MAKE "GREETING [HI! HOW ARE YOU?]	Declares a variable name and assigns one or more values to it.
FIRST	PR FIRST :M	Specifies the FIRST item in a list.
LAST	PR LAST :M	Specifies the LAST item in a list.
ITEM	PR ITEM 2 :M	Specifies a particular item in a list (in this case, the second item).
PONS	PONS	Prints the names and values of all variables in the workspace.
ERN	ERN "M ERN [NUM HOUSE M]	Erases the specified variables from the workspace.
ERNS	ERNS	Erases all the variables in the workspace.
POALL	POALL	Lists all the procedures and variables in the workspace.

A Logo Challenge

Write a procedure that creates :X as [ONE TWO THREE] and then uses :X in a REPEAT instruction to print:

```
THREE TWO ONE
```

Chapter 11

Procedures with Inputs

A Powerful Idea

No matter how good you've gotten in the creation of Logo procedures, you will still find a fundamental difference between those procedures and Logo primitives such as FORWARD and RIGHT. FORWARD and RIGHT allow you to specify how much the turtle should move or turn, but your procedures are all more static.

The BOX procedure, for example, draws only one size figure, even though you can modify the procedure to draw other sizes and you can write several similar procedures—BOX20, BOX30, BOX50, and so on—to produce boxes of different sizes. Wouldn't it be much better if you could write only one BOX program for all sizes and specify the size you want at the time you use it? You can.

How to Do It

One Input

Here's a modification of an old favorite, adjusted to take the desired size of the BOX as an input.

```
TO BOX :SIZE
REPEAT 4 [FD :SIZE RT 90]
END
```

This differs from the earlier version of BOX in two ways. First, notice :SIZE has been added to the title of the procedure. This tells the computer to expect an input to accompany BOX and instructs it to call that input :SIZE. You could name the input whatever you want, but it must begin with a colon.

Notice that in second line of the program the turtle is instructed to move :SIZE units forward. Why don't you EDIT your BOX procedure now, and then try different inputs to draw these boxes:

BOX 30

BOX 50

BOX 100

Recall now that you also created a procedure labeled BOXES, which created a windowlike design by repeating and rotating BOX. Since BOX now requires an input, BOXES needs to be revised slightly, as follows:

```
TO BOXES :SIZE
REPEAT 4 [BOX :SIZE RT 90]
END
```

You do not need to use the same name (:SIZE) in both programs, but it's probably less confusing that way. Once you've modified BOXES, why don't you try it out using different inputs.

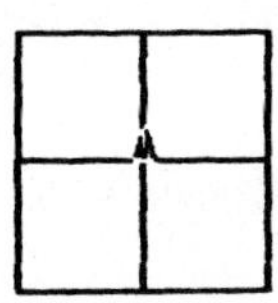

BOXES 50

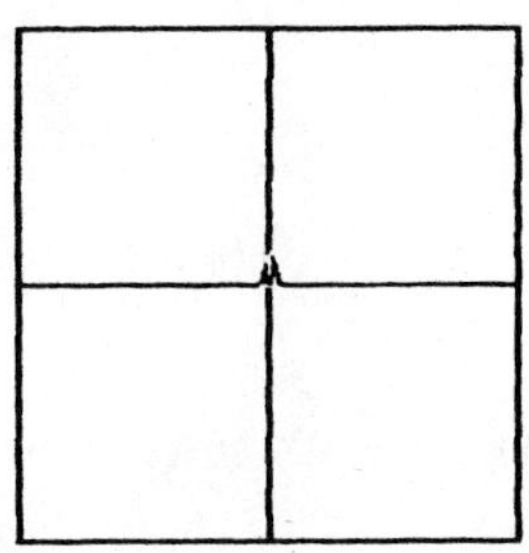

BOXES 100

Take some time now to modify some of your earlier procedures so that they take inputs. You might revise your TRIANGLE procedure, for example.

Two or More Inputs

Procedures can also be designed to expect more than one input. You'll recall from Chapter 4 that any polygon can be created using Logo. Now you can create a procedure that asks you to specify the number of sides of the polygon and also the length of a given side. Here's how:

```
TO POLY :SIDES :SIZE
REPEAT :SIDES [FD :SIZE RT 360/:SIDES]
END
```

Now try it out. For example:

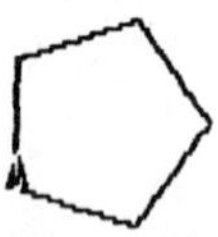

POLY 5 50

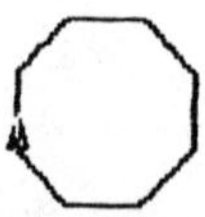

POLY 8 30

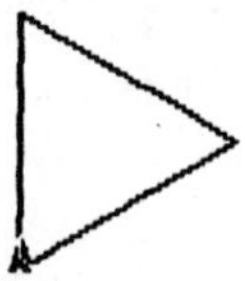

POLY 3 100

You can also create procedures that take more than two inputs. Your imagination is the only limit.

Writing New Procedures

Thus far, only revising old procedures by adding inputs on the title line and as appropriate elsewhere in the instructions has been considered. If you were to write a procedure with inputs from scratch, you could initiate it like this:

```
?TO POLY :SIDES :SIZE
```

or like this:

```
?TO POLY "SIDES "SIZE
```

or even this:

```
?TO POLY SIDES SIZE
```

In a rare tolerance for ambiguity, Logo lets you specify the inputs preceded by colons, by quotes, or by nothing at all. In each case it will begin each input with a colon in the title line of the program. However, you *must* use colons in input names elsewhere in the procedure.

Illustrations

Piling up Boxes

When you were asked to try different inputs for BOXES, you probably cleared the screen each time so the different designs wouldn't conflict with one another. That's usually a good idea, but this time you might also want to break the rule. For example:

```
BOXES 30
BOXES 40
BOXES 50
BOXES 60
BOXES 70
```

Better yet, why don't you write a procedure to superimpose BOXES 10 through BOXES 100 on one another. Here's what you'll get if you do.

Rotating BOXES

Here's a way to expand on MOREBOXES. Why not rotate the design each time before increasing the size? You can do it many ways; this is one of them. The results of a couple experiments with this procedure are shown here.

```
TO ROTABOXES :SIZE :TURNS
REPEAT :TURNS [BOXES :SIZE RT 360 / :TURNS
       MAKE "SIZE 10 + :SIZE]
END
```

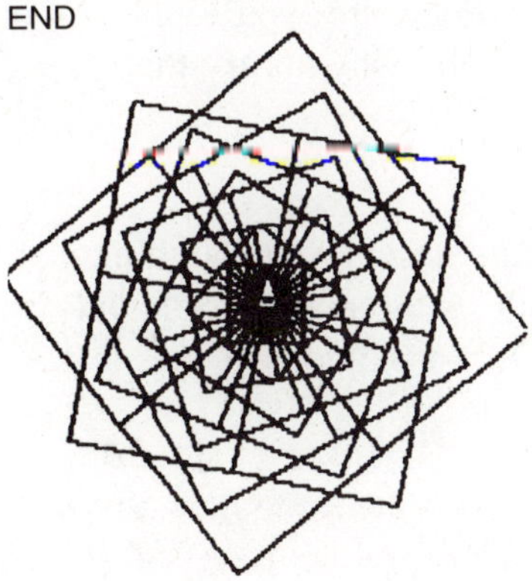

ROTABOXES 20 9

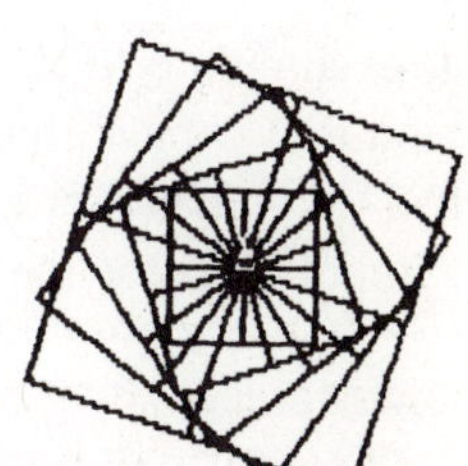

ROTABOXES 30 5

Playing with POLY

You might want to experiment with POLY along the same lines as with BOXES. Here are a few procedures to get you started, but you should be able to devise other experiments.

```
TO MOREPOLY :SIDES :SIZE
REPEAT 8 [POLY :SIDES :SIZE MAKE "SIZE 10 + :SIZE]
END
```

MOREPOLY 3 5

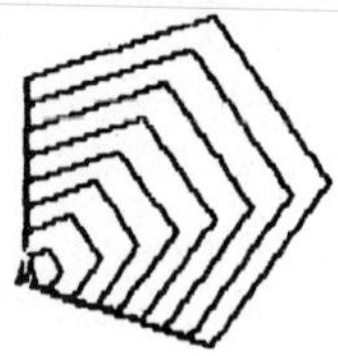

MOREPOLY 5 10

```
TO ROTAPOLY :SIDES :SIZE :TURNS
REPEAT :TURNS [POLY :SIDES :SIZE RT 360 / :TURNS
      MAKE "SIZE 10 + :SIZE]
END
```

ROTAPOLY 3 30 36

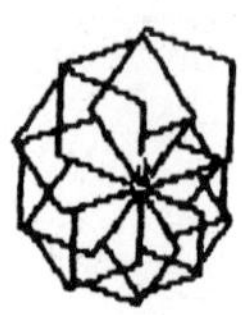

ROTAPOLY 5 20 10

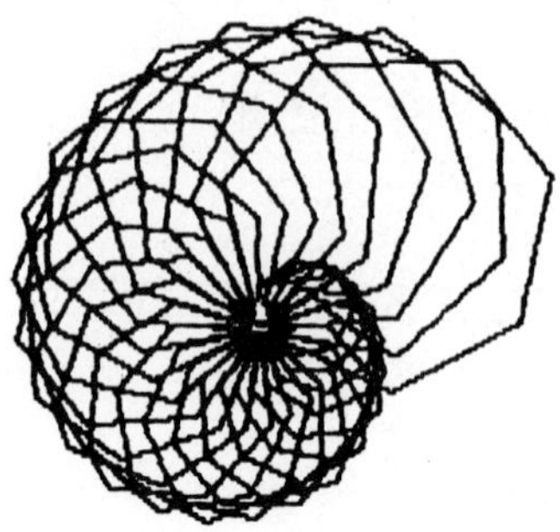

ROTAPOLY 7 20 25

Remember, you can use any of the procedures you've created in direct commands to Logo. For example, why not try this:

```
REPEAT 36 [POLY 3 80 RT 10].
```

Take a minute to look at the resulting design. Do you think you would ever have figured out how this was created if you only had the finished product? It looks like a religious or mystical symbol. (Maybe the Aztecs had Logo.)

Some Common Bugs

Colons and quotes. By now you will have discovered that any time you need to precede a name by either a colon or a quotation mark you have another opportunity to use the wrong one. You have already seen that Logo is quite tolerant about how you specify inputs on the title line of a procedure. It's not so tolerant otherwise. If you neglect the colon in an input name in the body of the procedure, the computer will respond in ways you have already seen earlier in the book. Thus, if you say FD SIZE, the computer will probably try to treat SIZE like a procedure, reporting:

```
I DON'T KNOW HOW TO SIZE
```

Not providing enough inputs. Once you've created a procedure properly, you may make errors in using it. You'll recall that POLY requires two inputs: SIDES and SIZE. Here's a common interaction:

```
?POLY 5
NOT ENOUGH INPUTS TO POLY
```

Providing too many inputs. If, on the other hand, you are overly generous with inputs, the computer will usually be able to carry out the procedure and then complain about the excess. If you entered POLY 5 50 5, for example, the computer would draw a pentagon with fifty-unit sides and then say

```
I DON'T KNOW WHAT TO DO WITH 5
```

Omitting inputs for subprocedures. Whenever you nest procedures that require inputs, there seems to be a better than even chance that you'll neglect to specify the input in calling up a subprocedure. The *incorrect* version of BOXES below illustrates this error.

```
TO BOXES :SIZE
REPEAT 4 [BOX RT 90]
END
```

If you run this version of BOXES, you'll get the following message from your silicon friend:

```
RIGHT DIDN'T OUTPUT TO BOX
JUST BEFORE LEAVING BOXES
```

Here, the computer is telling you that it needed an input for BOX, but RT didn't provide (OUTPUT) one. Thus, the computer folded up its tent and left BOXES.

Exploring Further

1. Review the procedures you have written previously and see which ones could be made more elegant if you converted them to take inputs.
2. Write a procedure that allows you to create these designs from the commands you've learned so far.

STAR 100 0

STAR 150 18

STAR 50 60

3. Revise the following procedure so it will function as shown in the illustration.

```
TO CIRCLE :SIZE :STEPS
REPEAT :SIZE [FD (4* :SIZE) / :STEPS RT 360 / :STEPS]
END
```

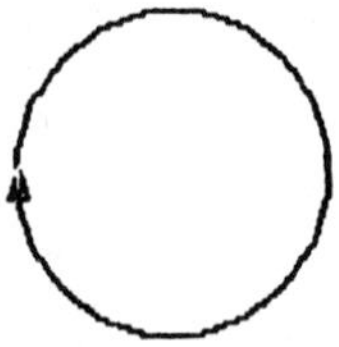
CIRCLE 100 20

Teaching Objectives

- ☐ Students will be able to modify a previously created procedure to take an input.
- ☐ Students will be able to create new procedures that take inputs.
- ☐ Students will be able to create procedures that require multiple inputs.
- ☐ Students will be able to understand error messages pertaining to inputs and make the necessary corrections.

Teaching Techniques and Materials

Concrete Learning

Piaget maintained that children learn abstract concepts best when they can relate those concepts to elements in their concrete reality. Papert has stressed the importance of computers as part of children's reality. Here's where you can take advantage of these two theoretical points.

By now, your students should be pretty comfortable with the fundamental Logo commands such as FORWARD and BACK. Because BACK is now a part of their concrete reality, your students might grasp the nature of inputs by creating a procedure that simulates BACK:

```
TO BAQ :DIST
RT 180 FD :DIST RT 180
END
```

BAQ produces the same result as BACK, although it does so somewhat differently. If your students play around with BACK and BAQ for awhile, they will see that the turtle spins around in the process of BAQ whereas it keeps facing in the same direction throughout an execution of BACK. Nonetheless, this simulation will be just what it takes for some of your students to grasp the logic and the potential of inputs.

Mind-size Bites—Simple to Complex

There's a fairly simple progression to follow in presenting inputs to students. Begin by drawing their attention to the role inputs play in Logo primitives such as FORWARD and RIGHT. Then show them how to modify a simple procedure like BOX so it will take an input.

Next, have them think of a new procedure that could profit from taking an input. As with all the other commands in Logo, the mastery of a command includes knowing when it would be useful. Once they have envisioned the new procedure, have them create and debug it. Probably they will then want to expand on it.

Once they have mastered procedures with single inputs, have them experiment with multiple inputs.

Student Exercises

Pencil and Paper Exercises

1. Revise this procedure so that it takes an input that specifies the size of the design.

```
TO BOX
REPEAT 4 [FD 50 RT 90]
END
```

2. Complete this procedure so that it will take an input to specify the number of sides of a polygon.

```
TO POLY :SIDES
REPEAT ______ [FD 50 RT __________]
END
```

3. What's wrong with this procedure?

```
TO STAR :SIZE
REPEAT 5 [FD SIZE RT 144]
END
```

4. Suppose there were no LEFT in Logo. Write a procedure using RT that would do the job of LEFT.
5. Write a procedure that requires two inputs.

At the Computer

1. Write a procedure that behaves like this:

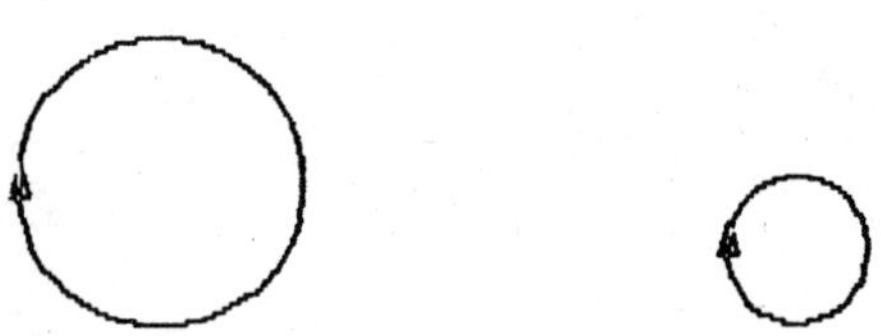

CIRCLE 10 CIRCLE 5

2. Write a procedure that behaves like this:

STAIRS 5

STAIRS 15

3. Enter this procedure and run it as indicated. Then find the bug in the procedure and correct it.

```
TO DESIGN :X
REPEAT :Y [FD :X RT 360 / :Y]
END

DESIGN 50 5
```

4. Enter this procedure and run it as indicated. Then find the bug in the procedure and correct it.

```
TO DESIGN :X :Y
REPEAT :X [FD 50 RT Y]
END

DESIGN 5 50
```

Lesson Plan Elements

- ☐ Using procedures that require inputs.
- ☐ Writing new procedures that require inputs.
- ☐ Modifying old procedures so that they require inputs.

A Logo Challenge

Write a procedure using three inputs that behaves like this:

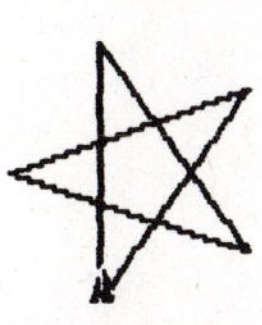

DESIGN 5 100 144

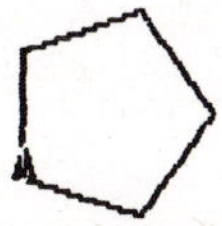

DESIGN 5 50 72

DESIGN 5 10 36

Chapter 12

Outputs from Procedures

A Powerful Idea

You have discovered that some Logo primitives require inputs and that you can write procedures with this same quality. Now you are going to focus on another quality of some primitives: **outputs.** SQRT is a good example.

If you enter SQRT 256 as a Logo command, the computer will respond:

```
I DON'T KNOW WHAT TO DO WITH 16.
```

This is because SQRT merely computes the square root; it doesn't specify what is to be done with the result. Thus, you should enter PR SQRT 16, indicating that you want the result PRinted. While this might seem inconvenient to you, it has a positive side as well.

Since SQRT merely computes a square root, you can use the result of that computation in other computations. Here's an example:

```
?PR (SQRT 1 + SQRT 4 + SQRT 9)
6
?
```

In this chapter you are going to learn how to write procedures having that property.

How to Do It

To start out, here is a fairly straightforward procedure—one that multiplies two numbers times each other. Take a minute to examine this procedure and figure out what it will do when run.

```
TO MULTIPLY :X :Y
PR :X * :Y
END
```

Once you have an idea what MULTIPLY will do, enter it and try it out. Here are some possibilities for testing it.

```
?MULTIPLY 3 4
12
?MULTIPLY 33 5
165
?MULTIPLY 8 (5/4)
10
?
```

Notice that MULTIPLY prints out the results of its calculations, as instructed. Now, consider this slight revision of the procedure:

```
TO MULTIPLY :X :Y
OUTPUT :X * :Y
END
```

If you try to run this new procedure—for example, MULTIPLY 4 5—Logo will respond with I DON'T KNOW WHAT TO DO WITH 20. Although the procedure has calculated the result, you have not told it what to do with the result. One way out is the following:

```
?PR MULTIPLY 4 5
20
?
```

Now the procedure prints out the result without protest. As discussed in regard to SQRT, this new version of MULTIPLY permits instructions such as these:

```
?PR 5 + MULTIPLY 4 5
25
?PR MULTIPLY (MULTIPLY 4 5) 7
140
?
```

As soon as the computer encounters an OUTPUT instruction in a procedure, it will execute the OUTPUT instruction—exiting the procedure in the process. This means that any instructions that appear following the OUTPUT command will be ignored.

Illustrations

Squares of Numbers

You've seen that Logo has a SQRT primitive for calculating the square roots of numbers. Now you can write a procedure to calculate the *squares* of numbers:

```
TO SQUARE :N
OUTPUT :N * :N
END
```

Here's how SQUARE would work in practice:

```
?PR SQUARE 2
4
?PR SQUARE 13
169
?PR SQUARE SQRT 37
37
?
```

Inverses of Numbers

The *inverse* of a number is the result of dividing that number into 1. Thus, the inverse of 2 is ½ or .5, the inverse of 4 is ¼ or .25, and so on. You can write a procedure that takes a number as input and OUTPUTs its inverse.

```
TO INVERT :N
OUTPUT 1 / :N
END
```

Here are some examples of INVERT in action:

```
?PR INVERT 2
.5
?PR INVERT 7.2
.138889
?PR INVERT SQRT 2
.707107
?
```

Areas of Squares and Circles

The following procedure, you'll recall, creates a box that measures :S on a side.

```
TO BOX :S
REPEAT 4 [FD :S RT 90]
END
```

Since the area of a square is the square of its side, you could write the following procedure, which would take an area as input and create a square having the specified area.

```
TO SQUAREA :A
MAKE "S SQRT :A
REPEAT 4 [FD :S RT 90]
END
```

Now do you suppose you could write a procedure that would take an area as input and draw both the square and the *circle* that enclosed the area? Actually, you now know enough Logo to do that rather handily. The following instructions will lead you through the process in case you don't recall the math involved, but you should try it on your own first if you think you can do it.

Drawing a circle that will have a specified area involves two formulas. Recall that to find the area of a circle you square the radius and multiply times pi. Turned around, this means that if you know the area and divide it by pi and then take the square root of the result, the answer will equal the radius of the circle. These Logo commands would accomplish that:

```
MAKE "PI 3.14159
MAKE "R SQRT(:A / :PI)
```

You could have simply included the value for pi in the second line instead of defining :PI, but pi will be used again later so it's easier to make it a variable here.

The circumference of a circle is calculated by doubling the radius and multiplying it times pi. Here's how to do that in Logo:

```
MAKE "C :R * 2 * :PI
```

Recall that in Logo circles are approximated in the form of many, very small sides. As a practical matter, thirty-six sides can look like a circle on the screen, and as a mathematical calculation it comes pretty close to a real circle. To draw a thirty-six-sided "circle" with a circumference of :C, then, each side would need to be :C / 36 units long. The following line draws such a circle:

```
REPEAT 36 [FD (:C / 36) RT 10]
```

Putting together the various pieces, here is a procedure that takes an area as input and draws the square and the circle that enclose that area.

```
TO CIRCAREA :A
MAKE "S SQRT :A
REPEAT 4 [FD :S RT 90]
MAKE "PI 3.14159
MAKE "R SQRT(:A / :PI)
MAKE "C :R * 2 * :PI
REPEAT 36 [FD (:C / 36) RT 10]
END
```

Alphabetical Outputs

You can OUTPUT alphabetical as well as numerical results. Here's a simple example.

```
TO INITIAL :NAME
OUTPUT FIRST :NAME
END
```

```
?PR INITIAL "EARL
E
?
```

Once you learn more about text processing in Chapters 17–19, the ability to output alphabetical materials will become more useful.

Some Common Bugs

Not specifying what to do with the result. The most common error you are likely to make in regard to OUTPUTs is a failure to specify what is to be done with the result when using it. As you saw in the chapter, if you enter MULTIPLY 3 4, the computer will respond:

```
I DON'T KNOW WHAT TO DO WITH 12
```

Programming past OUTPUT. Once the computer encounters and executes an OUTPUT in a procedure, the computer exits that procedure. Thus, any instructions you might place after OUTPUT in the procedure will be ignored.

Exploring Further

1. Recalling SQUARE earlier in the chapter, write CUBE to calculate the cubes of numbers and work like this:

```
?PR CUBE 3
27
?PR CUBE 4
64
?
```

2. Write a superprocedure using CUBE that will print the following Table of Cubes.

```
TABLE OF CUBES

1 CUBED IS 1
2 CUBED IS 8
3 CUBED IS 27
4 CUBED IS 64
5 CUBED IS 125
6 CUBED IS 216
7 CUBED IS 343
8 CUBED IS 512
9 CUBED IS 729
10 CUBED IS 1000
```

3. Write a procedure that changes the form of names, as follows:

```
?TURN [EARL BABBIE]
BABBIE, EARL
?
```

Teaching Objectives

- ☐ Students will be able to describe the similarity between primitives that produce outputs (such as SQRT) and procedures that do the same.
- ☐ Students will be able to create procedures that produce outputs.
- ☐ Students will be able to debug procedures designed to produce outputs.

Teaching Techniques and Materials

Mind-size Bites—Simple to Complex

The fundamental structure of OUTPUT is pretty simple in itself, so you'll have no trouble starting out simply. For the simplest example of OUTPUT, you could start your students with this:

```
TO PROC :IN
OUTPUT :IN
END
```

Once your students are comfortable with simply flowing numbers and words through this procedure, you can modify it so that the OUTPUT differs from the input. You might begin with a program to square numbers, since that only requires one input. Then, you can expand your procedures so as to process more than one input.

Students who are doing really well with this might be encouraged to nest procedures using OUTPUTs. Here's a simple example: a procedure that raises numbers to the fourth power, using another procedure that SQUAREs numbers.

```
TO SQUARE :X
OUTPUT :X * :X
END

TO QUAD :X
OUTPUT SQUARE SQUARE :X
END
```

Student Exercises

Pencil and Paper Exercises

1. Study the procedure shown below and then indicate what the computer's response would be in each of the interactions presented under the procedure.

```
TO CALC :X :Y
OUTPUT :X * :Y
END
```

a. PR CALC 3 4
b. PR CALC 33 2
c. PR CALC 5 5
d. PR CALC 17 3

2. Study the procedure shown below and then indicate what the computer's response would be in each of the interactions presented under the procedure.

```
TO CALC :X :Y
OUTPUT :X * :Y + :X / :Y
END
```

a. PR CALC 3 4
b. PR CALC 33 2
c. PR CALC 5 5
d. PR CALC 15 3

3. What's wrong with this procedure?

```
TO CALC :X :Y
OUTPUT (X + Y) / (X − Y)
END
```

4. What will be the computer's response at the end of these entries?

```
?TO CALC :X :Y :Z
>OUTPUT :X * :Y − :Z
>END
?CALC 3 4 5
```

____

At the Computer

1. Write a procedure that will produce the following interaction:

```
?PR CALC 3 4
7
?PR CALC 77 23
100
?
```

2. Write a procedure that will produce the following interaction:

```
?PR CALC 6 18
3
?PR CALC 4 64
16
?
```

3. Write a procedure that will produce the following interaction:

```
?PR CALC 43 27
16
?PR CALC 88 19
69
?
```

4. Write a procedure that will produce the following interaction:

```
?PR CALC 7 4
28
?PR CALC 18 3
54
?
```

5. Write a procedure that will take your full name as input and will OUTPUT your first name.

Lesson Plan Elements

- ☐ OUTPUT
- ☐ Writing new procedures to create numerical and alphabetical outputs.
- ☐ Modifying old procedures to create outputs.

Review of Logo Commands

NAME	EXAMPLE	FUNCTION
OUTPUT	OUTPUT :X / :Y	As a command within a procedure, OUTPUT causes the computer to exit the procedure, carrying the specified value with it. It is necessary to specify what is to be done with the value: PRinting it, for example.

A Logo Challenge

Write a procedure, POWER, that takes a number and a power as inputs and OUTPUTs the result of raising the specified number to the specified power. Here's what it would look like to square 6, cube 4, and raise 2 to the fifth power.

```
?PR POWER 6 2
36
?PR POWER 4 3
64
?PR POWER 2 5
32
?
```

Chapter 13

Interactive Procedures

A Powerful Idea

In the previous two chapters you learned how to write procedures with inputs and outputs. This chapter is going to add still another dimension to Logo; one that may represent a more radical shift in your experience of computers.

It is possible to write **interactive** procedures: those that ask for inputs from the keyboard while the procedure is operating. Thus, for example, you can write a procedure that will ask you how big a circle you want and will then follow your instructions. Here's how it works.

How to Do It

READCHAR

The Logo primitive READCHAR instructs the computer to stop and wait for a character to be entered at the keyboard. Typically, you will assign a name to that character. The following command illustrates how this primitive might be used:

```
MAKE "X READCHAR
```

Located in a procedure, this command tells the computer to wait until a key is struck on the keyboard; then whatever character is typed will be assigned to the name :X. Now, take a minute to consider the following procedure. What do you think it would do?

```
TO TURN
REPEAT 100 [MAKE "T READCHAR RT (:T * 10) FD 10]
END
```

Once you have some idea about what it will do, enter it and try it out. Enter the procedure; enter TURN; then start entering the numbers 0 through 9 and watch the screen.

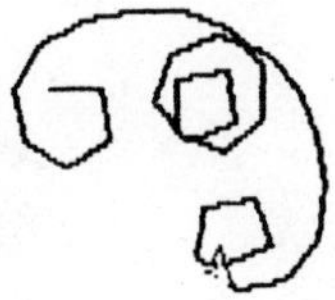

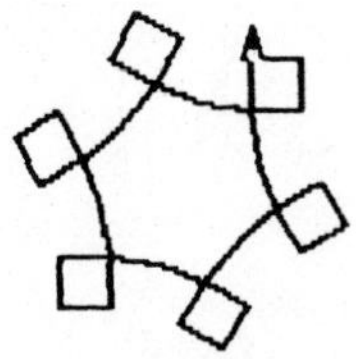

As you'll see, every time you enter a number, what you enter is assigned as the value of :T. Then, the turtle turns RIGHT (:T * 10) degrees and moves FORWARD 10 steps. The procedure is set up to handle one hundred such cycles (that is, REPEAT 100), although you can terminate the process early with CTRL-G. Shown are some examples of what you might create with this procedure.

READLIST

READLIST works a lot like READCHAR except it accepts longer inputs. It takes in whatever you type until it gets a RETURN. Here's an example of READLIST in action:

```
?MAKE "A READLIST
NOW IS THE TIME FOR ALL GOOD COMPUTERS
?PR :A
NOW IS THE TIME FOR ALL GOOD COMPUTERS
```

Once you've entered MAKE "A READLIST, the cursor moves to the beginning of the next line and waits for your input, which it takes in as the value of :A. You will find this function very useful whenever you create interactive procedures. Here's a simple example:

```
?TO HELLO
>PR [WHAT'S YOUR NAME?]
>MAKE "NAME READLIST
>TYPE [HI THERE] TYPE CHAR 32
>PR :NAME
>PR [HOW ARE YOU?]
>END
?HELLO
WHAT'S YOUR NAME?
EARL
HI THERE EARL
HOW ARE YOU?
?
```

Logo has a peculiar quirk whenever you use READLIST to get a number. Since the command structures your input as a *list,* even if you only type in one number you must use the FIRST command for any mathematical calculations using the input. Here's an example:

```
TO TRIPLE
PR [ENTER A NUMBER]
MAKE "X FIRST READLIST
PR :X * 3
END
```

Run this procedure and the computer will ask you for a number; once you enter it, the computer will triple it and PRint the result. Here's an example of how it works.

```
?TRIPLE
ENTER A NUMBER
22
66
?
```

If you omitted the FIRST in line 3 of the procedure, the computer would tell you that

```
* DOESN'T LIKE [22] AS INPUT
```

Using FIRST as shown will solve this problem.

IF

This little command is a very powerful one in Logo. It allows you to specify a condition and instruct the computer to take actions based on whether the condition is met or not. The following procedure lets you decide whether to have the computer say hello to you.

```
TO GREET
PR [DO YOU WANT ME TO SAY HELLO?]
MAKE "ANS FIRST READLIST
IF :ANS = "YES [PR "HELLO]
END
```

This is how it works.

```
?GREET
DO YOU WANT ME TO SAY HELLO?
YES
HELLO
?
```

```
?GREET
DO YOU WANT ME TO SAY HELLO?
NO
?
```

The IF command structure has two key elements. First, the condition is described: for example, IF :ANS = "YES. The action to be taken if the condition is met is contained in brackets following the description of the condition. In this case, the computer is to PRINT HELLO. If the condition isn't met, then the computer does not execute the instruction in brackets.

As an alternative, you can add a third element. You can specify some action to be taken if the condition is *not* met. This other action is simply presented with another set of brackets.

```
TO GREET
PR [DO YOU WANT ME TO SAY HELLO?]
MAKE "ANS READLIST
IF :ANS = "YES [PR HELLO] [PR "OKAY]
END
```

Here's how it would work:

```
?GREET
DO YOU WANT ME TO SAY HELLO?
NO
OKAY
?
```

STOP

The command STOP in a procedure instructs the computer to terminate its execution of the procedure. This is often used in the context of an IF statement. Consider this, for example:

```
TO BOX
PR [DO YOU WANT TO SEE A BOX?]
MAKE "ANS FIRST READLIST
IF :ANS = "NO [STOP]
REPEAT 4 [FD 100 RT 90]
END
```

If you say NO when the computer asks if you'd like to see a box, it will STOP execution of the procedure. If you say anything other than NO, it will proceed to draw the box.

Illustrations

Reversing Names

Here's a procedure that will take your name as an input and convert it to a last-name-first format:

```
TO REVERSE
PR [ENTER YOUR NAME]
MAKE "NAME READLIST
TYPE LAST :NAME TYPE ", TYPE CHAR 32 PR FIRST :NAME
END
```

```
?REVERSE
ENTER YOUR NAME
SARA STONE
STONE, SARA
?
```

Multiple Conditions

Often you will want to specify several conditions and actions to be taken in relation to a single input from the keyboard. For example, you can write a procedure that lets you ask for a variety of designs.

```
TO DESIGNS
PR [WHICH WOULD YOU LIKE?]
PR [BOX]
PR [CIRCLE]
PR [STAR]
MAKE "ANS FIRST READLIST
IF :ANS = "BOX [REPEAT 4 [FD 100 RT 90]]
IF :ANS = "CIRCLE [REPEAT 36 [FD 10 RT 10]]
IF :ANS = "STAR [REPEAT 5 [FD 100 RT 144]]
END
```

When you run this procedure, the computer will ask you which design you want, PRinting a list of options. If you respond by typing BOX, the computer will draw a box. If you type STAR, it will draw a star and so forth. If you had procedures for drawing each of the designs, you could enter those procedure names in the brackets, like this:

```
TO DESIGNS
PR [WHICH WOULD YOU LIKE?]
PR [BOX]
PR [CIRCLE]
PR [STAR]
MAKE "ANS FIRST READLIST
IF :ANS = "BOX [BOX]
IF :ANS = "CIRCLE [CIRCLE]
IF :ANS = "STAR [STAR]
END
```

You could streamline this procedure somewhat by using READCHAR instead of READLIST. Here's how:

```
TO DESIGNS
PR [WHICH WOULD YOU LIKE?]
PR [B — BOX]
PR [C — CIRCLE]
PR [S — STAR]
MAKE "ANS READCHAR
IF :ANS = "B [BOX]
IF :ANS = "C [CIRCLE]
IF :ANS = "S [STAR]
END
```

Now you indicate your preference by entering the appropriate letter—B, C, or S—instead of typing the whole word. You wouldn't even have to press RETURN.

Some Common Bugs

Failing to use input. Whenever you use READCHAR or READLIST, you must tell the computer what to do with the inputs it takes through the keyboard: PRINT it, assign it to a variable name, and so on. If you simply say READLIST, the computer will take your input at the keyboard and then complain that it doesn't know what to do with it. Here's an example:

```
?READLIST
TWO LEFT FEET
I DON'T KNOW WHAT TO DO WITH [TWO LEFT FEET]
?
```

Omitting FIRST *in connection with* READLIST. You've seen that when you use READLIST to get a number from the keyboard, it is necessary to specify FIRST or else the computer won't be able to use the number for mathematical calculations. Here's the format:

```
MAKE "NUM FIRST READLIST
```

Omitting parentheses. As you experiment with FIRST in connection with READLIST inputs that contain more than one number, you may have to use parentheses, like this:

```
PR (FIRST :NUMS) + (LAST :NUMS)
```

If you omit these parentheses, the computer will try to read :NUMS in full rather than the FIRST or LAST as specified. Enclosing them in parentheses solves the problem. As a general rule of thumb, when in doubt, use parentheses.

Exploring Further

1. Write a procedure that will let you carry on a conversation with the computer.
2. Write a procedure that will produce this kind of interaction:

```
ENTER A NUMBER
16
16 SQUARED IS 256
?
```

3. Write a procedure that will produce this kind of interaction:

```
ENTER YOUR NAME
LARRY LOGO
LARRY
LOGO
?
```

4. Write a procedure that uses IF and STOP.

Teaching Objectives

- ☐ Students will learn to create interactive procedures, using both READCHAR and READLIST.
- ☐ Students will learn to use IF commands in procedures.
- ☐ Students will learn to use STOP to halt the execution of procedures.
- ☐ Students will be able to identify uses for the interactive capability of Logo.

Teaching Techniques and Materials

Mind-size Bites—Simple to Complex

The simplest beginning for interaction is reading and PRinting back single characters. You might try this, for example.

```
TO BABBLE
PR [ENTER A LETTER]
MAKE "L READCHAR
REPEAT 100 [TYPE :L]
END
```

Next, show students how to use READLIST to get alphabetical inputs and PRint them back. Then you can have them do things with the inputs.

Finally, show them how to deal with numerical inputs. Remember, it is necessary to use FIRST in conjunction with READLIST. Once they become proficient with a single numerical input, show them how to get more than one number. Here's an example.

```
TO MULTIPLY
PR [ENTER TWO NUMBERS]
MAKE "NUMS READLIST
TYPE [THE PRODUCT OF]
TYPE CHAR 32
TYPE FIRST :NUMS TYPE CHAR 32
TYPE "AND TYPE CHAR 32
TYPE LAST :NUMS TYPE CHAR 32
TYPE "IS TYPE CHAR 32
PR (FIRST :NUMS) * (LAST :NUMS)
END
```

Note that it's necessary to use parentheses in the next-to-last line in this example. Omitting the parentheses will cause the procedure to crash, with an explanatory error message. Why not try it without the parentheses and see what happens?

In introducing the IF command, it is a good idea to have students start with a single condition. Then you can encourage them to begin adding more conditions.

Concrete Learning

Students may be able to grasp the logic of the IF command if you have them write the condition statement—such as IF :N = 1—on one side of an index card and the appropriate action—such as, STOP—on the other side. Then they can lay out several such cards in the column on a table, simulating the list of commands in a procedure. They can specify an input, test it against each IF statement in order, and turn over the card of whatever IF condition is met. Be sure to have them continue through the remaining cards after the specified action has been taken (unless the action is STOP).

Student Exercises

Pencil and Paper Exercises

1. What's wrong with these commands?
   a. MAKE "NUM LIST
   b. MAKE :NAME READLIST
   c. IF :ANS "YES [STOP]
2. What will the computer do if you enter YES in response to its question?
```
TO DESIGN
PR [WANT A DESIGN?]
MAKE "ANS READLIST
IF :ANS = "YES [REPEAT 4 [FD 50 RT 90]]
END
```
3. There is a bug in this procedure. What is the bug? What will the computer do if you enter YES?
```
TO BOX
PR [WANT TO SEE A BOX?]
MAKE "ANS READCHAR
IF :ANS = "YES [REPEAT 4 [FD 50 RT 90]]
END
```
4. Revise the procedure shown in (3) above so that the computer will accept and act on Y or N as inputs.

At the Computer

1. Write a procedure that will ask you what size STAR you want and will then draw it.
2. Write a procedure that will ask for two numbers and will then divide the first by the second.
3. Write a procedure that will ask you to enter your full name and will then print your last name one hundred times.
4. Modify the procedure in (3) above so that entering FORGET IT will cause the computer to terminate operations without printing your name.

Lesson Plan Elements

- ☐ READCHAR
- ☐ READLIST
- ☐ IF
- ☐ STOP

Review of Logo Commands

NAME	EXAMPLE	FUNCTION
READCHAR	MAKE "X READCHAR	Computer waits for a character to be entered at the keyboard and then assigns that value to the name indicated. In the case of the present example, whatever key is hit will be assigned to the name :X.
READLIST	MAKE "X READLIST	Computer waits for one or more characters followed by a carriage return. In this case, whatever is entered is assigned to the name :X.
STOP	STOP	Causes procedure to STOP.
IF	IF :X = "R [RT 90]	IF the condition specified is satisfied, then the instructions contained in the brackets are executed. IF the condition is not met, then the whole statement is simply ignored.

A Logo Challenge

Write a procedure that will produce the following interaction:

?**DESIGNS**
HOW MANY SIDES DO YOU WANT?
5
HOW LONG DO YOU WANT THEM?
100
WHAT ANGLE DO YOU WANT?
144

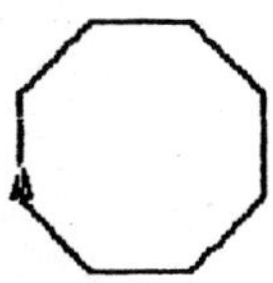

?**DESIGNS**
HOW MANY SIDES DO YOU WANT?
8
HOW LONG DO YOU WANT THEM?
40
WHAT ANGLE DO YOU WANT?
45

Chapter 14

Recursive Procedures

A Powerful Idea

In this chapter, one of the most powerful ideas in Logo will be examined: **recursion.** To understand what this means, recall first that it is possible for one procedure to call another into action. Here's a simple example.

```
TO STEP1
PR [THIS IS STEP1]
STEP2
END

TO STEP2
PR [THIS IS STEP2]
END
```

In this example, entering STEP1 causes that procedure to be executed. As you can see, it prints THIS IS STEP1 and then causes the computer to execute STEP2, which PRints the statement shown.

Take a moment now to examine these two procedures. What will happen now if we enter STEP1?

```
TO STEP1
PR [THIS IS STEP1]
STEP2
END
```

```
TO STEP2
PR [THIS IS STEP2]
STEP1
END
```

If you examine these procedures carefully, you'll realize that you have created an endless **loop**. STEP1 will cause STEP2 to execute, and STEP2 calls up STEP1, which calls up STEP2, and so on. If you were to create these procedures and enter STEP1, the computer would begin printing:

```
THIS IS STEP1
THIS IS STEP2
THIS IS STEP1
THIS IS STEP2
THIS IS STEP1
THIS IS STEP2
THIS IS STEP1
THIS IS STEP2
```

and would continue doing so forever, or until you entered CTRL-G to stop it.

But to take this peculiar process one step further, what would this procedure do?

```
TO STEP1
PR [THIS IS STEP1]
STEP1
END
```

If you were to run this procedure, it would also launch itself into an endless loop. It would begin to execute STEP1, which would cause the computer to execute STEP1, which would cause the computer to execute STEP1, and so forth. Once again, this process would continue endlessly.

Switching to a physical illustration of recursion, suppose you want to go east endlessly. (Since the world is round, you can do that.) Here is a set of instructions for going east; there are two instructions.

☐ To GO EAST

1. Take one step east
2. GO EAST

Notice that once you begin following the instructions of GO EAST, you will continue going east forever. This is another example of recursion.

As you will see shortly, this simple technique can be used with great power, especially in conjunction with commands such as IF and STOP. Moreover, recursion brings out the true power of variables, which were first examined in Chapter 10. Ultimately, you will be able to create very compact but sophisticated and potent procedures.

How to Do It

Recursive Graphics

Return for a moment to the first procedure. You'll recall that you first created BOX by entering FD 50 RT 90 four times. Later the process was simplified through the use of REPEAT. Now you are going to accomplish the same result in still another way.

```
TO BOX
FD 50 RT 90
BOX
END
```

Enter this procedure and run it, and the turtle will rush into an endless frenzy of BOX making. Follow the procedure step by step and you'll see it works like this: It executes FD 50 RT 100, then it runs BOX, which executes FD 50 RT 90, and then executes BOX, and so on. Once again, the turtle will continue running around the BOX forever until you enter CTRL-G.

You can do the same with a STAR.

```
TO STAR
FD 100 RT 144
STAR
END
```

Now you can get a little more complicated, returning to another familiar procedure.

```
TO BOXES
REPEAT 4 [FD 90 RT 90]
RT 10
BOXES
END
```

Start this procedure going and it will continue on and on, eventually retracing its earlier path.

Recursive Mathematics

Recursion also has mathematical applications. Here's a simple example.

```
TO KOUNT :X
PRINT :X
KOUNT :X + 1
END
```

The name KOUNT is used because Logo has reserved the name COUNT for its own purposes. (It counts the number of items in a list.) Before running this procedure, however, take a minute to examine the procedure and see what it would do.

The first thing to note is that KOUNT has an input named :X. The second line of the procedure asks Logo to print :X. So far so good. The third line, however, calls up KOUNT, giving as input a number one higher than :X. Thus, if you begin by entering KOUNT 1, Logo will print 1 on the screen. Line 3, in effect, says KOUNT 2—setting :X equal to 2. Now Logo will print 2 on the screen, and line 3 says KOUNT 3, and so on. Now enter the program and run it.

As expected, the procedure begins counting and continues indefinitely—until stopped with a CTRL-G. Here's a way to make the procedure a little more elegant. What do you think this will do?

```
TO KOUNT :X :Y
PRINT :X
IF :X = :Y [STOP]
KOUNT :X + 1 :Y
END
```

Notice that the new version has another input, indicating the highest number to be printed. The new line 3 in the procedure does exactly what it says: If :X (getting larger each time) equals :Y (the highest wanted), then the process should STOP. It is also necessary to add the second input to line 4. Try it out.

Illustrations

Spirals

You have only scratched the surface of possibilities for recursion, however. The technique is also used for graphics. Here's a simple illustration:

```
TO SPI.A :DIST
FD :DIST
RT 10
SPI.A :DIST + .03
END
```

Enter this program and try it out with the instruction SPI.A .01.

SPI.A .01

You see that each iteration of the procedure sends the turtle ahead an ever-greater distance and turns it 10 degrees to the right. The result is a spiral. Adding the same increment (.03) each time results in a steady growth of the design. Now, see what would result from expanding the distance through multiplication rather than addition. For example:

```
TO SPI.M :DIST
FD :DIST
RT 10
SPI.M :DIST * 1.02
END
```

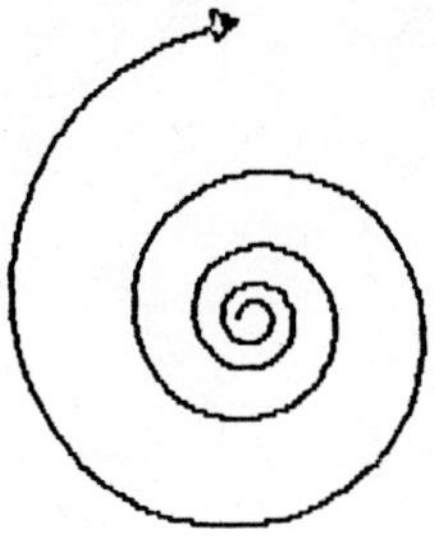

SPI.M 1

Now initiate it with SPI.M 1.

Papering Your Way to the Moon

Here's a math problem that involves the issue of recursion. It also illustrates the phenomenon of doubling, an important model used in studies of population and environment. Take a simple example.

A piece of bond paper is about 1⁄254 of an inch thick (or thin). If you fold it in half, the resulting double layer is twice as thick or about 1⁄127 of an inch—not a very big difference. Fold it again and the resulting four layers of paper equal approximately 1⁄64 of an inch thick.

Now here's the question: How many times would you have to fold the piece of paper for the resulting thickness to be something you might notice? For example, you may have a gut sense that if you folded the paper a million times, it would probably amount to something. But see if it would take that much.

Start with a piece of paper 1⁄254 inches thick. Here's a procedure that would fold it and report the resulting thickness.

```
TO FOLD :TIMES :THICK
TYPE [FOLDED:] TYPE CHAR 32
TYPE :TIMES TYPE CHAR 32
TYPE [TIMES =] TYPE CHAR 32
TYPE :THICK TYPE CHAR 32
PR [INCHES THICK]
PAUSE
PR [ ]
FOLD :TIMES + 1 :THICK * 2
END
```

There's one new feature in this procedure: PAUSE. This works a lot like STOP. When the computer reaches this command, it will terminate the operation and type the procedure name (FOLD, in this case) on the screen, as a reminder to you that it is pausing in the middle of a procedure. Once this happens, you will be able to review what's printed on the screen at your leisure. Whenever you're ready for more, typing CO (for COntinue) will cause the procedure to resume operating.

Let's try the procedure out with FOLD 0 1/254. This means that when the paper is folded 0 times, it is 1/254 inches thick. Once you run the procedure, Logo will respond with:

```
FOLDED 0 TIMES = 3.93701N3 INCHES THICK
PAUSING. . . IN FOLD:
PAUSE
FOLD?
```

This tells you that when the paper is folded 0 times, it is 3.93701N3 inches thick. 3.93701N3!?! Recall that this is the computer's scientific notation when presenting very large or very small numbers. In this case, the N3 indicates that the decimal point in this number should be moved three places to the left, resulting in .00393701.

To get back to the paper-folding procedure, enter CO to get past the PAUSE in the procedure. Logo responds with:

```
FOLDED 1 TIMES = 7.87401N3 INCHES THICK
PAUSING. . . IN FOLD:
PAUSE
FOLD?
```

Now enter CO a few more times to see what happens to the thickness of the paper. Notice that you need to fold the paper eight times before it gets more than an inch thick (1.00787 inches, but who's counting?).

Folded thirteen times, the paper is almost a yard thick (32.252 inches). Folded twenty times, it is 4128.25 inches thick, or about 344 feet. Now the paper is beginning to amount to something, but it's getting a little hard to conceive of in inches. Try modifying the program as follows:

```
TO FOLD :TIMES :THICK
TYPE [FOLDED:] TYPE CHAR 32
TYPE :TIMES TYPE CHAR 32
TYPE [TIMES =] TYPE CHAR 32
TYPE :THICK/(12*5280) TYPE CHAR 32
PR [MILES THICK]
PAUSE
PR [ ]
FOLD :TIMES + 1 :THICK * 2
END
```

In the revised program, :THICK (in inches) is divided by (12 times 5280)—which converts it to miles. Miles? Isn't that a bit much for a folded piece of paper? You'll see in a moment.

When you start the program again, we notice that the paper begins as 6.21371N8 (.0000000621371) miles thick. See what happens as you progress, entering CO each time the procedure pauses.

Once you've folded the paper twenty-one times, you lose the scientific notation when the paper reaches .13 miles. Folded twenty-four times, the paper is a mile thick. Folded thirty-six times, the hypothetical paper's thickness would reach across the United States. That's significant, but you're on a roll now. Folded another six times, the paper would be thick enough to reach the moon; another nine folds (totaling fifty-one) would take the paper past the sun.

You'll recall this examination began with the question of how many times you'd have to fold the paper to have its thickness amount to something interesting. You probably agreed that folding the paper a million times would be pretty thick. You have now discovered that folding it fifty-one times would create something 139,920,000 miles thick—reaching to the sun and about halfway back to earth.

While the PAUSE-CO cycle has made it possible to move through iterations of the procedure step-by-step, it has also created a problem. No matter what you do, the FOLD ? doesn't go away. The computer keeps pausing in FOLD and waiting to continue. Trying to start the procedure from scratch by entering FOLD 0 1/254 only makes matters worse. The first time the computer PAUSEs now, you'll be looking at FOLD FOLD ? every time. The computer is now keeping track of two suspended operations, ready to go back to the latest one and, presumably, once the latest one is completed it will return to the earlier one. Unfortunately, this recursive procedure is never going to complete itself.

Here's a command that will break you out of the cycle. Enter THROW "TOPLEVEL. That's all it takes, and you are back to the ? prompt. Think of all the suspended operations as forming a stack filling up from the bottom. Every time you COntinue, the computer goes to the suspended operation at the bottom of that stack. The command THROW "TOPLEVEL takes you to the top level of the stack. If you enter CO now, the computer will respond YOU'RE AT TOPLEVEL.

Just for fun, take the PAUSE line out of FOLD and run it. My computer folded the paper 134 times before reporting NUMBER TOO BIG—with the hypothetically folded paper 1,353,220,000,000,000,000,000,000,000,000,000 miles thick.

You can cause the computer to pause in another way than that just discussed. If you press CTRL-W while a procedure is operating, that will interrupt the procedure; then pressing any other key will cause the procedure to resume its operations.

Some Common Bugs

Not using enough inputs. Here's a common problem in recursive procedures:

```
TO BOX :LEN
FD :LEN RT 90
BOX
END
```

In the first line, BOX is declared as a procedure that requires an input :LEN. Even though the size of :LEN will not be changed, it is necessary to specify *some* input in the third line of the procedure, such as BOX :LEN.

Also, be careful whenever the procedure requires more than one input and you are only changing one of them. Here's an example:

```
TO POLYSPI :LEN :ANGLE
FD :LEN RT :ANGLE
POLYSPI :LEN + 2
END
```

The third line of this procedure is going to cause an error message: NOT ENOUGH INPUTS. The line should read: POLYSPI :LEN + 2 :ANGLE.

Failing to increment inputs in recursive line. As you've seen, recursive procedures often involve the incrementing of some variable, such as a distance to be moved or an angle to be turned. Thus, the recursive line in a procedure called PROC might look like this: PROC :DIST + 5. If you forgot the + 5, the DISTance would remain the same with each iteration of the procedure rather than growing.

Preceding ? prompt by procedure name. When the FOLD procedure is run, once it hits the first PAUSE command the prompt looks like this:

```
FOLD ?
```

If you try to run the procedure from scratch, the prompt will look like this:

```
FOLD FOLD ?
```

The way out of this situation is to enter THROW "TOPLEVEL.

Exploring Further

1. Write recursive procedures like BOXES that rotate other designs, such as triangles or pentagons.
2. Write a recursive procedure to draw a triangular spiral like this one.

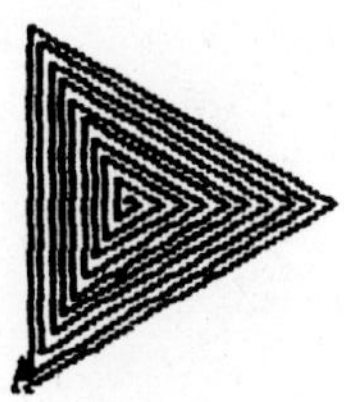

SPI.T 1

3. Write recursive procedure that will keep lengthening the string of X's as follows:

```
X
XX
XXX
XXXX
XXXXX
XXXXXX
XXXXXXX
```

4. How many times would you have to fold the paper discussed in this chapter for it to be one light year thick? (Note: Light travels 286,000 miles a second, and a light year is the distance light travels in a year. Use Logo to find out how many miles light travels in a year.)

5. Take a moment to examine this procedure and figure out what it will do. Enter it into the computer. Run it. Tinker with it. If you let it run long enough, what kind of display will you have on your screen?

```
TO RANDLINE
MAKE "DIST RANDOM (100)
MAKE "ANGLE RANDOM (360)
FD :DIST RT :ANGLE
RANDLINE
END
```

Teaching Objectives

- ☐ Students will be able to explain the logic of recursive procedures.
- ☐ Students will be able to create recursive procedures that draw graphic designs.
- ☐ Students will be able to create recursive procedures that handle numerical or alphabetical outputs.
- ☐ Students will be able to write procedures that include PAUSE.
- ☐ Students will be able to use COntinue and THROW "TOPLEVEL.

Teaching Techniques and Materials

Concrete Learning

To illustrate recursion concretely, have a group of five or six students form a circle, with each student facing the back of the person in front of him or her. Then have one student *gently* push the one in front forward, having that student push the one in front of him or her, and so forth until the original student is pushed and again pushes. This should give them a sense of how an endless process is initiated and proceeds thereafter.

Here's a less physical illustration. On a card, write the following: "Tell me to read my instructions aloud." Give the card to one of your students, say, Hannah. Now instruct another student as follows: "I want to you to tell Hannah to read the written instruction aloud. From then on, you are to do whatever you are told." When they begin, here's what happens:

Second student: Read your instructions aloud.
First student: Tell me to read my instructions aloud.
Second student: Read your instructions aloud.
First student: Tell me to read my instructions aloud.
Second student: Read your instructions aloud. . . .

While the two students are repeating this cycle, you might ask the rest of the class how to stop them. See if someone eventually shouts "CTRL-G."

Mind-size Bites—Simple to Complex

Start students off with very simple recursive procedures; those that merely type a letter are probably best. Here's an example:

```
TO X
TYPE "X
X
END
```

Next, move to procedures that do something different with each iteration. You might start with a simplified version of KOUNT.

```
TO KOUNT :N
PR :N
KOUNT :N + 1
END
```

Then they should be ready to start experimenting with recursive graphics. The recursive BOX would be a good start. From here on, you can move to more and more complex uses of this powerful capability.

Student Exercises

Pencil and Paper Exercises

1. What would happen on your screen if you ran this procedure?

```
TO XXX
XXX
END
```

2. What will happen if you run this procedure by typing DOUBLE 1?

```
TO DOUBLE :N
PR :N * 2
DOUBLE :N * 2
END
```

3. Correct this procedure so that it will draw a star recursively.

```
TO STAR
FD 100 RT 144
END
```

4. Now revise the procedure so that you can specify the size of the star as an input.

At the Computer

1. Write a recursive procedure to draw a simple triangle endlessly.
2. Modify the procedure created in question 4 above so that the star keeps growing, as shown.

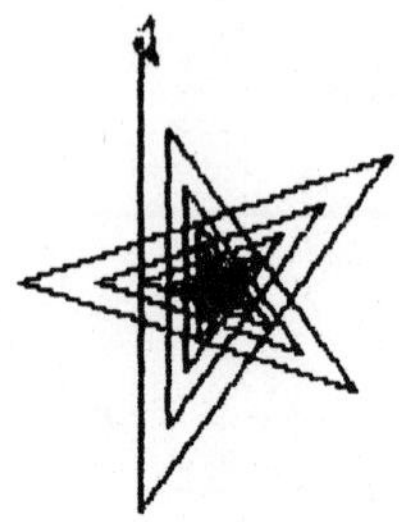

GROWING. STAR 1

3. Write a procedure that creates a pentagonal spiral like the one shown.

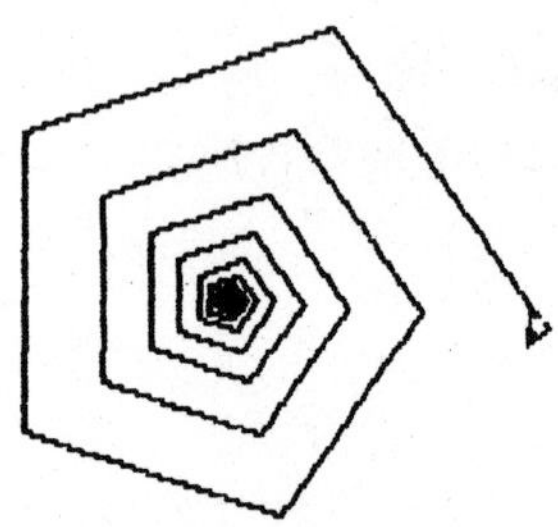

PENTSPI 1

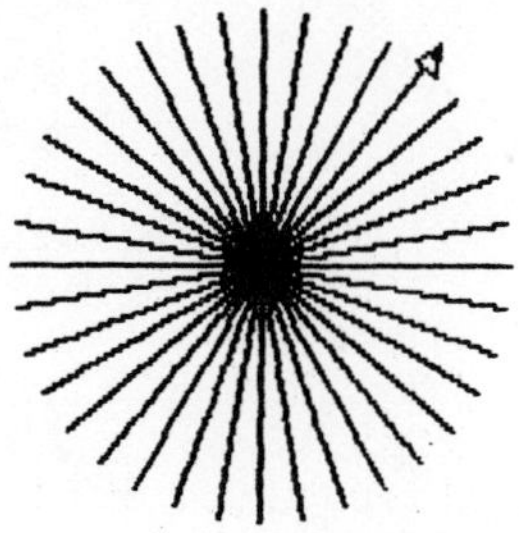

RAYS

4. Write a recursive procedure, RAYS, that will draw this design.

RAYS 10

5. Modify RAYS so that it creates this design.

Lesson Plan Elements

- ☐ The logic of recursion
- ☐ PAUSE
- ☐ COntinue
- ☐ THROW "TOPLEVEL

Review of Logo Commands

COMMAND	FUNCTION
PAUSE	Causes the computer to terminate operations on the current procedure.
CO	Causes the computer to resume operations following a PAUSE.
THROW "TOPLEVEL	Takes computer out of PAUSE-CO mode.
CTRL-W	Causes computer to PAUSE.

A Logo Challenge

Write a recursive procedure that behaves as follows in response to the commands shown.

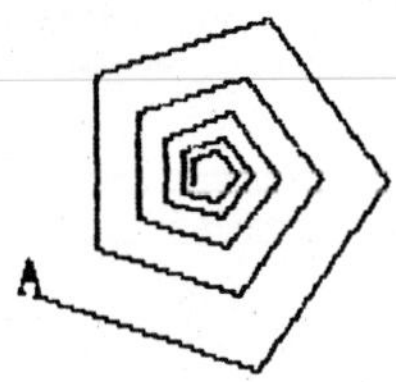

DESIGN 10 5 1.1

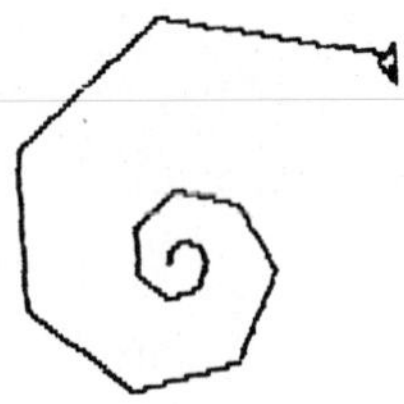

DESIGN 5 7 1.2

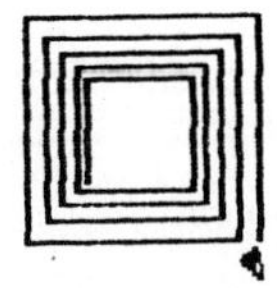

DESIGN 40 4 1.05

Chapter 15

Junior Logo

A Powerful Idea

Though simple in comparison to other computer languages, Logo is still not accessible to young children who have not learned to read and write. Two-year-old children are simply not going to learn to FORWARD 50, RT 90, or REPEAT 4. This is not to say they cannot use Logo, however.

You now know enough Logo to create a subset of Logo that even the youngest children can use and enjoy. The **Junior Logo** system that will be discussed in this chapter has been tested on children one year old and younger. While their graphic designs are not as elaborate as others that have been created in this book, the children are delighted nonetheless.

How to Do It

In order to illustrate how you are likely to create your own systems, Junior Logo will be developed and presented in stages—even though some of the methods used first will be abandoned later. You'll get an idea of how to proceed, try it out, find it less than perfect, redesign what you've done, and so on.

A False Start

What if you could create a system in which typing single letters would produce a result? Suppose a young child could type F and have the turtle move forward ten spaces. Type R and it would turn, say, 30 degrees to the right. That would make Logo available to children who were too young to learn commands such as FORWARD 50.

Before reading on, take a few minutes to see if you can figure out how to create such a system by yourself. Specifically, can you create a procedure that will let you type F and have the turtle move ten spaces forward? Here's one way to do it:

```
TO F
FD 10
END
```

This is pretty straightforward, and it's obvious how you could create procedures to make the turtle move back, turn right or left, or any of the other simple procedures you have already created.

While you could build a full system like this, it still has a few shortcomings as far as preschoolers are concerned. First, they will have to know that F stands for FORWARD, R stands for RIGHT, and so forth. The problem of children not reading has been reduced, but not solved. Second, the system is unnecessarily clumsy in that it is necessary to press RETURN after each letter command.

"Unnecessarily" clumsy was used here because you've already learned a command that can streamline matters: READCHAR. Take a minute to consider the following procedure. What do you think it would do?

```
TO JRL
MAKE "RK READCHAR
IF :RK = "O [FD 50]
IF :RK = ", [BK 50]
IF :RK = "K [LT 90]
IF :RK = "L [RT 90]
JRL
END
```

After you've had a chance to study the procedure and guess what it will do, enter it and try it out. As you'll discover, typing O causes the turtle to move forward fifty units, typing L turns it 90 degrees to the right, and so forth. Since the program is recursive, it starts looking for a new command as soon as it acts on the previous one. You (or a little friend) can keep entering one-stroke commands to your heart's content. CTRL-G will interrupt the program.

Notice that the four keys selected form a diamond on the keyboard, as follows:

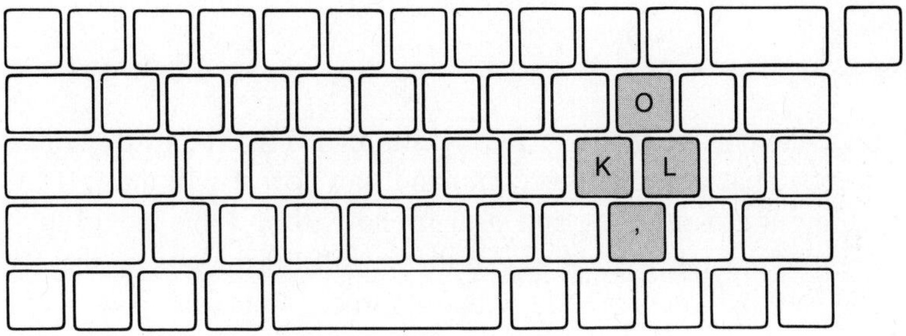

This solves the literacy problem, since the keys have been selected so their locations correspond to the turtle movements.

If you are creating Junior Logo for a young child, it would be a great idea to mark these four keys on the keyboard. There are several ways of doing that. You might cut up some masking tape and stick little pieces on the tops of these four keys. Or you could use some typewriter correction fluid to make white dots on the tops of the four keys. (This is, of course, a more permanent solution.)

Why don't you enter the program and start it going by typing JRL. Now all you need to do is hit any of the four keys to move the turtle around the screen in single keystrokes.

Once you've gotten JRL working, you can make it a little fancier.

```
TO JRL
MAKE "RK READCHAR
IF :RK = "O [FD 50]
IF :RK = ", [PE BK 50 PD]
IF :RK = "K [LT 90]
IF :RK = "L [RT 90]
IF :RK = "Q [PU]
IF :RK = "A [PD]
IF :RK = "W [HT]
IF :RK = "S [ST]
IF :RK = "Z [CS]
JRL
END
```

Notice the change made to the BK command (,). The turtle will still move backward at this command, but now it will erase (PE) anything it crosses. You and your friend will find this useful in correcting mistakes. Notice also that Q will lift the pen so the turtle can be moved around without a trace; A puts the pen down again. W hides the turtle and S brings it back again. Finally, Z will erase the screen (CS) so you can start over whenever things get out of hand.

Finally, to add some elegance to the system, you can write a procedure to clean up the screen and get things set for JRL:

```
TO JRLOGO
CS
FULLSCREEN
JRL
END
```

Now, you can simply type JRLOGO and begin teaching your young friend to use these few keys:

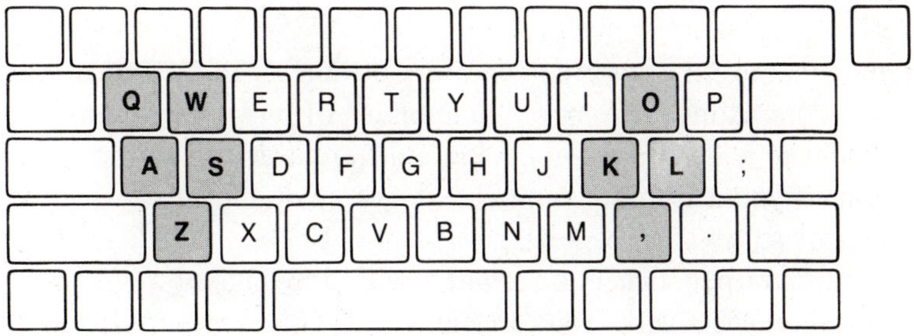

This is just the beginning, however. There is nothing sacred about this way of constructing Junior Logo. You can do whatever you want with it. You may, for example, want to have the turns occur in 10-degree increments. Or you may want to add some more Logo primitives to the list that READCHAR checks for. Ideally, you should tailor your system to your own interests and/or the needs of the young people who will be using it. As an example, however, you might want to consider these additional possibilities.

Junior Logo Extended

Remember the BOX and the CIRCLE? You can add them to the Junior Logo repertoire by adding these lines to the procedure:

```
IF :RK = "X [REPEAT 4[FD 30 RT 90]]
IF :RK = "C [REPEAT 36[FD 3 RT 10]]
```

Notice that X has been used as the symbol for the box and C for the circle, which keeps them alongside each other near the QAWS cluster. Now you can move the turtle around and create boxes and circles with a single keystroke. (Although only a right-turn circle has been provided, you can draw a circle to the left by turning the turtle 180 degrees first.)

Notice also that the procedures for the box and circle have been written in, rather than calling up subprocedures. Either way will work, but this way JRL is self-contained and you don't have to keep track of the subprocedures required by the main procedure.

You can make the system even more powerful. In the following procedure listing, two more "diamonds" of movement commands are added, each producing a different degree of movement. If you add these commands to JRL, you may also want to mark these keys on the keyboard. It might be a good idea, for example, to put stickers on X and C with drawings of a box and a circle, respectively. You can figure out whatever would work best for your particular situation.

```
TO JRL
MAKE "RK READCHAR
IF :RK = "O [FD 50]
IF :RK = ", [PE BK 50 PD]
IF :RK = "K [LT 90]
IF :RK = "L [RT 90]
IF :RK = "U [FD 30]
IF :RK = "N [PE BK 30 PD]
IF :RK = "H [LT 45]
IF :RK = "J [RT 45]
IF :RK = "T [FD 10]
IF :RK = "V [PE BK 10 PD]
IF :RK = "F [LT 30]
IF :RK = "G [RT 30]
IF :RK = "Q [PU]
IF :RK = "A [PD]
IF :RK = "W [HT]
IF :RK = "S [ST]
IF :RK = "Z [CS]
IF :RK = "X [REPEAT 4[FD 30 RT 90]]
IF :RK = "C [REPEAT 36[FD 3 RT 10]]
JRL
END
```

These suggestions for expanding on Junior Logo were not meant to dictate a system to you. Now that you have learned the basic format of the system, you should feel free to expand the system in any direction that suits you.

Illustrations

Here are a few designs some friends and I made using Junior Logo. These should serve as a jumping off place for you.

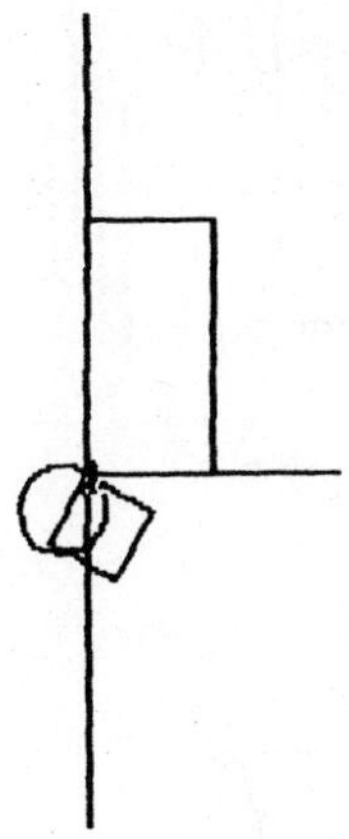

Justin, age 1

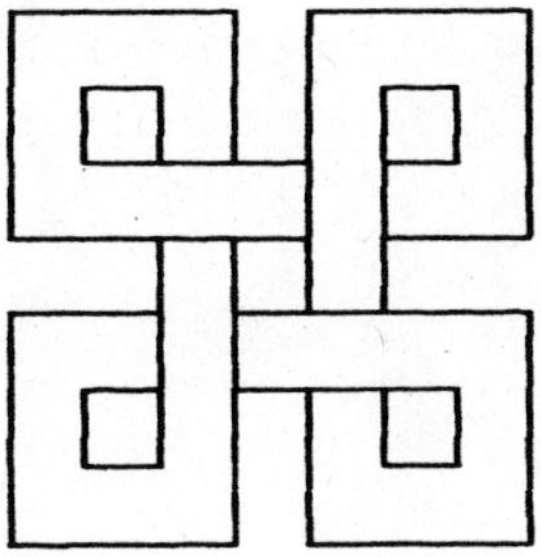

Earl, age 45

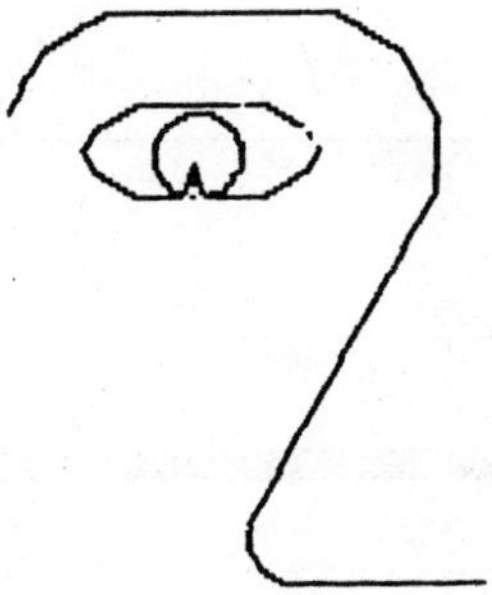

St. John, age 15

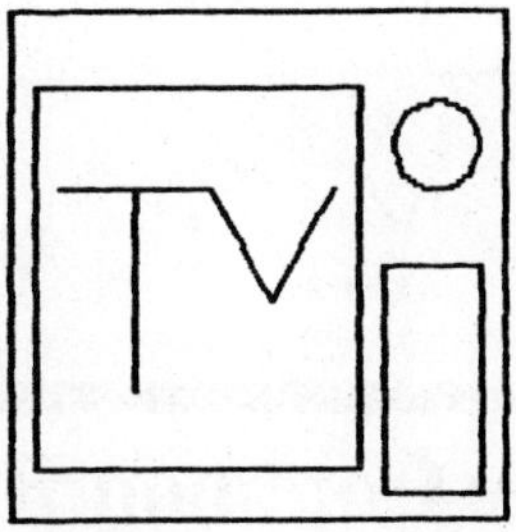

Aaron, age 14

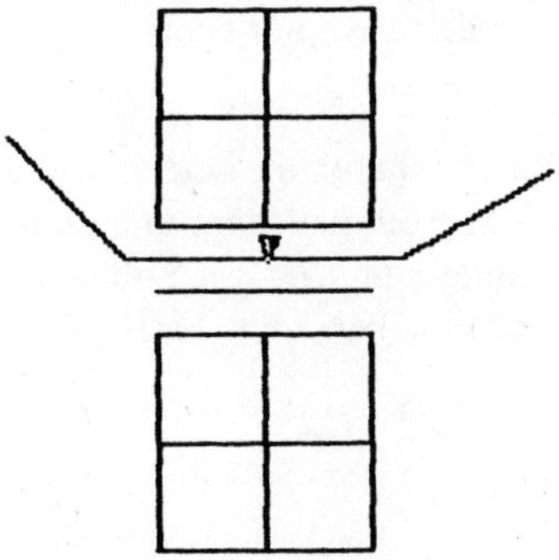

Warren, age 14

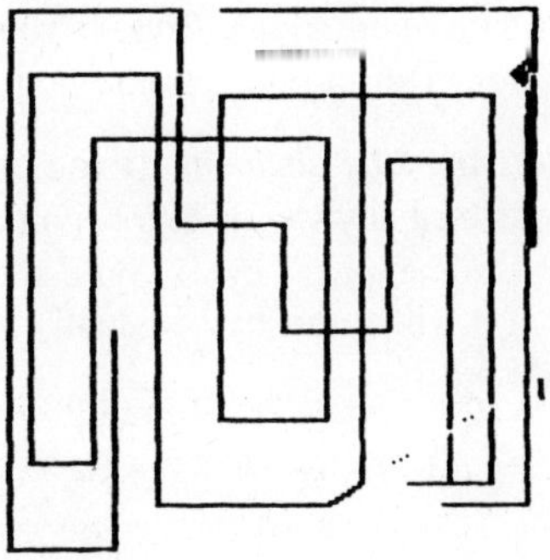

Joy, age 12

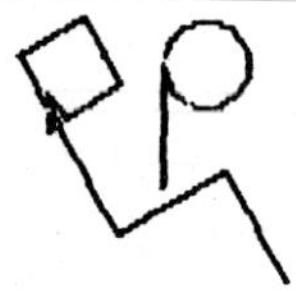

Marissa, age 1

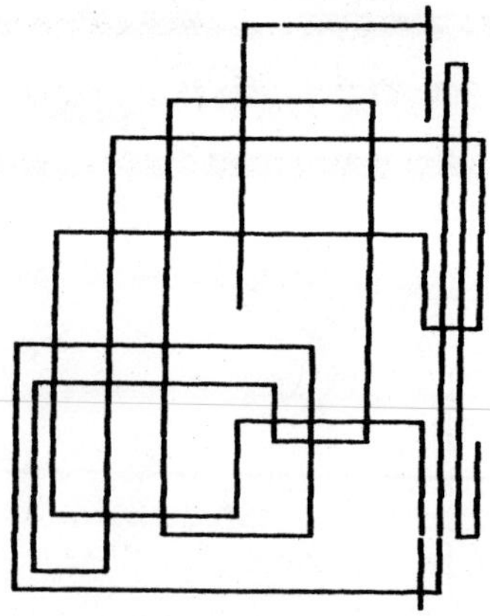

Diane, age 41

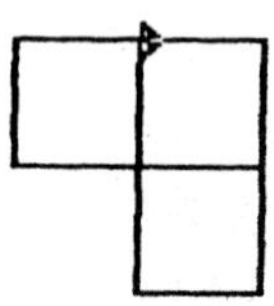

Adam, age 4

Aaron, age 14

Some Common Bugs

Pressing unassigned keys. If you press keys that have not been assigned any Logo actions, nothing will happen.

Pressing Z *by accident.* If you press Z unintentionally, the screen will be erased anyway. If this becomes a problem, you may want to assign it to some other key. If you use, say, the dollar sign ($), it is unlikely that it will be hit by accident, since that requires two keys: SHIFT and 4.

Exploring Further

1. Modify JRL so that pressing R will result in a triangle being drawn.
2. Use Junior Logo to draw letters of the alphabet.
3. Use Junior Logo to create a maze.

Teaching Objectives

- ☐ Young children will grasp the connection between their pressing keys on the computer keyboard and what the computer presents on the video screen.
- ☐ Young children will be able to create Logo designs.

Teaching Techniques and Materials

Concrete Learning

Some young children will profit from using a model turtle with a hole drilled through it for a pen or pencil. As discussed earlier, these can be made out of wood, walnut shells, clay, or any number of other materials.

To relate the turtle to keyboard commands, try this: On a large piece of cardboard, draw a picture of the OL,K diamond. Now have one child hold the model turtle and have another touch one of the keys on the drawing. The game is for the child holding the turtle to move it in accordance with the keys the other child touches on the keyboard. Have them take turns giving and following commands.

Mind-size Bites—Simple to Complex

With very young children, you will need to begin with the link between the keyboard and the video screen. One-year-old Justin, who contributed one of the designs presented earlier in this chapter, was originally more interested in pounding on the keys and picking the tape off than with the video screen. As his mother and I began exclaiming with great glee whenever he made the turtle move, Justin seemed to enjoy watching us more than what was happening on the screen. If you have this experience, don't worry. It's a start.

Begin with the OL,K command diamond. You might want to cut out a stiff template that covers all the keys except these four. When I cut up a manila folder so that it covered all the keys except OL,K Justin immediately zeroed in on them and did much better.

Once students have pretty much mastered the use of the OL,K command diamond, you should show them the BOX and CIRCLE command keys and any other complex function keys you've created. You'll find they really get a kick out of being able to set the turtle off on its circuit by pressing only one key.

Finally, you can add the other command diamonds, one at a time. Show them how the UJNH diamond works as a new set of commands. Before long they will discover that they can use both command diamonds: turn RT 45 with J, then move FD 50 with O, and so on. It's important to let them discover this for themselves if possible, since it will support their natural discovery process and encourage them to experiment.

Student Exercises

In the case of Junior Logo, it doesn't make sense to have students work on pencil and paper problems. Here are some exercises for them to try at the computer.

1. With the initial version of Junior Logo:
    a. Make the turtle move: FORWARD, BACKward, RIGHT, and LEFT.
    b. Make a square.

c. Make a rectangle.
d. Make these designs:

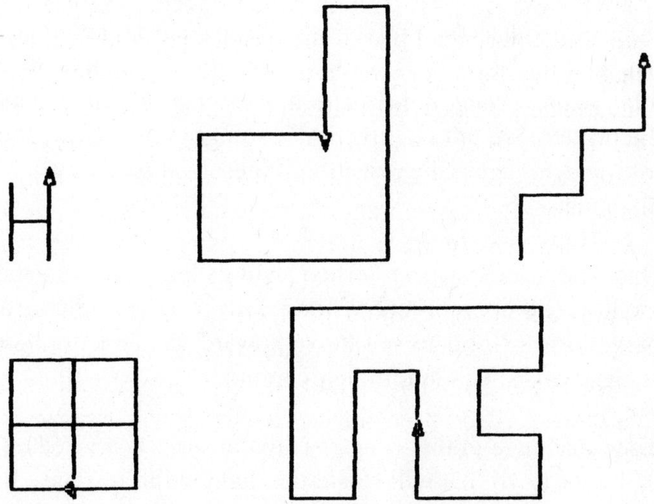

2. With the extended version of Logo, create these designs:

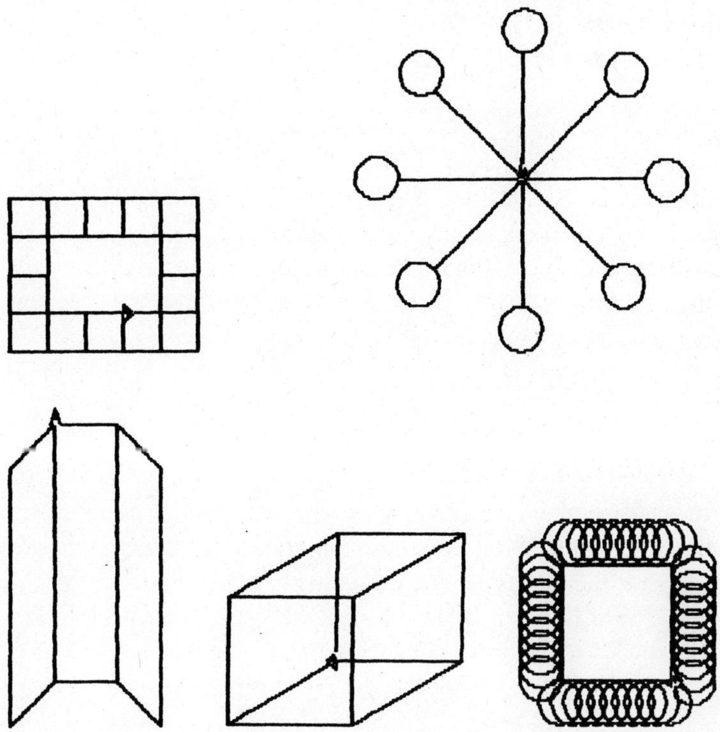

A Logo Challenge

Junior Logo has one problem that keeps it from being as effective as it might be. When you first begin, the OL,K diamond is totally appropriate to the turtle movements. Pressing O makes the turtle move in that direction—straight up. Pressing L makes it turn right, again the direction represented by L in the diamond.

Once the turtle has been turned right or left, however, the diamond is less appropriate. While O will still cause the turtle to move forward, it does not move upward, as the letter would suggest by its location in the diamond.

Your challenge in this chapter is to construct a revised version of Junior Logo that will rotate the diamond in response to turns right and left. For example, whenever the turtle is facing to the right on the screen, L will cause it to move FORWARD, O will cause it to turn LEFT, and so forth.

Chapter 16

Advanced Graphics

A Powerful Idea

As discussed earlier in the book, turtle graphics differs from most other computer graphing systems. Whereas most other systems are based on Cartesian coordinates, turtle graphics operates on the basis of direction and distance.

As it turns out, Logo offers two graphing systems. In this chapter, you are going to see how to work with Cartesian coordinates. In addition, you will be introduced to a number of other powerful commands.

How to Do It

Screen Positions

Imagine that the video screen is a grid composed of numerous horizontal and vertical lines, like a piece of graph paper. Each point on the screen, therefore, lies on a particular horizontal and a particular vertical line. If you were to number the two sets of lines, you could specify the location of any point on the screen with two numbers. That's exactly how this Logo system works.

Logo identifies each screen position by a pair of numbers, with the first indicating positions on the *x* dimension (left-right) and the second indicating positions on the *y* dimension (up-down). Logo defines the center of the screen as position [0 0]. The diagram illustrates the boundaries of the screen, using this notational system.

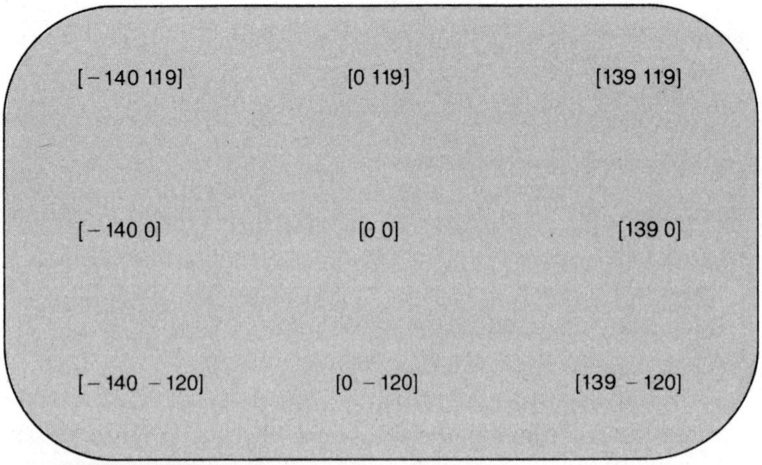

Cartesian coordinates of the Logo screen

DOT To experiment with this notation, plot dots on the screen with the command DOT[*x y*], as in:

```
DOT[50 50]
DOT[75 −30]
DOT[−20 0]
```

Notice that DOT does not move the turtle. Take a few minutes to experiment with this.

POS This command reports the turtle's current location, expressed in the notational system just described. For example, if you clear the screen (CS) and then enter PR POS, the computer will print out the current position of the turtle as 0. 0.

SETPOS You can also place the turtle wherever you like with the command SETPOS[x y]. Try these, for example.

```
SETPOS[50 50]
SETPOS[−100 120]
```

If you try these out, you will discover that the turtle leaves a track when you change its position (if the pen is down). If you want to move the turtle without creating a line, all you need to do is PU.

The brackets are essential in this command, signaling the computer that the two numbers should be considered as a set, since SETPOS requires two numbers as input.

You can also specify positions using variables. Here's a simple example:

```
MAKE "X 100
MAKE "Y 50
SETPOS (SE :X :Y)
```

This procedure contains a new command: SE or SENTENCE. This is an extremely useful command. The SE and the parentheses tell the computer that it should consider the two variables as a set, just as the brackets do with numerical inputs.

Sometimes you may only want to change the horizontal or the vertical position of the turtle, along the *x* and *y* dimensions, respectively. This is accomplished by the commands SETX and SETY. Here are sample commands:

```
SETX 50
SETY −100
```

If you try these commands, you'll see that the turtle draws a line (if PD) when you move it about like this.

SETHEADING (SETH) You can change the turtle's direction with this simple command, using the 360 degrees of the circle to indicate the desired directional headings: for example, SETH 120. Both 0 and 360 point straight up, and you can also use negative numbers. Here are a few commonly used headings:

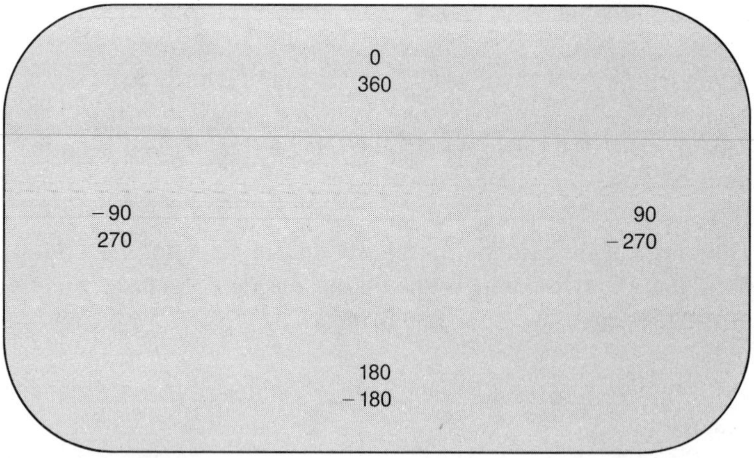

This command is especially useful whenever you have taken the turtle through numerous heading changes (using RT and LT) and then want to have it face in a particular direction. You may also want to use it in connection with subprocedures that should begin with the turtle facing in a particular direction, even though you may use it in a variety of situations.

The command HEADING reports the turtle's current heading, just as POS tells you its position. (Remember, you need to enter PR HEADING if you want the heading printed out.)

HOME The command HOME returns the turtle to the center of the screen, heading straight up. It takes the most direct route, and you'll know what that is if you have the PENDOWN.

Some More New Commands

Here is a miscellaneous collection of additional commands that may be of use to you.

- ☐ CLEAN. This command is like CLEARSCREEN except that it leaves the turtle in its current position, pointing in its current direction, whereas CLEARSCREEN brings the turtle to the center of the screen, pointing straight up.

  Example: CLEAN

- ☐ WRAP. This is the condition in which Logo begins: If the turtle moves beyond the screen, it reappears at the opposite side from where it disappeared. You can see this with a command such as FD 200. See also WINDOW and FENCE.

  Example: WRAP

- ☐ WINDOW. This cancels out the WRAP feature of Logo. Once you've entered this command, the turtle simply disappears when you go past a border of the screen. Future commands will be followed as though the turtle were wandering around a much bigger surface than the one you can see. Thus, you can maneuver the turtle around out of sight and bring it back into view. See also FENCE.

  Example: WINDOW

- ☐ FENCE. This command forces you to keep the turtle within the boundaries of the screen. It will reject any command that would take the turtle too far, responding with the statement TURTLE OUT OF BOUNDS.

  Example: FENCE

- ☐ WAIT. This is a useful command in a variety of situations. It lets you instruct the computer to pause momentarily in its operations and then resume. In using the command, you must specify how long you want operations delayed, in units of 1/60 of a second.

  Example: WAIT 60 (This will cause a one-second delay.)

Now you will see some of the ways you can use these various new commands.

Illustrations

Sowing Boxes

With SETPOS, SETX, and SETY, you can create the accompanying design easily. Here are the procedures that created the design:

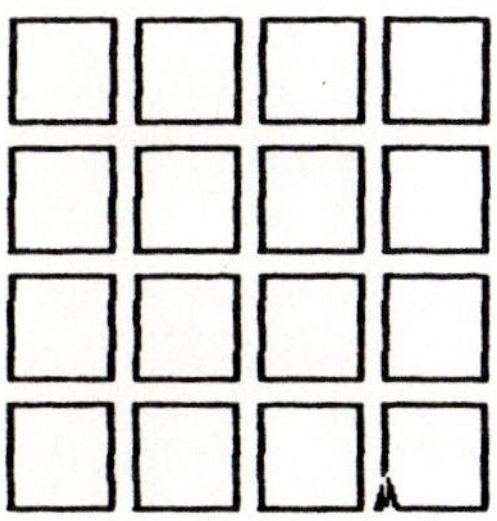

```
TO BOX
REPEAT 4 [FD 40 RT 90]
END

TO BOXES
PU SETPOS [-100 50] PD BOX
```

(Continued on next page)

(*Continued*)

```
PU SETX −50 PD BOX
PU SETX 0 PD BOX
PU SETX 50 PD BOX
PU SETPOS [−100 0] PD BOX
PU SETX −50 PD BOX
PU SETX 0 PD BOX
PU SETX 50 PD BOX
PU SETPOS [−100 −50] PD BOX
PU SETX −50 PD BOX
PU SETX 0 PD BOX
PU SETX 50 PD BOX
PU SETPOS [−100 −100] PD BOX
PU SETX −50 PD BOX
PU SETX 0 PD BOX
PU SETX 50 PD BOX
END
```

Take a minute to read through BOXES and figure out what it will do. Then enter it into the computer and try it out.

As you examine the procedure, you will notice that the same steps are repeated on several occasions. In Logo, this usually signals an opportunity for greater efficiency. Here's one way of streamlining these procedures.

```
TO BOXROW
PU SETX −50 PD BOX
PU SETX 0 PD BOX
PU SETX 50 PD BOX
END

TO BOXES
PU SETPOS [−100 50] PD BOX
BOXROW
PU SETPOS [−100 0] PD BOX
BOXROW
PU SETPOS [−100 −50] PD BOX
BOXROW
PU SETPOS [−100 −100] PD BOX
BOXROW
END
```

Drawing Lines Point to Point

As you've seen, the turtle can leave a trail when it moves around the screen. You can use that feature in the creation of designs. Here's a procedure that will produce a simple design.

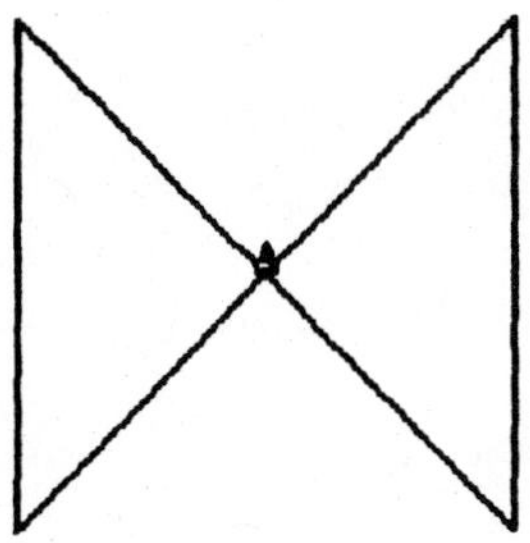

```
TO DESIGN
CS
SETPOS [−100 100]
SETPOS [−100 −100]
SETPOS [100 100]
SETPOS [100 −100]
HOME
END
```

Cartesian graphing like this allows the treatment of location as a variable. Take a look at this procedure, decide what it will do, and then take it for a test drive. The accompanying design is the result.

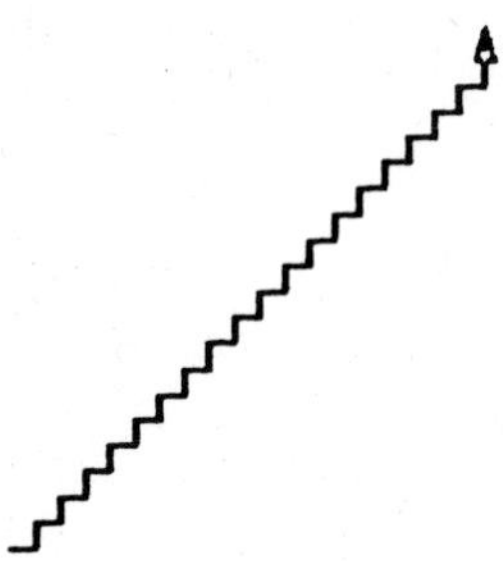

```
TO DESIGN
MAKE "X −100
PU SETPOS[−100 −100] PD
REPEAT 20 [SETX :X SETY :X MAKE "X :X + 10]
END
```

In case the turtle whips through too quickly for you to see what it's doing, you can remedy that as follows:

```
TO DESIGN
MAKE "X −100
PU SETPOS[−100 −100] PD
REPEAT 20 [SETX :X SETY :X WAIT 30 MAKE "X :X + 10]
END
```

Try it out to see how WAIT works.

Here's a slightly more complicated example of essentially the same technique. This one draws a parabola.

```
TO PARABOLA
PU SETPOS [−100 100]
MAKE "Q −100
REPEAT 21 [SETPOS (SE :Q ((:Q * :Q) / 100)) PD MAKE "Q :Q + 10]
END
```

As you can see, the procedure increases the value of Q from −100 to 100 in 21 steps. At each step along the way, a point is plotted that is located at Q on the horizontal scale and at Q squared and divided by 100 (to keep it on the screen) on the vertical scale. Notice the use of SE in the procedure.

Random Specks

Here's a procedure your students may like.

```
TO SPECKS
HT
MAKE "X RANDOM 200
MAKE "Y RANDOM 200
DOT (SE :X – 100 :Y – 100)
SPECKS
END
```

As you'll notice, this procedure uses RANDOM, first introduced in Chapter 9. Two numbers have been selected at random from the range 0 through 199. Those numbers are used to place a DOT on the screen—subtracting 100 from each of the numbers to bring them into line with the dimensions of the screen.

Notice also that this is a recursive procedure. It will continue running until the screen is totally white—and keep running even after that. This is a good time to recall that CTRL-G will stop such procedures in their tracks.

Some Common Bugs

Failing to lift the pen. Whenever you move the turtle around using SETPOS, SETX, or SETY, it will leave a trail unless you raise the pen (PU) before moving.

Failing to lower the pen. Any time you lift the turtle's pen, you create an opportunity to watch the turtle subsequently roar around the screen, leaving no trail. If you raise the pen in moving the turtle to a new location, you must put it down again (PD) before drawing designs.

Forgetting brackets. DOT and SETPOS require that the numerical specifications be contained within brackets. If you omit the brackets, the computer will try to carry out the command with only one of the numbers and will complain as follows:

```
?DOT 50 50
DOT DOESN'T LIKE 50 AS INPUT
?SETPOS 50 50
SETPOS DOESN'T LIKE 50 AS INPUT
?
```

Using extra brackets. To make your life interesting, other commands—SETX, SETY, and SETH—should *not* have their numerical specifications in brackets. Placing them so will result in this kind of response:

```
?SETX [50]
SETX DOESN'T LIKE [50] AS INPUT
```

Forgetting PR. POS, which tells you the turtle's location, must be preceded by PR. Otherwise, the computer will react like this:

```
?POS
I DON'T KNOW WHAT TO DO WITH [O. O.]
?
```

Using WAIT *without specification.* When you wish to use WAIT to cause the computer to pause for a time in midstream, you must specify how long it should pause, in units equal to 1/60 of a second each. Failure to do this will result in an error message saying NOT ENOUGH INPUTS TO WAIT.

Exploring Further

1. Write a one-line command that will draw a clock's hour hand pointing to 7 o'clock. Write another command to indicate where the hour hand would point at 7:15, as in these illustrations.

7:00

7:15

2. Write a procedure that takes two inputs (hour, minute) and creates a clock with both the hour and minute hands.

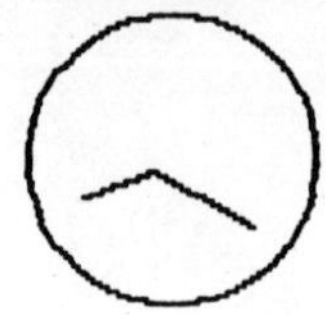

8:20

3. Write a procedure with a random star burst like the one shown. Have the computer select the direction and length of the rays at random.

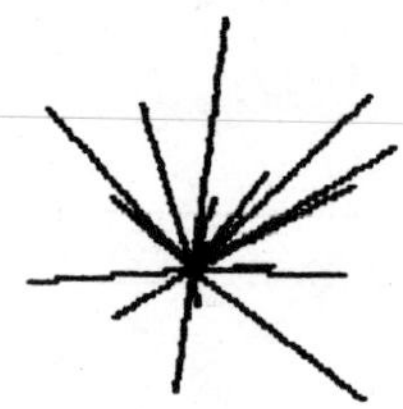

Teaching Objectives

- ☐ Students will be able to plot DOTs within a Cartesian space.
- ☐ Students will be able to determine the turtle's location.
- ☐ Students will be able to place the turtle at a specified point within a Cartesian space.
- ☐ Students will be able to determine the direction the turtle is heading.
- ☐ Students will be able to shift the turtle's heading to a specified direction.
- ☐ Students will be able to change the nature of the screen boundaries.
- ☐ Students will be able to cause the computer to pause for a specified period of time, using WAIT.

Teaching Techniques and Materials

Concrete Learning

In introducing Cartesian graphing in Logo, the obvious teaching aid is graph paper. Most older children have used it.

The most straightforward use of graph paper in this context is to have students begin by numbering the lines in both the horizontal and vertical directions. Number the center lines 0, and number the rest with positive or negative numbers in the same fashion as the Logo screen:

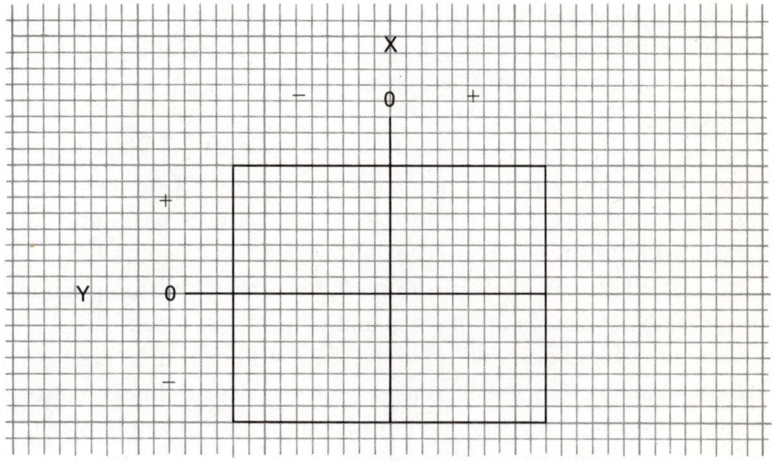

Don't worry about having fewer lines on the graph paper than on the video screen; the logic is more important than the concrete numbers in this respect.

Once they have numbered the lines, have the students plot some designs they might like to create. Then have them write out the Logo instructions that would cause the turtle (or DOTs) to create the designs.

The central structure of Cartesian graphing is the matrix or grid, and there are other physical aids you might use, such as a chess- or checkerboard, checkered table cloth, wire screen, rattan mat, tiled floor, or chalkboard with a grid on it.

Mind-size Bites—Simple to Complex

The fundamental concept for students to grasp concerns the logic of Cartesian coordinate systems as a device for creating designs. Here's a logical progression of elements with which to take students from the simple to the complex.

1. The structure of the grid is one of horizontal and vertical lines.
2. Lines can be identified by numbering them.

3. Points are located at the intersections of horizontal and vertical lines.
4. Points can be identified numerically with reference to the lines they lie on.
5. Lines to be drawn can be identified by specifying their two end points.
6. Designs are sets of such lines.
7. Thus, graphic designs can be specified in the form of a series of numbers, and the computer can be taught to create those designs.

This is one of those situations in which the abstract ideas to be understood are extremely powerful, and yet their true power lies in individuals discovering those ideas for themselves. Some students will use these materials as an avenue for grasping the logic of other technologies around them. The television pictures they watch are made up of rows and columns of black and white or colored dots. So are magazine and newspaper photos. Some students may use the insights they get from this aspect of Logo to see how the sounds of a rock concert or symphony can be stored as long strings of numbers.

While you may want to open the way to these kinds of insights, be careful not to explain too much. Support your students in making the discoveries for themselves. Explaining too much can rob them of the power and joy of discovery.

Student Exercises

Pencil and Paper Exercises

1. Get a piece of graph paper. Identify the middle horizontal line and write a 0 on the left end of that line. Identify the middle vertical line and write a 0 on the bottom end of that line. Now, number the rest of the lines in the pattern used by Logo.
2. On your graph paper, identify the points that would be marked by the following Logo commands:

```
DOT[−5 5]
DOT[10 10]
DOT[3 −4]
DOT[−7 −6]
```

3. On your graph paper, draw the design that would be created by these Logo commands:

```
CS
SETPOS[−5 5]
```

```
SETX 5
HOME
SETY −5
```

4. Draw a star on your graph paper. Now write the set of Logo commands—using SETPOS—that would cause the turtle to draw your star.

At the Computer

1. Write a Logo procedure to create this design using SETPOS, SETX, and SETY.

2. Write a Logo procedure to create this design using only SETPOS.

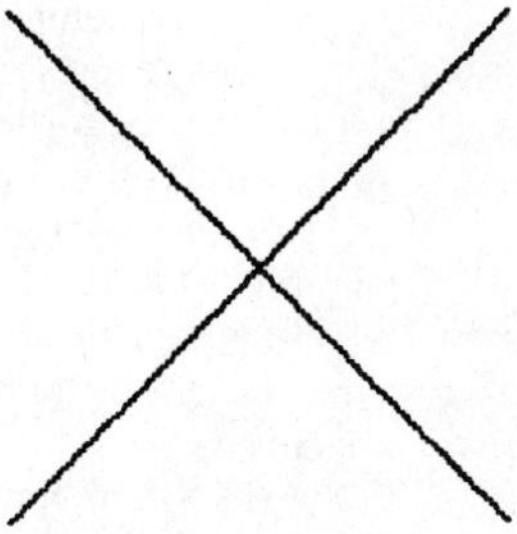

3. Revise this procedure so it will create the design shown.

```
TO DESIGN
SETPOS [—50 50]
SETY 50
HOME
SETY 50
END
```

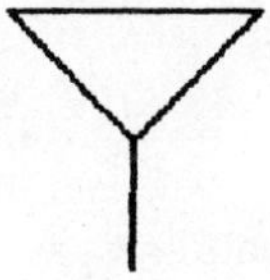

4. Write a Logo procedure to create this design.

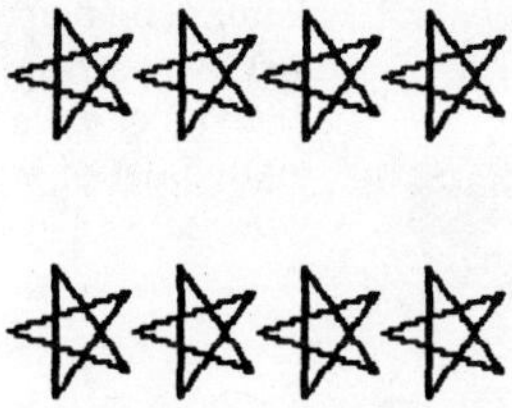

Lesson Plan Elements

☐ DOT	☐ HEADING
☐ POS	☐ HOME
☐ SETPOS	☐ CLEAN
☐ SE	☐ WRAP
☐ SETX	☐ WINDOW
☐ SETY	☐ FENCE
☐ SETH	☐ WAIT

Review of Logo Commands

NAME	EXAMPLE	FUNCTION
DOT	DOT[50 50]	Tells the computer to put a dot at the location specified; the turtle does not move.
POS	PR POS	Asks the computer to report the turtle's location on the screen, expressed in terms of its *x* and *y* coordinates.
SETPOS	SETPOS [50 50]	Moves the turtle to the location specified.
SE	(SE :X :Y)	Instructs the computer to consider the variables specified as a set.
SETX	SETX −100	Moves turtle along the *x* axis.
SETY	SETY 75	Moves turtle along the *y* axis.
SETH	SETH 90	Changes turtle's direction to the heading specified (in degrees).
HEADING	PR HEADING	Asks the computer to report the turtle's current heading.
HOME	HOME	Moves turtle to the center of screen without changing its heading.
CLEAN	CLEAN	This command is like CLEARSCREEN except that it leaves the turtle in its current position and pointing in its current direction, whereas CLEARSCREEN brings the turtle to the center of the screen, pointing straight up.
WRAP	WRAP	This is the condition that Logo is in when you first log on: If the turtle moves beyond the screen, it reappears at the opposite side from where it disappeared. You can see this with a command such as FD 200. See also WINDOW and FENCE .
WINDOW	WINDOW	This cancels out the WRAP feature of Logo. Once you've entered this command, the turtle simply disappears when you go past a border of the screen. Future commands will be followed as though the turtle were wandering around a much bigger surface than the one you can see. Thus, you can maneuver the turtle around out of sight and bring it back into view. See FENCE.

NAME	EXAMPLE	FUNCTION
FENCE	FENCE	This command forces you to keep the turtle within the boundaries of the screen. It will reject any command that would take the turtle too far, responding with the statement, TURTLE OUT OF BOUNDS.
WAIT	WAIT 3600	This lets you instruct the computer to pause momentarily in its operations and then resume. In using the command, you must specify how long you want operations delayed in units of 1/60 of a second.

A Logo Challenge

There was one fundamental problem with the clock you created in Exercise 2 in the Exploring Further section of the chapter: It didn't work.

Your challenge is to modify the procedures so they will create a clock on your screen that *actually keeps time*. Both the hour and minute hands should advance once a minute.

Once you have the clock working, you might want to spend some extra time on the clock case. You might put it in a box and decorate it with stars and anchors, for example.

Chapter 17

Elementary Text Processing

A Powerful Idea

Thus far the examination of Logo has focused on its graphics capabilities. In addition, Chapters 8 and 9 examined some of the mathematical power of Logo. In this chapter and the two that follow, another domain in which Logo functions powerfully will be examined.

Logo can also be used in the processing of text materials. While it is not a word-processing system like those used for writing books and articles, Logo does offer some powerful techniques. First some of the commands appropriate to text processing will be examined; then some of the ways those techniques can be employed will be discussed.

How to Do It

You have already been using some of Logo's text-processing techniques. To begin, here is a quick review of the most elementary commands.

TYPE and PRINT (PR) can be used to cause the computer to print text materials. The difference between these two commands is that PRINT causes a carriage return to be added at the end of the materials, whereas TYPE does not.

The format for printing single words, you'll recall, is as follows:

```
PR "HELLO
TYPE "HOWDY
```

Longer passages can be set up for printing by enclosing them within brackets.

```
PR [WELCOME TO THE WORLD OF LOGO]
```

Now here are some additional text-processing commands.

WORD

This instruction makes one word out of two or more inputs. Here's an example:

```
?PR WORD "HELLO "FELLAH
HELLOFELLAH
```

WORD only works with quotation marks, not with brackets. It will work with TYPE as well as with PRINT, however. If you have more than two inputs, you should use this format:

```
?PR (WORD "HI "THERE "BIG "FELLAH)
HITHEREBIGFELLAH
```

This command also works on defined variables, as the following example shows:

```
?MAKE "H "HI
?MAKE "T "THERE
?MAKE "B "BIG
?MAKE "F "FELLAH
?PR WORD :H :T :B :F
HITHEREBIGFELLAH
```

In my experience I have not had many uses for WORD, but it's useful to have available. Here's one situation where WORD comes in handy.

THING

This function takes a word as input and treats it as though it were the name of a variable. Here's a simple example:

```
?MAKE "NAME [THIS IS THE DEFINITION]
?PR :NAME
THIS IS THE DEFINITION

?PR THING "NAME
THIS IS THE DEFINITION
```

But now look at this:

```
?PR THING (WORD "NA "M "E)
THIS IS THE DEFINITION
```

Consider a practical application of this feature. Suppose you have three separate variables as follows:

```
?MAKE "NUM1 [THIS IS NUMBER 1]
?MAKE "NUM2 [THIS IS NUMBER 2]
?MAKE "NUM3 [THIS IS NUMBER 3]
```

Now suppose you want to create a recursive procedure that will run through values of :N and print :NUM1, :NUM2, and :NUM3. You can accomplish this feat with the following PRINT statement:

```
?PR THING (WORD "NUM :N)
```

Whatever the current value of :N, it will be tacked on the end of NUM, and THING will read the result as though it were the name of a variable (which it is).

SENTENCE (SE)

This command, which was introduced earlier, lets you string inputs together into a meaningful sentence. It uses the same format as WORD. Here's an example that uses the inputs used in the previous example.

```
?PR (SE :H :T :B :F)
HI THERE BIG FELLAH
```

SENTENCE (and also WORD) will work on extensive, complex lists of words.

```
?PR (SE :H :T ", "YOU'RE "SURE "A :B :F)
HI THERE , YOU'RE SURE A BIG FELLAH
```

Handling Lists of Words

So far, variables have been defined as single words (for example, MAKE "T "THERE). As you know, however, variables can be defined as lists of words as well. Here's a reminder of how:

```
?MAKE "VAR [HERE'S A LONG VARIABLE]
```

If you simply ask Logo to PRINT this variable, it will print the whole list, like this:

```
?PR :VAR
HERE'S A LONG VARIABLE
```

You can combine list variables with single-word variables also. Here's an example:

```
?PR (SE :VAR :B :F)
HERE'S A LONG VARIABLE BIG FELLAH
```

COUNT

Whenever you have a list, Logo is ready and willing to tell you how many elements it contains. Use COUNT this way:

```
?PR COUNT :VAR
4
```

This tells us there were 4 words in :VAR.

Now, what do you suppose would happen if you asked Logo to COUNT a single word variable, such as :F (FELLAH)? Here's the surest way to find out:

```
PR COUNT :F
COUNT DOESN'T LIKE FELLAH AS INPUT
```

The point here is that COUNT only works on lists. (Actually, PRINT COUNT SE :F works, producing 1 as an answer.)

ITEM

COUNT is often used in connection with ITEM, which lets you specify a particular element in a list. Here's a review of how it works:

```
?PR :VAR
HERE'S A LONG VARIABLE

?PR COUNT :VAR
4

?PR ITEM 3 :VAR
LONG
```

FIRST and LAST

These functions, as you have seen earlier, select the first and last elements in a list. Here are some examples of how they would work in the processing of text materials:

```
?PR FIRST :VAR
HERE'S

?PR LAST :VAR
VARIABLE
```

BUTFIRST and BUTLAST

These two do exactly what they say: They select all elements in a list *except*, respectively, for the first and last elements. Look at these:

```
?PR BUTFIRST :VAR
A LONG VARIABLE

?PR BUTLAST :VAR
HERE'S A LONG
```

Here now are some of the ways you might use these several commands.

Illustrations

Slide Shows and Lessons

One of the more potent uses of text processing for your students combines text and graphics, allowing them to create slide shows, stories, lessons, and the like. By alternating between the text and graphics screens, rather sophisticated presentations can be created. Start with some simple examples that your students will be able to recreate and modify, and then present some examples that will expand their vision of what is possible.

It would be useful to begin with a superprocedure that will bring together some of the graphics designs your students have created, held together with text screen commentaries. Here's an example:

```
TO SLIDESHOW
NOTE1
PICTURE1
NOTE2
PICTURE2
END

TO NOTE1
TEXTSCREEN
CLEARTEXT
SETCURSOR [6 6]
PR [THIS IS A BOX]
WAIT 120
END

TO PICTURE1
CLEARSCREEN
REPEAT 4 [FD 80 RT 90]
WAIT 120
END
```

```
TO NOTE2
TEXTSCREEN
CLEARTEXT
SETCURSOR [6 6]
PR [THIS IS A TRIANGLE]
WAIT 120
END
```

```
TO PICTURE2
CLEARSCREEN
REPEAT 3[FD 80 RT 120]
WAIT 120
END
```

And so on.

As a variation on this theme, you can pull together designs created by different children, using the text screen displays to identify who created each design.

As another example, you can intersperse comments throughout the course of a complex graphics design. The superprocedure might begin by drawing the first portion of the design; then you stop the design to comment on it. Then the drawing could resume, followed by more comments. This might be a good way of providing automatic instruction to students, letting Logo teach your students Logo.

Recursion and Lists

Some of the most powerful uses of Logo's more complex list-processing techniques involve the kinds of recursive loops constructed in earlier chapters. Consider this:

```
?MAKE "VAR [HERE'S A LONG VARIABLE]
```

```
?TO ABC :V
>PRINT FIRST :V
>IF BUTFIRST :V = [ ] [STOP]
>ABC BUTFIRST :V
>END
```

```
?ABC :VAR
HERE'S
A
LONG
VARIABLE
```

You should take a few minutes to "walk through" the procedure until you fully understand how it does what it does. Then take a few more minutes to discover other uses for this capability. Once you get some ideas, try them out.

Random Stories

Here's a use of Logo's text processing that students often enjoy. It has a silliness value that appeals to children from 8 to 80. Here's a simplified version; you and your students should elaborate on it. The procedure will be explained as it is developed.

```
TO RANDSTORY
MAKE "ADJ [SWEET SOUR SMELLY BEAUTIFUL HAPPY DUMB CRUMMY]
MAKE "NOUNS [DOG CAR FLOWERPOT TROLLEY SEWERPIPE
      MAGAZINE HANDKERCHIEF]
MAKE "VERBS [RUN JUMP DIVE LAUGH SMILE CRY BARK]
```

These lines define sets of adjectives, nouns, and verbs for future use. This is a section your students will want to play with later on. They should think up words they want to have show up in their stories.

```
CLEARTEXT PR[ ] PR [ ] PR[ ] PR [ ]
PR [ONCE UPON A TIME, THERE WAS A]
```

This clears the screen for the story, moves the cursor down several lines, and begins the gripping drama.

```
PR (SE ITEM (1 + RANDOM 7) :ADJ ITEM (1 + RANDOM 7) :NOUNS
     [THAT DECIDED TO])
```

This is a multipart line, so take it a piece at a time. To begin, the PR indicates that you want the computer to PRINT something. The SE indicates there are several pieces you want strung together in a sentence. The expression RANDOM 7 selects a number at random from 0 through 6; adding 1 makes it a random number from 1 through 7. (There are seven items in each of the lists, so 7 has been specified. Change this if the number of items changes.) If this process selects 3 as a random number, you will have told the computer to PR ITEM 3 in :ADJ. In other words, you have said "Pick an adjective at random." Then it picks a noun at random and adds some additional language.

```
PR (SE ITEM (1 + RANDOM 7) :VERBS [AT A] ITEM (1 + RANDOM 7)
    :ADJ ITEM (1 + RANDOM 7) :NOUNS
```

This latest instruction adds more to the story, using a randomly selected verb, adjective, and noun.

```
PR READCHAR
```

The purpose of this line is to stop the procedure so you will have time to read the story the computer has created. Once you press any key, the procedure goes on to

```
RANDSTORY
END
```

which starts the whole process over again.

Here are some sample runs of the procedure:

```
ONCE UPON A TIME, THERE WAS A
DUMB DOG THAT DECIDED TO
RUN AT A HAPPY HANDKERCHIEF

ONCE UPON A TIME, THERE WAS A
BEAUTIFUL MAGAZINE THAT DECIDED TO
CRY AT A HAPPY TROLLEY

ONCE UPON A TIME, THERE WAS A
SOUR FLOWERPOT THAT DECIDED TO
JUMP AT A BEAUTIFUL CAT
```

Here are some of the ways you and your students may want to modify the procedure.

- ☐ Change the lists of adjectives, nouns, and verbs.
- ☐ Change and/or add to the story.
- ☐ Add adverbs or other kinds of words.
- ☐ Improve the procedure, writing subprocedures to handle expressions that are frequently repeated.

Some Common Bugs

Misplacing the parentheses with SE *and* WORD. Putting the commands SE and WORD inside the same parentheses as the materials they address seems somehow unusual. However, if you should enter either of these instructions:

```
PR SE("HI "THERE)
PR WORD("HI "THERE)
```

the computer will respond with:

```
TOO MUCH INSIDE ( )'S
```

Remember, the correct format is:

```
?PR (SE "HI "THERE)
HI THERE
```

or

```
?PR (WORD "FAB "ULOUS)
FABULOUS
```

Specifying too large an ITEM *number.* ITEM is a useful command, but you have to limit your requests to the range set by the number of items in the list. Here's an example of what happens if you make an error:

```
?PR ITEM 4 [ONE TWO THREE]
TOO FEW ITEMS IN [ONE TWO THREE]
```

Using READLIST *with* WORD. Perhaps this warning will save you the hour it took me to discover my error and correct it. Here's an example of how the problem might crop up:

```
?MAKE "H "HELLO
?MAKE "N READLIST
HARRY
?PR :H
HELLO
?PR :N
HARRY
?PR (WORD :H :N)
WORD DOESN'T LIKE [HARRY] AS INPUT
```

What's wrong here? Clearly, the computer knows the values assigned to :H and :N, since it can print them back individually, but it will not put them together using WORD. (If you can see the answer, where were you when I really needed you?)

The problem is that WORD only puts together single words (or letters or numbers), while READLIST creates variables as *lists* even when only assigned a single word. The clue is in the *brackets* in [HARRY]; brackets always indicate a list.

The example given, then, asks WORD to combine a word with a list. The solution is simple enough: MAKE "N FIRST READLIST converts the list into a word. Or you could handle it later with PR (WORD :H FIRST :N).

Exploring Further

1. Write a procedure to produce this result:

```
?PROC1 "ABCDEFGHIJKLMNOPQRSTUVWXYZ
ABCDEFGHIJKLMNOPQRSTUVWXYZ
BCDEFGHIJKLMNOPQRSTUVWXY
CDEFGHIJKLMNOPQRSTUVWX
DEFGHIJKLMNOPQRSTUVW
EFGHIJKLMNOPQRSTUV
FGHIJKLMNOPQRSTU
GHIJKLMNOPQRST
HIJKLMNOPQRS
IJKLMNOPQR
JKLMNOPQ
KLMNOP
LMNO
MN
```

2. Modify the procedure to produce the following:

```
PROC2 1 "ABCDEFGHIJKLMNOPQRSTUVWXYZ
 ABCDEFGHIJKLMNOPQRSTUVWXYZ
  BCDEFGHIJKLMNOPQRSTUVWXY
   CDEFGHIJKLMNOPQRSTUVWX
    DEFGHIJKLMNOPQRSTUVW
     EFGHIJKLMNOPQRSTUV
      FGHIJKLMNOPQRSTU
       GHIJKLMNOPQRST
        HIJKLMNOPQRS
         IJKLMNOPQR
          JKLMNOPQ
           KLMNOP
            LMNO
             MN
```

3. Write a procedure that will take a list of words as input and will print the middle word in the list, *regardless of the length of the list*. (If the list contains an even number of words, the procedure should select the second of the two middle words.)
4. Write a slide show procedure that will show students, step by step, how to create a procedure that draws a star.

Teaching Objectives

- ☐ Students will be able to discuss the logic of lists.
- ☐ Students will become proficient with PRint and TYPE.
- ☐ Students will be able to use FIRST, LAST, BUTFIRST, and BUTLAST separately and in combination.
- ☐ Students will be able to COUNT the number of items in a list.

Teaching Techniques and Materials

Concrete Learning

An effective way to communicate the logic of lists of words concretely is through the use of index cards. Write words on individual cards, and then arrange the cards in a horizontal list on a table or desk. Now you can make a game out of identifying what cards would be selected by Logo commands such as.

```
PR LAST :LST
PR BUTFIRST :LST
PR FIRST BUTFIRST :LST
```

As an alternative, you can address the logic of lists by using alphabetical building blocks, using lists of letters rather than words. Arrange a set of blocks in a row and ask students to identify the blocks that would be selected by various Logo commands.

Mind-size Bites—Simple to Complex

Here are some suggestions for introducing students to the commands that operate on *lists* of words, after they have grasped the logic of such lists.

- ☐ Create a list variable.

```
MAKE "NUM [ONE TWO THREE FOUR FIVE]
```

- ☐ Introduce FIRST and LAST.

```
?PR FIRST :NUM
ONE
?PR LAST :NUM
FIVE
```

- ☐ Introduce BUTFIRST and BUTLAST.

```
?PR BUTFIRST :NUM
TWO THREE FOUR FIVE
?PR BUTLAST :NUM
ONE TWO THREE FOUR
```

- ☐ Combine commands.

```
PR FIRST BUTFIRST :NUM
TWO
PR LAST BUTLAST :NUM
FOUR
```

- ☐ Introduce WORD with single words rather than with lists; that makes it simpler. Here's an example:

```
?MAKE "L "LO
?MAKE "G "GO
?PR (WORD :L :G)
LOGO
```

- ☐ Introduce SEntence with single words also. Here's an example:

```
?MAKE "H1 "HIP
?MAKE "H2 "HOORAY
?PR (SE :H1 :H1 :H2)
HIP HIP HOORAY
```

- ☐ THING is for your older, more advanced students.

Student Exercises

Pencil and Paper Exercises

1. What word or words would be selected by these Logo commands?

```
MAKE "LST [ONE TWO THREE FOUR FIVE SIX SEVEN]
PR FIRST BUTFIRST :LST
```

2. What word or words would be selected by these Logo commands?

```
MAKE "LST [RED YELLOW GREEN BLUE PINK BLACK WHITE]
PR BUTLAST BUTLAST :LST
```

3. What would the computer respond as a result of these instructions?

```
MAKE "N "NEW
MAKE "Y "YE
MAKE "H "HAP
MAKE "A "AR
MAKE "P "PY
PR (SE(WORD :H :P)(WORD :N :Y :A))
```

4. What is the missing command that would result in the computer response shown?

```
?MAKE "CODE [THIS IS A SECRET]
?MAKE "C "CO
?MAKE "D "DE
?PR __________ (WORD :C :D)
THIS IS A SECRET
```

5. Break your first name into two parts and assign each part to a variable name. Do the same with your last name. Now, write the instruction, using the variable names, that will cause the computer to print your full name.

At the Computer

1. Write a procedure to produce the following results:

```
PICK [ONE TWO THREE FOUR FIVE]
FIVE

PICK [ONE TWO THREE FOUR FIVE SIX]
SIX
```

2. Write a procedure to produce the following results:

```
PICK [ONE TWO THREE FOUR FIVE]
FOUR

PICK [ONE TWO THREE FOUR]
THREE
```

3. Write a procedure that takes your name as input and says things to you, using your name.
4. Write a "slide show" that combines text and graphics to explain some aspect of Logo.
5. Write a procedure, ALPHIE, that behaves like this:

```
?ALPHIE "ABCDEFGHIJKLMNOPQRSTUVWXYZ
ABCDEFGHIJKLMNOPQRSTUVWXYZ
BCDEFGHIJKLMNOPQRSTUVWXYZ
CDEFGHIJKLMNOPQRSTUVWXYZ
DEFGHIJKLMNOPQRSTUVWXYZ
EFGHIJKLMNOPQRSTUVWXYZ
FGHIJKLMNOPQRSTUVWXYZ
GHIJKLMNOPQRSTUVWXYZ
HIJKLMNOPQRSTUVWXYZ
IJKLMNOPQRSTUVWXYZ
JKLMNOPQRSTUVWXYZ
KLMNOPQRSTUVWXYZ
LMNOPQRSTUVWXYZ
MNOPQRSTUVWXYZ
NOPQRSTUVWXYZ
OPQRSTUVWXYZ
PQRSTUVWXYZ
QRSTUVWXYZ
RSTUVWXYZ
STUVWXYZ
TUVWXYZ
UVWXYZ
VWXYZ
WXYZ
XYZ
YZ
Z
```

6. Revise ALPHIE so it behaves like this:

```
?ALPHIE "ABCDEFGHIJKLMNOPQRSTUVWXYZ
ABCDEFGHIJKLMNOPQRSTUVWXYZ
ABCDEFGHIJKLMNOPQRSTUVWXY
ABCDEFGHIJKLMNOPQRSTUVWX
ABCDEFGHIJKLMNOPQRSTUVW
ABCDEFGHIJKLMNOPQRSTUV
ABCDEFGHIJKLMNOPQRSTU
ABCDEFGHIJKLMNOPQRST
ABCDEFGHIJKLMNOPQRS
ABCDEFGHIJKLMNOPQR
ABCDEFGHIJKLMNOPQ
```

```
ABCDEFGHIJKLMNOP
ABCDEFGHIJKLMNO
ABCDEFGHIJKLMN
ABCDEFGHIJKLM
ABCDEFGHIJKL
ABCDEFGHIJK
ABCDEFGHIJ
ABCDEFGHI
ABCDEFGH
ABCDEFG
ABCDEF
ABCDE
ABCD
ABC
AB
A
```

Lesson Plan Elements

- ☐ WORD
- ☐ THING
- ☐ COUNT
- ☐ BUTFIRST
- ☐ BUTLAST

Review of Logo Commands

NAME	EXAMPLE	FUNCTION
WORD	PR (WORD :VAR1 :VAR2)	Squeezes variables together. If VAR1 in this example is "HEL and VAR2 was "LO, the instruction will produce HELLO.
THING	PR THING "NAME	Takes a literal text as input and converts it to a variable name. You might recall it as converting the quotation mark into a colon. In this example, it converts "NAME to :NAME.
COUNT	PR COUNT :ALPHA	Counts the number of items in a list. Thus if :ALPHA were [RED BLUE GREEN], the answer to this instruction would be 3.
BUTFIRST	PR BUTFIRST :ALPHA	Selects all items in a list *except* the first one.
BUTLAST	PR BUTLAST :ALPHA	Selects all items in a list *except* the last one.
CLEARTEXT	CLEARTEXT	Clears the text screen just as CLEARSCREEN clears the graphics screen.

A Logo Challenge

Write a procedure that will produce the following kind of interaction:

```
?NAMING 1
ENTER NAME1 OR 'END'
JAN BROWN
ENTER NAME2 OR 'END'
ROBIN WHITE
ENTER NAME3 OR 'END'
PAT BLACK
ENTER NAME4 OR 'END'
END
?PR:NAME2
ROBIN WHITE
?PR:NAME1
JAN BROWN
?PR:NAME3
PAT BLACK
?NAMING 4
ENTER NAME4 OR 'END'
ANDY GREEN
ENTER NAME5 OR 'END'
END
?PR:NAME2
ROBIN WHITE
?PR:NAME4
ANDY GREEN
```

You must write the procedure in such a way that you can enter as many names as you want. You must be able to terminate the procedure and start it again, indicating the number (4, in the example above) you want to start with.

Chapter 18

Intermediate Text Processing

A Powerful Idea

Until now, the characters you type on the keyboard have been treated in a pretty straightforward, uncomplicated fashion. You type an A and an A appears on the screen. In this chapter you will get under the surface of the way the computer deals with characters. By complicating matters slightly, you will gain a lot of power in dealing with text materials in Logo. You are going to be able to do things you didn't think possible.

In addition, you're going to learn how to gain a new level of mastery over the placement of materials on the text screen of Logo, similar to the placement of DOTs and the turtle on the graphics screen.

How to Do It

ASCII

The letters, numbers, and other characters that you use in dealing with your computer are handled by the machine in the form of numerical codes known as the **American Standard Code**

for Information Interchange (ASCII). It's as though you used the numbers 1 through 26 to represent the twenty-six letters of the alphabet, although ASCII is a little more involved than that. Here are some of the ASCII assignments that will be of interest to you.

ASCII 1–26 These are devoted to CTRL-A through CTRL-Z. Some of the control characters have special functions. For example:

ASCII	CHARACTER	FUNCTION
7	CTRL-G	Bell, beep
8	CTRL-H	Backspace
13	CTRL-M	Carriage return

You can test these codes at the keyboard. For example, type CTRL-M several times. As you can see, the result is the same as pressing RETURN. Or do this: space the cursor halfway across the screen and then enter a series of CTRL-Hs. You'll see that the cursor backspaces across the screen.

CTRL-G, which rings the computer's bell, has another function, as you have already seen: It will interrupt a procedure in midstream. Because of this latter function, if you enter CTRL-G at the keyboard the computer will respond STOPPED!. There is a way to access the other meaning of CTRL-G.

You can print out any ASCII character, using the Logo primitive CHAR and the ASCII code number. To ring the bell, for example, enter this:

```
PR CHAR 7
```

Or, how about this procedure:

```
TO BELL
PR CHAR 7
BELL
END
```

When you run this procedure, don't forget that you can interrupt it by typing CTRL-G.

ASCII 48–57 These codes are dedicated to the numbers 0 through 9.

ASCII 65–90 These are the twenty-six letters of the alphabet, in capital letters. You can experiment with these, using CHAR. Try the following instruction, using WORD.

```
PR (WORD CHAR 76 CHAR 79 CHAR 71 CHAR 79)
```

You can learn the ASCII code of any character that interests you as follows:

```
PR ASCII "!
33
PR ASCII " "
34
PR ASCII "#
35
PR ASCII "$
36
PR ASCII "%
37
```

Each of these instructions will get you the ASCII code for the character specified. Thus, A is 65, # is 35, and " is 34.

One important ASCII character that cannot be discovered in this fashion is 32: *space*. You can examine this character with the following command:

```
REPEAT 20 [TYPE CHAR 32]
```

Notice that this command moves the cursor to the center of the line.

ASCII 97–122 These ASCII codes are dedicated to the alphabet in lower-case letters, for those computers with a lower-case capacity. If your computer doesn't have lower-case letters, these will appear the same as ASCII 65–90.

ASCII 129–154 Although the normal character display on the Apple screen is white on black, this alphabet is displayed in *inverse:* black on white. To see what this means, you might want to PR CHAR some of the numbers in this range. You will use this soon to create a program to convert regular letters to inverse ones.

ASCII 193–218 This alphabet is displayed in a *flashing* format. You can PR CHAR some of the characters in this range to check it out. Or consider the procedures in the following section.

INVERSE and FLASH

If you take a look at the ASCII codes assigned to the regular alphabet and compare them to the inverse alphabet, you'll see there's a constant difference of 64. For example, regular A is 65, whereas *inverse* A is 129.

You know how to discover the ASCII code of a character using the ASCII command, and you know how to print an ASCII code using the CHAR command. You can put those two capacities together to create a procedure that translates regular letters into inverse ones, as follows:

```
TO INVERT :T
TYPE CHAR (64 + ASCII(FIRST :T))
INVERT BUTFIRST :T
END
```

The second line is the key to this procedure. Notice that :T is the string of characters (a word, for example) that you want to convert to inverse. The expression FIRST :T selects the first character of the string. ASCII(FIRST :T) determines the ASCII code for that character, adding 64 generates the code of the inverse equivalent, and the TYPE CHAR portion of the statement prints the new (inverse) character. The third line causes INVERT to run again, dropping off the character just converted.

The procedure has some flaws as first constructed. If you create and run it, you will see the procedure has no capacity for ending without a fuss. The following additional line solves that problem. Before sending the computer off to invert the next BUTFIRST :T, check to see if it is blank ("). If it is, have the computer PR [ ], which simply moves the cursor to the beginning of the next line, at which point have it STOP.

```
TO INVERT :T
TYPE CHAR (64 + ASCII(FIRST :T))
IF (BUTFIRST :T) = " [PR [ ] STOP]
INVERT BUTFIRST :T
END
```

Why not try the program now by entering something like:

```
INVERT "WOW
```

The procedure thus constructed is limited to single words. There are a number of ways of remedying that shortcoming. For example, the additional lines shown here will convert nonalphabetical characters, such as periods, into blanks. The second line checks whether the character being examined has an ASCII code lower than 65. If it does, the third line causes the computer to print a blank (CHAR 32); if not, the fourth line prints the inverse of the character.

```
TO INVERT :T
TEST ASCII (FIRST :T) < 65
IFTRUE [TYPE CHAR 32]
IFFALSE [TYPE CHAR (64 + ASCII(FIRST :T))]
IF (BUTFIRST :T) = " [PR [ ] STOP]
INVERT BUTFIRST :T
END
```

Notice that the additional lines in the procedure involve some new commands: TEST, IFTRUE, and IFFALSE. These operate as an extension of the logic of the IF command examined previously. Line 2 of the procedure TESTs whether the first character of :T has an ASCII code of less than 65. If it does (IFTRUE), the computer is to skip a space (CHAR 32) and proceed. If the ASCII code isn't less than 65 (IFFALSE), it should invert the character as discussed earlier.

Here's an example of an instruction using this procedure:

```
INVERT "LOGO.IS.THE.GREATEST
```

Now that you have INVERT working the way you want, you can create a comparable program that will convert regular letters to a flashing format. One simple way of doing this is to:

```
COPYDEF "FLASH "INVERT
```

As used here, COPYDEF will create a duplicate copy of INVERT and call it FLASH. Then you:

```
EDIT "FLASH
```

and edit the new procedure as follows:

```
TO FLASH :T
TEST ASCII (FIRST :T) < 65
IFTRUE [TYPE CHAR 32]
IFFALSE [TYPE CHAR (128 + ASCII(FIRST :T))]
IF (BUTFIRST :T) = " [PR [ ] STOP]
FLASH BUTFIRST :T
END
```

Why not take some time now to experiment with these new procedures. See if you can find ways you might use them within other procedures that you want to create.

Cursor Positions

As we've seen, Logo operates two screens simultaneously: a graphics screen and a text screen. You can see the graphics screen by entering CTRL-L and the text screen by entering CTRL-T. And, as you'll recall, CTRL-S gives you a combination of the two, reserving the bottom four lines of the screen for text.

The turtle lives (and moves) on the graphics screen; the cursor moves on the text screen. The text screen is organized along *x* and *y* dimensions similar to those discussed in connection with the graphics screen, although the numbering is different, as indicated in this diagram:

As you can see, the text screen is twenty-four lines by forty columns in size. The lines are numbered from 0 to 23, starting at the top; whereas the columns are numbered from 0 to 39, starting at the left margin. (One of these spaces is what it takes for a single alphabetical or numerical character to occupy, whereas the graphics spaces are only the size of a dot.)

You can learn the position of your cursor by simply entering PR CURSOR. If you clear the screen first and then ask for the cursor location, the computer will respond with 0 23. You can move the cursor's position with the command SETCURSOR, as in SETCURSOR[25 23]. This will place the cursor at the twenty-fifth column of the bottom line of the screen. If you set the cursor higher than line 20, you will not see it (if you are in a SPLITSCREEN condition). CTRL-T will let you see where it is.

You can also place the cursor by using defined variables. Instead of brackets, in that case, use the SE function, as follows:

```
MAKE "H 12
MAKE "V 10
SETCURSOR (SE :H :V)
```

Now you can put some of these new tricks into practice. Instead of several illustrations, this chapter will present one long one. I think you'll get a kick out of it.

Illustration

The song "Old McDonald Had a Farm" provides an excellent opportunity to experiment with some of the text-processing techniques you've learned.

REFRAIN

To begin, recall the familiar old refrain:

> Old McDonald had a farm.
> E I E I O

You can recreate that refrain through Logo with the following procedure:

```
TO REFRAIN
PR [OLD MCDONALD HAD A FARM]
PR [E I E I O]
END
```

If you enter this and try it out, you'll find that it prints out the right words, but something is lacking. There's no soul in it. It's matter-of-fact, not cheery and musical. It doesn't swing. The following will make it a little fancier:

```
TO REFRAIN
PR [OLD MCDONALD HAD A FARM]
WAIT 60
PR [ ]
EIEIO
WAIT 60
END

TO EIEIO
REPEAT 14 [TYPE CHAR 32]
TYPE [E  I] WAIT 20
TYPE CHAR 32
TYPE [E  I] WAIT 20
TYPE CHAR 32
PR "O WAIT 60
END
```

Enter the procedures and try them out by typing REFRAIN. Notice that the EIEIO part of the refrain has been fancied up by the creation of a separate subprocedure. It prints a bit, pauses, prints some more, and so on. Also, EIEIO has been indented to put a little variation in the display.

FARM

Now you can create the superprocedure. It's a pretty simple procedure and contains the data of the song—the animals and the sounds they make. After you're all done, you can edit this procedure and change the data.

```
TO FARM
CLEARTEXT
MAKE "ANIMAL [[DUCKS QUACK] [COWS MOO] [PIGS OINK] [SHEEP BAA]
        [CHICKENS CLUCK] [TURKEYS GOBBLE]]
MCDONALD 1
END
```

You'll see that the data have been stored as a *list of lists*, which Logo allows with no problems. At the lowest level, a list consists of an animal name and its sound, such as [DUCKS QUACK]. The name :ANIMAL has been assigned to represent the list of lists. The next-to-last line in the superprocedure moves you on to MCDONALD, one of the procedures that does the real work. As you'll see, MCDONALD requires an input that refers to a particular animal in the list. Notice that MCDONALD starts with the first animal; as you'll see, MCDONALD will then proceed to move through the list.

MC DONALD

Before looking at the new procedure, review the structure of the song you are simulating. There are some regional variations, but this is the version you'll be working with. Here is the beginning:

> Old McDonald had a farm.
>   E I E I O
> And on that farm he had some ducks.
>   E I E I O

With a quack quack here,
A quack quack there,
Here a quack,
There a quack,
Everywhere a quack quack.

Old McDonald had a farm.
E I E I O

And on that farm he had some cows.
E I E I O

With a moo moo here,
A moo moo there,
Here a moo,
There a moo
Everywhere a moo moo.

A quack quack here,
A quack quack there,
Here a quack,
There a quack,
Everywhere a quack quack.

Old McDonald had a farm.
E I E I O

Then, as you'll recall, each successive verse adds a new animal (and its sound) to the head of the list—and proceeds to run through the list of all previous animals and sounds.

MCDONALD moves through the list of animals and sets up the ever-lengthening chorus of the song. A separate procedure, CHORUS, handles the chorus itself. Look at MCDONALD now.

```
TO MCDONALD :N
CLEARTEXT
REFRAIN PR [ ]
PR [AND ON THAT FARM]
WAIT 20 PR [ ]
TYPE [HE HAD SOME]
TYPE CHAR 32
INVERT (FIRST (ITEM :N :ANIMAL))
WAIT 60 PR [ ]
EIEIO
```

```
PR [WITH . . .]
PR [ ]
CHORUS :N
IF :N = COUNT :ANIMAL [REFRAIN STOP]
MCDONALD :N + 1
END
```

Notice the line INVERT (FIRST (ITEM :N :ANIMAL)) uses the procedure INVERT, which was created earlier in the chapter. If you didn't create INVERT, you can simply change INVERT to PR in this line, and it will work just fine. Either way, see what this line does.

The variable :N was specified as 1 by FARM. Thus, the phrase (ITEM :N :ANIMAL) refers to item number 1 in the list :ANIMAL. If you recall the way that list was structured, you'll see that the first item in that list was [DUCKS QUACK], itself a list containing two items. The addition of FIRST to this line specifies that you want the computer to INVERT (or PR) DUCKS. As a bottom line, then, the instructions up to this point will result in:

```
OLD MCDONALD HAD A FARM
      E I E I O
AND ON THAT FARM
HE HAD SOME DUCKS.
```

The next portion of the procedure adds another EIEIO. Then MCDONALD calls up CHORUS, which you'll see in a moment. (It handles the "quack quack here," "quack quack there" business.)

Skip to the next-to-last line for a moment:

```
MCDONALD :N + 1
```

This is the recursive instruction that runs MCDONALD again, but with :N equal to 2. Thus, for example, it will print HE HAD SOME COWS the second time through. Each progressive pass through this loop will move one more animal through the list.

As you may have imagined, however, you are going to run out of animals eventually. If that happens, the procedure will fall apart and send you an error message. To avoid that, add the line:

```
IF :N = COUNT :ANIMAL [REFRAIN STOP]
```

The phrase COUNT :ANIMAL will return the number of items in the main list. The remainder of the line says that once :N has increased to the full length of the list, the computer should [REFRAIN STOP]. That is, it should print the refrain one more time and quit.

Now you can turn to CHORUS and its quack-quacks and moo-moos.

CHORUS

Here's the hardest working procedure on Old McDonald's farm:

```
TO CHORUS :N
MAKE "S LAST (ITEM :N :ANIMAL)
PR (SE "A :S :S "HERE)
WAIT 90
PR (SE "A :S :S "THERE)
WAIT 90
PR (SE [HERE A] :S)
WAIT 45
PR (SE [THERE A] :S)
WAIT 45
PR (SE [EVERYWHERE A] :S :S)
WAIT 90 PR [ ]
IF :N > 1 [CHORUS :N - 1]
END
```

To start, note that CHORUS takes the same input as MCDONALD, representing the number of the latest animal added to the song. To simplify matters, it has been called :N again, but don't forget you could call it something else if you wish.

The second line in the procedure is also a simplifying step. The phrase (ITEM :N :ANIMAL) again selects the most recent animal/sound pair; the first time through, this is [DUCKS QUACK]. Adding LAST selects the sound, which has been assigned as the value for :S. From now on, :S can be used for the sound rather than for the complex statement that defined it.

Most of the lines in this procedure are straightforward PR statements: "here a quack," "there a quack," and so on. But here's a powerful, though simple, statement:

```
IF :N > 1 [CHORUS :N - 1]
```

The first time through CHORUS, :N will equal 1, so Logo will fail the test IF :N > 1 and pass on to END. The next time through, however, :N will equal 2 (having mooed here and there). Since :N is greater than 1, Logo will rerun CHORUS, reducing :N to 1. Having mooed, it will set to quacking.

The third time through, with :N equal to 3, CHORUS will oink, reduce :N to 2 and moo, and reduce :N to 1 and quack. With :N once again equal to 1, CHORUS will send the computer back to MCDONALD.

While using :N as a counter in both MCDONALD and CHORUS simplifies matters in one sense, it can be a source of confusion also. If you study these procedures long enough, you will eventually ask yourself why the reduction of :N to 1 during the iterations of CHORUS doesn't interfere with MCDONALD's count. The reason is simply that when you use the same input name in different procedures, they do not interfere with each other. Therefore, changing :N in CHORUS doesn't affect :N in MCDONALD.

That pretty much completes Old McDonald's farm. In fact, you can run it now by simply typing FARM. Why don't you try it out? If it doesn't work, check your procedures to make sure they are the same as the ones here in the book.

If you run the procedure, you'll find that it still has one minor snag in it. It shows up this way:

```
A OINK OINK HERE
A OINK OINK THERE
HERE A OINK
THERE A OINK
EVERYWHERE A OINK OINK
```

ARTICLE

Clearly you can't expose young people to such blatant disregard for proper use of *a* and *an*. Though it takes a little work, you can remedy this problem fairly easily. All it takes is a new procedure and some modifications to CHORUS.

```
TO ARTICLE :S
MAKE "ART "A
IF FIRST :S = "A [MAKE "ART "AN]
IF FIRST :S = "E [MAKE "ART "AN]
IF FIRST :S = "I [MAKE "ART "AN]
IF FIRST :S = "O [MAKE "ART "AN]
IF FIRST :S = "U [MAKE "ART "AN]
OUTPUT :ART
END

TO CHORUS :N
MAKE "S LAST (ITEM :N :ANIMAL)
PR (SE (ARTICLE :S) :S :S "HERE)
WAIT 90
PR (SE (ARTICLE :S) :S :S "THERE)
WAIT 90
PR (SE "HERE (ARTICLE :S) :S)
WAIT 45
PR (SE "THERE (ARTICLE :S) :S)
WAIT 45
PR (SE "EVERYWHERE (ARTICLE :S) :S :S)
WAIT 90 PR [ ]
IF :N > 1 [CHORUS :N - 1]
END
```

The purpose of ARTICLE is to select the appropriate article—either *a* or *an*—to use with the animal sound :S. Ultimately, the procedure will output the correct article under the name :ART. Begin (on the second line) by defining :ART as A. The next five lines of the procedure check to see if that definition should be changed. (FIRST :S) is the first letter of the sound. If the sound begins with any of the five vowels, :ART will be changed to AN. Finally, the procedure outputs the result.

Notice in CHORUS that the old A has been replaced with ARTICLE :S. This will replace the offensive A OINK with AN OINK.

Old McDonald's farm is now complete. At the same time, I encourage you to tinker with it yourself. That's one of the best ways to learn how to write procedures. You might want to play with the timing of the pauses or with the spacing of words and sentences. At the very least, you should get into FARM and modify the list of animals and sounds.

Some Common Bugs

Not using space with CHAR. You must always put a space between CHAR and the number specified. If you to fail to, something like this will happen:

```
?PR CHAR65
I DON'T KNOW HOW TO CHAR65
?PR CHAR 65
A
```

Not using brackets with SETCURSOR. Like SETPOS, SETCURSOR requires a list of two values as its input; therefore, you need to use brackets, as follows:

```
SETCURSOR [10 15]
```

If, on the other hand, you want to set the cursor using defined variables, you need to use the SE function instead of brackets. Here's an example:

```
SETCURSOR (SE :H :V)
```

Setting cursor outside its range. The horizontal range for the cursor is 0 to 39; its vertical range is 0 to 23. Here's what happens if you try to place the cursor outside those limits:

```
?SETCURSOR [20 39]
SETCURSOR DOESN'T LIKE 39 AS INPUT]
```

Sometimes, you will make this error by reversing the horizontal and vertical specifications. Remember, the horizontal comes first, the vertical second. (You can remember that horizontal and vertical are in alphabetical order in this instance.)

Exploring Further

1. Write some slide show procedures that will instruct students in the logic of ASCII and how to use it.
2. Create a procedure using SETCURSOR to create the letter X as shown. Then create other letters.

```
X   X
 X X
  X
 X X
X   X
```

3. Write an interactive procedure that asks you to enter some word, asks if you want it converted to an inverse or flashing format, and then does whichever is asked for.
4. Write a procedure that uses the TEST-IFTRUE-IFFALSE combination.

Teaching Objectives

- ☐ Students will explain the logic of the ASCII system of notation.
- ☐ Students will PRint characters by using CHAR and their ASCII codes.
- ☐ Students will determine the ASCII codes of characters by using the ASCII command.
- ☐ Students will write a simple procedure to print the inverse of flashing versions of single letters. (The procedures illustrated in the chapter took words and sentences as input.)
- ☐ Students will create TEST-IFTRUE-IFFALSE units in a procedure.
- ☐ Students will determine the position of the cursor on the text screen.
- ☐ Students will place the cursor at specified locations on the text-screen, using the SETCURSOR command.

Teaching Techniques and Materials

Concrete Learning

ASCII codes can usefully be introduced to some students by using index cards. Here's one way to structure the cards:

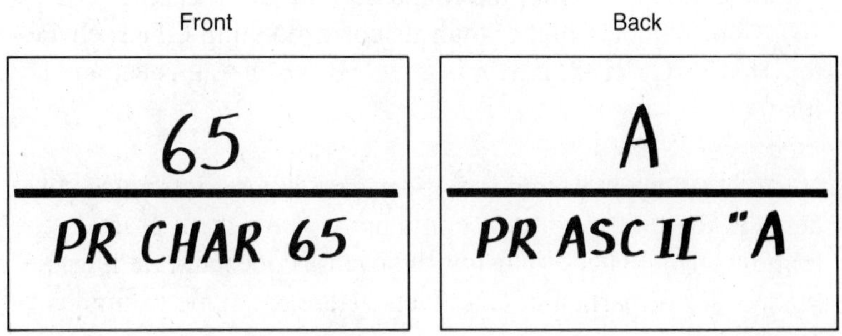

As you can see, the cards link characters with their ASCII code numbers. In addition, they present the format for using the CHAR and ASCII commands in connection with that linkage.

You can create numerous games in connection with the ASCII codes, and your students will be able to think of many more. For example, you can encourage them to use ASCII to send each other coded messages.

Cursor position commands can be introduced concretely with graph paper. In fact, this will be easier than was the case with the graphics screen, since the text screen is composed of fewer lines. Have students rule off the appropriate portion of a piece of graph paper and label the vertical lines 0–23 and the horizontal lines 0–39. Once they have done that, students can practice identifying specific locations based on SETCURSOR specifications.

Mind-size Bites—Simple to Complex

Begin the introduction of ASCII codes with the observation that the letters of the alphabet can simply be numbered from 1 to 26. Once students are comfortable with that, point out that ASCII uses that range of numbers for the control characters CTRL-A to CTRL-Z. Remind them of what some of those control characters do: for example, CTRL-G stops procedures from operating.

Next, indicate that the regular (upper-case) letters of the alphabet are contained within the range 65–90. Each capital letter is sixty-four numbers higher than its corresponding CTRL character. Hence, CTRL-A is 1, A is 65; CTRL-B is 2, B is 66; and so forth.

Once they have mastered the upper-case letters, introduce students to the CHAR and ASCII commands. Have them practice both PRINTing letters by using their ASCII codes and finding the ASCII codes of particular characters. Here are some examples:

```
?PR CHAR 65
A
?PR CHAR 66
B
?PR ASCII "A
65
?PR ASCII "B
66
```

Once students are able to use CHAR and ASCII effectively, introduce them to the other keyboard characters, such as !"#. Be sure to include CHAR 32 (space). For many students, the best way of handling this is in the form of a challenge. Either challenge them to discover the ASCII codes for each of a specified set of characters, or ask them to determine what the ASCII codes 27–63 (and other ranges) represent.

Student Exercises

Pencil and Paper Exercises

1. What is your name, as represented in ASCII codes?
2. What do these ASCII codes translate into?

   70 65 78 84 65 83 84 73 67

3. Create a secret coding system, based on ASCII, that you could use to code and decode messages.
4. Rule off thirty-nine by twenty-four boxes on a section of graph paper and number the lines the way the Logo text screen is organized for the cursor. Show where the cursor would be in response to the command SETCURSOR [10 12].
5. Create a procedure that will make a large letter L on the text screen, using SETCURSOR and a bunch of L's.

At the Computer

1. Using the CHAR command, determine what characters have been assigned to the ASCII codes 27–63.
2. Write a procedure that will take a word as input and respond with the ASCII codes, as shown here:

   ```
   ?CODE "LOGO
   76 79 71 79
   ```

3. Write a procedure that will take a string of ASCII codes and respond with the characters they represent, as in this example:

   ```
   ?DECODE [76 79 71 79]
   LOGO
   ```

4. Write a Logo procedure that will fill the first line of the text screen with X's.
5. Modify the procedure in (4) so that it will fill the entire text screen with X's.

Lesson Plan Elements

- ☐ CHAR
- ☐ ASCII
- ☐ TEST
- ☐ IFTRUE
- ☐ IFFALSE
- ☐ INVERT
- ☐ FLASH
- ☐ CURSOR
- ☐ SETCURSOR

Review of Logo Commands

NAME	EXAMPLE	FUNCTION
CHAR	PR CHAR 65	Specifies a character by using its ASCII code number. This example will cause the computer to print A.
ASCII	PR ASCII("A)	Learns the ASCII code number for the character specified. In this case, the computer will return the number 65.
TEST	TEST :X < :Y	Asks the computer to conduct a test of whether the condition specified (here, :X < :Y) is true or false. Used in conjunction with IFTRUE and IFFALSE.
IFTRUE	IFTRUE [PR :X]	Tells the computer what to do if the result of a TEST is true.
IFFALSE	IFFALSE [STOP]	Tells the computer what to do if the result of a TEST is false.
CURSOR	PR CURSOR	Asks the computer to report the current location of the cursor on the text screen, in the form of horizontal and vertical locations.
SETCURSOR	SETCURSOR [10 10]	Moves the cursor to the location specified, with the numbers in brackets indicating first the horizontal and then the vertical locations.
	SETCURSOR (SE :H :V)	Use this format when variable names (for example, :H :V) are used instead of numbers.

A Logo Challenge

Now that you've seen how Logo can be used to recreate Old McDonald's farm, try your hand at "The Twelve Days of Christmas," which you'll find a little simpler.

In case you're not familiar with the Christmas carol, it goes like this:

On the first day of Christmas,
My true love gave to me:
A partridge in a pear tree.

On the second day of Christmas,
My true love gave to me:
Two turtledoves and
A partridge in a pear tree.

On the third day of Christmas,
My true love gave to me:
Three French hens,
Two turtledoves, and
A partridge in a pear tree.

Successive verses add the following presents:

Four calling birds
Five gold rings
Six geese a-laying
Seven swans a-swimming
Eight maids a-milking
Nine ladies dancing
Ten lords a-leaping
Eleven pipers piping
Twelve drummers drumming

Write procedures to recreate the twelve verses of the song.

Chapter 19

Advanced Text Processing

A Powerful Idea

In this final chapter on Logo programming, three illustrations will be presented that should expand your ideas about what you can do with Logo. In addition to developing your use of text-processing techniques, you will find new ways of combining text and graphics.

While this chapter will not introduce any new Logo commands, it will raise the idea of **computer simulation:** using the computer to mimic real-life processes. The three procedures illustrated in this chapter reflect different aspects of simulation. Although ways for you to explore further in connection with these procedures will be suggested, the pedagogical sections used throughout the book are not appropriate here.

Illustrations

Simulating the Recursive Wage-Price Spiral

One of the things that makes recursive procedures particularly interesting is that many life processes are recursive. Take a minute to think of someone you know fairly well. Think of three or four characteristics of that person: outgoing personality, intelligence, friendliness—things like that. These characteristics can be called your "picture" of the person.

Your picture of the person you are thinking of is based in large part on your actual observations of that person during the time you have known each other. This picture provides a basis for your expectations about the person—how he or she is likely to act in particular situations, for example.

It is by now well known that the pictures we all have of people strongly affect our observations of them. If you are certain that the person you are thinking of would become frantic and irrational in a crisis and a crisis occurs, you are likely to perceive the person acting frantically and irrationally. What you "observe," however, will further confirm your pictures. All of this represents a recursive process.

Another real-life example of recursion is the much-discussed wage-price spiral. To demonstrate the use of recursions in Logo, you are now going to create three Logo procedures that will produce a computer simulation of the wage-price spiral. To keep it as simple as possible, the example will focus on the bread industry. You'll consider the wages paid those involved in the production of the bread and also the cost of a loaf of bread. You want to look at the impact of price changes on wages and the impact of wage changes on prices.

Begin by creating a procedure to determine wage levels based on prices. For the sake of simplicity, assume that when the price of bread increases—by 10 percent, for example—it is necessary for workers' wages to increase by the same percentage, so the workers are able to buy bread at the new price. The construction of the procedure will be demonstrated step by step.

```
TO LABOR :NEWPRICE
```

The first line declares the name of the procedure, LABOR, and specifies an input, :NEWPRICE, which represents the current price of a loaf of bread. As you'll see, this is only meaningful in relation to the previous price of bread, which can be called :OLDPRICE. In this model, LABOR needs to know price changes in order to determine the wage changes required by workers.

```
MAKE "INC :NEWPRICE / :OLDPRICE
```

Now you are establishing a variable, :INC, which represents the degree of increase, if any, in the price of bread. It is calculated by dividing the :NEWPRICE by the :OLDPRICE. (Don't worry where :OLDPRICE came from; you will handle that shortly.) Notice that if there has been no increase—if old and new prices are the same—:INC equals 1.

```
MAKE "PERCENT (100 * (:INC - 1 ))
```

To determine the percentage increase, create a new variable by subtracting 1 from :INC and then multiplying the result times 100. You can test the logic of this step by trying it on different possible increases. Notice, for example, where :INC equals 1, :PERCENT equals 0; where :INC equals 1.1, :PERCENT equals 10.

```
PR [THIS IS LABOR SPEAKING]
PR [SINCE PRICES HAVE INCREASED]
SP 3 (PR SE :PERCENT "PERCENT)
PR [IT WILL BE NECESSARY TO RAISE WAGES]
SP 3 PR [BY THAT SAME PERCENT]
```

These are primarily PRINT statements, but notice that the second line reports the :PERCENT of increase in price that was calculated. Notice there is an unfamiliar command in two of the lines: SP. It is a short procedure:

```
TO SP :N
REPEAT :N [TYPE CHAR 32]
END
```

CHAR 32, as you'll recall, is the ASCII character representing a blank space. This short procedure takes some number as its input and indents the next printed line by that amount. With that aside, return to LABOR:

```
MAKE "NEWWAGE (:INC * :OLDWAGE)
```

Now calculate the increase in wages needed if the workers are to continue buying the bread being produced. :NEWWAGE is created by multiplying :INC and :OLDWAGE. Now wages have been increased by the same percentage as prices. (Note: This is commonly referred to as "keeping up with inflation.")

```
(PR SE [THE NEW WAGE IS] :NEWWAGE)
```

This line simply reports the new wage level.

```
MAKE "OLDPRICE :NEWPRICE
PR [ ]
```

As you continue this process, the new price becomes history, so you are making it the :OLDPRICE. The next time this procedure is run, the starting wages and prices will be higher than they were the previous time around. PR [ ], as you recall, simply prints a blank line.

```
WAIT 900
```

This command causes the program to pause for 900/3600 of a minute, or fifteen seconds. The purpose of this is simply to give you time to read what the computer has just printed. You may want to raise or lower the amount—increasing or decreasing the delay, respectively.

```
MANAGEMENT :NEWWAGE
END
```

This tells the computer to run the procedure called MANAGEMENT, which you will create shortly, giving it an input of :NEWWAGE.

Here's the whole procedure:

```
TO LABOR :NEWPRICE
MAKE "INC :NEWPRICE / :OLDPRICE
MAKE "PERCENT (100 * (:INC - 1))
PR [THIS IS LABOR SPEAKING]
PR [SINCE PRICES HAVE INCREASED BY]
SP 3 (PR SE :PERCENT "PERCENT)
PR [IT WILL BE NECESSARY TO RAISE]
```

(continued on next page)

(continued)
```
SP 3 PR [OUR WAGES BY THAT PERCENT]
MAKE "NEWWAGE (:INC * :OLDWAGE)
(PR SE [THE NEW WAGE IS] :NEWWAGE)
MAKE "OLDPRICE :NEWPRICE
PR [ ]
WAIT 900
MANAGEMENT :NEWWAGE
END
```

To review, LABOR is a procedure that calculates the wages workers need in order to keep up with cost of living, which has been represented here by the price of a loaf of bread. The procedure takes :NEWPRICE as an input, compares it with :OLDPRICE, and calculates the wage increase, which would correspond to the price increase. Finally, as you've seen, it reports the wage increase to MANAGEMENT. Now, what does MANAGEMENT do with the new information?

```
TO MANAGEMENT :NEWWAGE
```

This declares the procedure and specifies the input it requires.

Similar to what you've just seen in LABOR, MANAGEMENT checks to see how much wages have increased . . .

```
MAKE "INC :NEWWAGE / :OLDWAGE
```

. . . and calculates the increase as a percentage.

```
MAKE "PERCENT (100 * (:INC − 1))
```

These lines are similar to the same ones in LABOR:

```
PR [THIS IS MANAGEMENT SPEAKING]
PR [SINCE WAGES HAVE INCREASED BY]
SP 3 (PR SE :PERCENT "PERCENT)
PR [IT WILL BE NECESSARY TO RAISE THE PRICE]
SP 3 PR [OF BREAD BY THAT PERCENT]
```

So are these:

```
MAKE "NEWPRICE (:INC * OLDPRICE)
(PR SE [THE NEW PRICE IS] :NEWPRICE)
MAKE "OLDWAGE :NEWWAGE
```

```
PR [ ]
WAIT 900
```

Finally, MANAGEMENT reports the increased price of bread back to LABOR.

```
LABOR :NEWPRICE
END
```

Here's the whole procedure:

```
TO MANAGEMENT :NEWWAGE
MAKE "INC :NEWWAGE / :OLDWAGE
MAKE "PERCENT (100 * (:INC - 1))
PR [THIS IS MANAGEMENT SPEAKING]
PR [SINCE WAGES HAVE INCREASED BY]
SP 3 (PR SE :PERCENT "PERCENT)
PR [IT WILL BE NECESSARY TO RAISE THE PRICE]
SP 3 PR [OF BREAD BY THAT PERCENT]
MAKE "NEWPRICE (:INC * OLDPRICE)
SP 3 PR [OF BREAD BY THAT PERCENT]
MAKE "NEWPRICE (:INC * OLDPRICE)
(PR SE [THE NEW PRICE IS] :NEWPRICE)
MAKE "OLDWAGE :NEWWAGE
PR [ ]
WAIT 900
LABOR :NEWPRICE
END
```

Now you have two procedures, one representing management and the other representing labor. While grossly oversimplified, these procedures nonetheless reflect the functions of these two segments of industry.

What you need now is a superprocedure to organize and initiate the two procedures already created. Call it INFLATION. The procedure begins:

```
TO INFLATION
```

and continues thus:

```
MAKE "OLDWAGE 5
MAKE "OLDPRICE .65
```

These numbers are arbitrary. Assume wages start at $5.00 an hour and the price of bread is sixty-five cents ($.65) a loaf. Assume further that these two amounts are in balance. That is, if the workers earn $5.00 an hour, they can afford to buy the bread at $.65 a loaf. On the other hand, as long as labor costs $5.00 an hour, management can afford to sell the bread for $.65 a loaf.

```
LABOR .65
END
```

This launches the interaction between MANAGEMENT and LABOR. LABOR has been informed that bread now costs $.65 a loaf. Here's the whole procedure:

```
TO INFLATION
MAKE "OLDWAGE 5
MAKE "OLDPRICE .65
LABOR .65
END
```

Notice that LABOR has been told that the price of bread is the same as before. What do you suppose will happen if you run INFLATION? Try it and see.

If you enter and run these procedures, you will find that prices and wages stay in balance over time. The procedures will keep grinding away: MANAGEMENT announces the price of bread as $.65 a loaf and LABOR responds by announcing wages need to be $5.00 an hour.

```
THIS IS LABOR SPEAKING
SINCE PRICES HAVE INCREASED BY 0. PERCENT
IT WILL BE NECESSARY TO RAISE OUR WAGES BY THAT PERCENT
THE NEW WAGE IS 5.

THIS IS MANAGEMENT SPEAKING
SINCE WAGES HAVE INCREASED BY 0. PERCENT
IT WILL BE NECESSARY TO RAISE THE PRICE OF BREAD BY THAT
      PERCENT
THE NEW PRICE IS .65
```

```
THIS IS LABOR SPEAKING
SINCE PRICES HAVE INCREASED BY 0. PERCENT
IT WILL BE NECESSARY TO RAISE OUR WAGES BY THAT PERCENT
THE NEW WAGE IS 5.

THIS IS MANAGEMENT SPEAKING
SINCE WAGES HAVE INCREASED BY 0. PERCENT
IT WILL BE NECESSARY TO RAISE THE PRICE OF BREAD BY THAT
      PERCENT
THE NEW PRICE IS .65
```

Not much of a wage-price spiral.

But now suppose management raises the price of bread just a little. Maybe the cost of wheat increased slightly one year. Or perhaps the investors demanded higher dividends, or maybe the company's executives wanted higher salaries. For whatever reason, assume that management increases the price of bread to $.75 a loaf. Do this by editing INFLATION as follows:

```
TO INFLATION
MAKE "OLDWAGE 5
MAKE "OLDPRICE .65
LABOR .75
END
```

Now what do you suppose will happen?

- ☐ Will the price increase have no effect?
- ☐ Will wages rise one time and then flatten out?
- ☐ Will this one tiny increase begin a wage-price spiral?

Again, the best way to find out is to try it.

If you try out the program, you will find the third possibility above is what happens. Once the price is increased, wages increase to catch up. Once wages rise, however, management must increase the price of bread again. The process is unending.

```
THIS IS LABOR SPEAKING
SINCE PRICES HAVE INCREASED BY 15.3846 PERCENT
IT WILL BE NECESSARY TO RAISE OUR WAGES BY THAT PERCENT
THE NEW WAGE IS 5.76923
```

```
THIS IS MANAGEMENT SPEAKING
SINCE WAGES HAVE INCREASED BY 15.3846 PERCENT
IT WILL BE NECESSARY TO RAISE THE PRICE OF BREAD BY THAT
       PERCENT
THE NEW PRICE IS .865385

THIS IS LABOR SPEAKING
SINCE PRICES HAVE INCREASED BY 15.3846 PERCENT
IT WILL BE NECESSARY TO RAISE OUR WAGES BY THAT PERCENT
THE NEW WAGE IS 6.65681

THIS IS MANAGEMENT SPEAKING
SINCE WAGES HAVE INCREASED BY 15.3846 PERCENT
IT WILL BE NECESSARY TO RAISE THE PRICE OF BREAD BY THAT
       PERCENT
THE NEW PRICE IS .998521

THIS IS LABOR SPEAKING
SINCE PRICES HAVE INCREASED BY 15.3846 PERCENT
IT WILL BE NECESSARY TO RAISE OUR WAGES BY THAT PERCENT
THE NEW WAGE IS 7.68093

THIS IS MANAGEMENT SPEAKING
SINCE WAGES HAVE INCREASED BY 15.3846 PERCENT
IT WILL BE NECESSARY TO RAISE THE PRICE OF BREAD BY THAT
       PERCENT
THE NEW PRICE IS 1.15214
```

Now things are moving swiftly. The process will continue on and on, with both prices and wages getting higher and higher, each trying to keep up with the other.

This set of procedures will demonstrate to your students that Logo (and computers in general) are good for something more than just entertainment. What Papert has described as "powerful ideas" can be powerful indeed!

The procedures are open to numerous modifications if you are interested in making them more realistic or useful. First, you can experiment with different initial increases. What would happen if the price of bread were initially increased to $.51 a loaf? To a dollar a loaf?

Also, the display formats of the procedures can be made more elegant in any number of ways.

A little more ambitiously, you might replace WAIT 900 with:

```
PR [PRESS ANY KEY TO CONTINUE] MAKE "X READCHAR
```

After printing the instruction, the computer will wait for you to press some key on the keyboard. Notice that the keyboard entry is assigned as X, even though you aren't going to do anything with it. Now you can control the pace at which the process continues. You can make this substitution in both LABOR and MANAGEMENT or simply omit WAIT 900 in one of them.

In the Exploring Further section of this chapter are some other suggested modifications you might want to experiment with. At this point, however, take a look at a very different application of Logo.

A Logo Bomb

Here's a more elaborate set of procedures that should expand the horizons of what can be done with Logo. As you'll see, it combines text and graphics to good effect.

This procedure simulates an exploding bomb. You'll see how to construct it step by step. The first procedure, BOMB, announces itself, pauses for a bit, and then draws the body of the bomb.

```
TO BOMB
CLEARTEXT TEXTSCREEN
SETCURSOR [10 10]
PR [THIS IS A BOMB]
WAIT 120
CS FULLSCREEN
PU LT 90 FD 50 RT 90 BK 20 PD
REPEAT 42 [FD 15 RT 10]
REPEAT 10 [FD 8 LT 90 FD 1 LT 90 FD 8 RT 90 FD 1 RT 90]
FUSE
END
```

Notice that BOMB ends by calling for FUSE to run. This procedure lays out a long, curving fuse from the bomb, and makes its clever comment.

```
TO FUSE
FD 2 LT 90
REPEAT 18 [FD 5 LT 10]
REPEAT 9 [FD 10 RT 10]
HT
CLEARTEXT
TEXTSCREEN
SETCURSOR [10 10]
PR [CAN YOU MATCH THAT?]
WAIT 120
FULLSCREEN
END
```

Now the plot thickens. In response to the challenge to "match" the bomb, a match appears, ignites, and starts the fuse burning. All this is interspersed with textual comments.

```
TO MATCH
RT 30 PU FD 50 PD
REPEAT 10 [BK 5]
REPEAT 36 [FD 2 BK 2 RT 10]
RT 60
CLEARTEXT
TEXTSCREEN
SETCURSOR [18 12]
PR [OH NO!!!]
WAIT 60
CLEARTEXT
SETCURSOR [10 12]
PR [NOT THAT KIND OF MATCH]
WAIT 120
FULLSCREEN
WAIT 30
REPEAT 6 [FD 15 BK 15 RT 10]
PE REPEAT 6 [LT 10 FD 15 BK 15]
LT 90
CLEARTEXT
TEXTSCREEN
SETCURSOR [15 10]
```

```
PR [RUN FOR COVER!!!]
WAIT 60
REPEAT 9 [LT 10 BK 10 LIGHT]
REPEAT 18 [RT 10 BK 5 LIGHT]
END
```

Notice that MATCH uses a procedure called LIGHT, which simulates bursts of flame as the fuse burns toward the bomb. Here's how LIGHT works:

```
TO LIGHT
RT 20 PD
REPEAT 5 [FD 6 BK 6 LT 10]
PE REPEAT 5 [RT 10 FD 6 BK 6]
LT 20
END
```

At last, the fuse burns all the way down and the bomb explodes, making good use of alternations between the text and graphics screens. The illusion of an explosion is produced by shifting the background color between black and white.

```
TO EXPLODE
SETBG 1
CLEARTEXT
TEXTSCREEN
SETCURSOR [21 12]
PR [B O O M]
WAIT 7
FULLSCREEN
SETBG 1 SETBG 0 CS
REPEAT 2 [SETBG 1 SETBG 0]
CLEARTEXT
TEXTSCREEN
SETCURSOR [33 23]
PR [WHOOPS]
END
```

Finally, here's a superprocedure to hold it all together:

```
TO BOOM
BOMB
MATCH
EXPLODE
END
```

Once all this has been entered, it is initiated by typing BOOM. Here's what follows:

THIS IS A BOMB

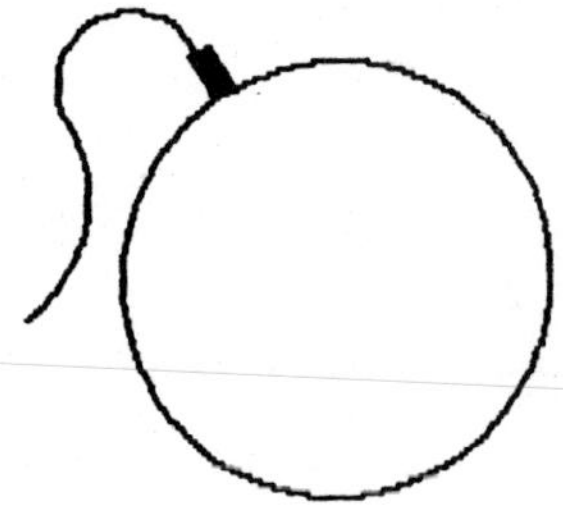

CAN YOU MATCH THIS?

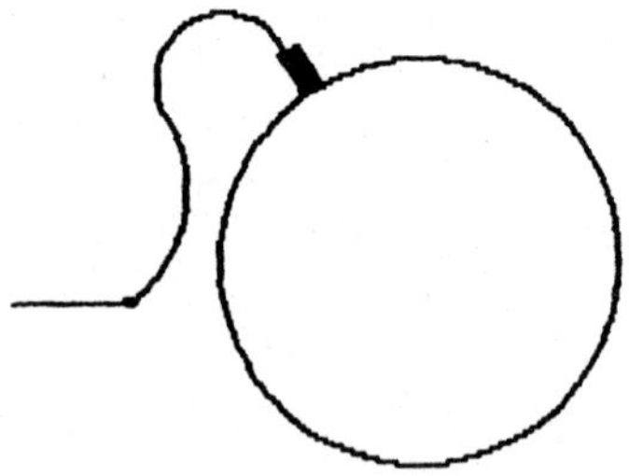

OH NO!!!
NOT THAT KIND OF MATCH

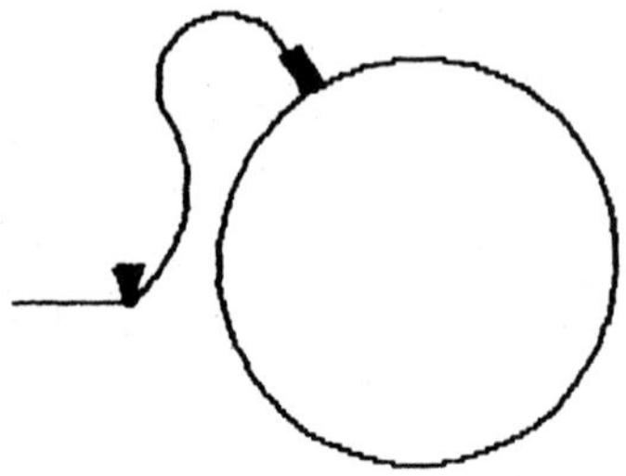

RUN FOR COVER!!!

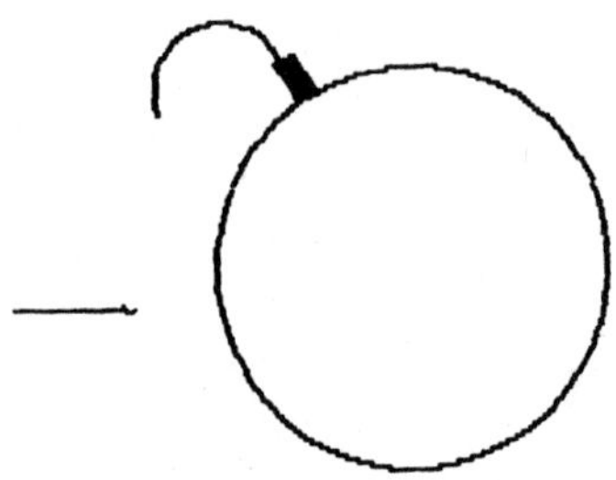

Bomb explodes.

These illustrations cannot do justice to the procedures in action. They are presented here just to give you a guide in debugging the procedures, if necessary, after you enter them. These procedures should suggest new possibilities that might not otherwise be obvious.

Arms Race

Here's a more sober view of bombs, which will interest any of your students who are concerned about the nuclear arms race. It has been calculated that the total of all explosives used in World War II by all countries equaled 3 megatons, or 3 million tons of TNT. This seems like a pretty big bang, except that it has also been estimated that the weapons currently being held in reserve by the USA and the USSR total 18,000 megatons—or 6,000 times the total firepower of World War II.

What follows is a set of procedures that presents this information, using both the graphics and text capacities of Logo. As you will see, the procedures are not polished; you or your students may want to improve them.

Here are the parts of the package. It begins with an introductory text passage. (This is an excellent place to make changes.)

```
TO INTRO
TEXTSCREEN
CLEARTEXT
PR [IN ALL OF WORLD WAR TWO, WHICH KILLED]
PR [FIFTY MILLION PEOPLE AND INVOLVED]
WAIT 240
PR [ ]
PR [ALMOST EVERY COUNTRY IN THE WORLD]
PR [FOR AROUND FOUR YEARS, THE TOTALITY]
PR [OF ALL THE EXPLOSIVES EXPLODED]
WAIT 240
PR [ ]
PR [EQUALED 3 MEGATONS OF TNT]
WAIT 120
PR [ ]
PR [OR . . . 3,000,000 TONS OF TNT]
WAIT 120
PR [ ]
PR [OR . . . 6,000,000,000 POUNDS]
WAIT 180
CLEARTEXT
PR [TO UNDERSTAND THE SCOPE OF THE]
```

(continued on next page)

(continued)

```
PR [CURRENT ARMS RACE BETWEEN THE USA]
PR [AND THE USSR, LET'S LET THIS DOT]
WAIT 180
PR [ ]
REPEAT 17 [TYPE CHAR 32] PR ".
WAIT 60
PR [ ]
PR [EQUAL THE 3 MEGATONS EXPLODED IN WWII]
WAIT 240
PR [ ]
PR [HERE'S THE "STRENGTH" OF THE USA AND]
PR [THE USSR TODAY]
WAIT 120
END
```

Following the text introduction, you create a sketch of the earth on the graphics screen. When you run this, you will see there is plenty of room for improvement, and your students may enjoy taking that on.

```
TO EARTH
HT
PU SETPOS [-50 0]
PD REPEAT 36 [RT 10 FD 10]
PU SETPOS [-10 30] PD
SETPOS [-10 10] SETPOS [-12 15]
SETPOS [-25 15] SETPOS [-28 5]
SETPOS [-20 -10] SETPOS [-15 -12]
SETPOS [-20 -40] SETPOS [-30 -12]
SETPOS [-28 5] SETPOS [-32 15]
SETPOS [-34 32] SETPOS [-28 35]
SETPOS [-5 34] SETPOS [-10 30]
PU SETPOS [10 30] PD
SETPOS [10 20] SETPOS [15 28]
SETPOS [15 20] SETPOS [13 3]
SETPOS [18 3] SETPOS [18 1]
SETPOS [30 0] SETPOS [10 -5]
SETPOS [13 -40] SETPOS [30 -10]
SETPOS [25 -5] SETPOS [30 -10]
SETPOS [40 -20] SETPOS [60 -15]
PU SETPOS [10 30] SETPOS [55 23]  PD
END
```

Since this is going to present a sort of nuclear scoreboard, the next two procedures create the labels USA and USSR. Notice that each of these procedures uses subprocedures that draw the individual letters: YEW (U), ESS (S), AYE (A), and ARE (R).

```
TO USANAME
PU SETPOS [-20 100] PD YEW
PU SETPOS [0 100] PD ESS
PU SETPOS [20 100] PD AYE
END

TO USSRNAME
PU SETPOS [-30 -80] PD YEW
PU SETPOS [-10 -95] PD ESS
PU SETPOS [30 -95] PD ARE
END

TO YEW
PU LT 45 FD 10 PD SETH 180
FD 15 REPEAT 18 [LT 10 FD 1]
FD 15
END

TO ESS
PU RT 45 FD 5 LT 45 PD
REPEAT 27 [LT 10 FD 1]
REPEAT 27 [RT 10 FD 1]
END

TO AYE
PU FD 10 PD RT 20 BK 25 FD 25
LT 40 BK 25 FD 10 LT 70 FD 10
END

TO ARE
PU LT 150 FD 15 RT 150 PD
FD 20 RT 90 FD 5
REPEAT 18 [RT 10 FD .8] FD 3
LT 135 FD 15
END
```

Having created the background for the graphics display, you offer a quick reminder of how the world's arms are going to be displayed, with one DOT equaling 3 megatons of TNT, the total of all explosives used in WWII (World War II).

```
TO REMINDER
CLEARTEXT TEXTSCREEN
SETCURSOR [0 6]
PR [REMEMBER, EACH DOT EQUALS]
PR [ALL THE FIREPOWER OF WWII]
WAIT 500
END
```

Now here's the superprocedure: ARMS.RACE. You'll see that it begins by calling up the INTRO procedure; then it prepares the graphics screen and puts the map and names on it. After running the reminder, the procedure defines two variables: :X is set at −118 and :Y is set at 115. Next the procedure runs USA, giving :X and :Y as inputs.

```
TO ARMS.RACE
INTRO
HT
FULLSCREEN
EARTH
USANAME
USSRNAME
REMINDER
MAKE "X −118 MAKE "Y 115
USA :X :Y
CS
END
```

USA is one of two procedures that place a DOT on the display for every 3 megatons of explosives in the world's military arsenals. As you can see, this procedure is a model of simplicity. A DOT is placed at position :X :Y. (Note: It is essential to use SE when giving defined variables as the inputs to DOT.) The first time USA is run, a DOT will be placed near the upper-left corner of the screen, at −118 115.

```
TO USA :X :Y
DOT SE :X :Y
USSR :X :Y
END
```

Notice that USA's last step is to run USSR, giving the same inputs that it received from ARMS.RACE. USSR begins by placing another DOT on the display. Notice that :Y is multiplied by −1, thereby placing the first DOT in the *lower*-left corner of the screen (at −118 −115). The next-to-last line in USSR sends returns to USA, to be rerun with :X increased by 1. This will have the effect of producing two horizontal lines of DOTs; one for the USA and one for the USSR. The two middle lines move the process from line to line and conclude it when the lines of DOTs converge in the middle of the display.

```
TO USSR :X :Y
DOT AE :X (:Y * −1)
IF :X > 118 [(MAKE "Y :Y −3) (MAKE "X − 121)]
IF :Y < 0 [EXPLODE STOP]
USA :X + 3 :Y
END
```

Once the rows of dots have converged, the whole process concludes when USSR goes to EXPLODE and then STOPs. As you can see, the procedure simulates an explosion by alternating between black and white backgrounds for the display.

```
TO EXPLODE
WAIT 120
REPEAT 4 [SETBG 1 SETBG 0]
END
```

Here's a sample of what the screen looks like in the midst of the graphics display.

These diverse examples should give you some ideas for projects you can undertake using Logo's text and graphics capabilities, and there are some specific suggestions in the following section. While the graphics aspect may seem more exciting at the start, the most professional products combine both graphics and text.

Exploring Further

1. Modify INFLATION so you can enter the initial increase in the price of bread as an interactive input rather than by editing the procedure.
2. Build a counter to keep track of how many cycles of wage-price increases have taken place.
3. Find other recursive processes in real life and write some Logo procedures to simulate them.

A Logo Challenge

In connection with the wage-price spiral simulation, create a new procedure, RESOURCE, which lets you make changes in the cost of resources over the course of the process. On each cycle, MANAGEMENT could run RESOURCE, which would ask whether resource costs have changed and further increase (or decrease) :NEWPRICE before returning to LABOR.

Chapter 20

Teaching Logo in the Classroom

You'll recall from earlier discussions in this book that Papert and his colleagues were motivated to create Logo partly in response to their unhappiness with conventional educational forms and practices. In Papert's view, schools often destroy the natural enthusiasm children have for learning. While this is perhaps most evident in regard to mathematics and foreign languages, Papert suggested in *Mindstorms* that conventional teaching techniques could easily create "dancophobia" if dancing were taught the way mathematics is taught.

One of Papert's persistent fears has been that Logo might be taught in the same way as other school topics. In particular, he has been concerned that computers will be used to program children rather than children learning to program computers. So this concluding chapter will draw your attention to some of the fundamental principles involved in having Logo be a positive, empowering experience for young people.

In addition, some logistical issues involved in teaching Logo—such things as managing the computer hardware—will be discussed. This is a topic about which little has been written previously, and I am especially grateful to the Logo instructors who were willing to share their teaching discoveries with you.

The Spirit of Logo

Learning versus Teaching

While I have spoken of *teaching* Logo, Logo is really more fundamentally a matter of *learning* than of teaching. In its most joyous sense, learning is a matter of discovery. We often speak of the **Aha! experience** in this respect: that moment in which something previously murky, unclear, and puzzling, even frustratingly so, suddenly becomes clear. "Now I see!" we may exclaim. At its most powerful, this experience has a sense of something being revealed to us, almost in a religious sense. We may speak of "all the pieces falling into place."

Other times, such Aha! experiences may be unrelated to any particular problem we were grappling with. We may simply see a new possibility that was not previously evident. For example, imagine the excitement of the first person who saw the potential of computers for word processing. Whatever their form or history, these are among the headiest moments of life.

Computers, perhaps because they are new and unfamiliar to most of us, can provide a seemingly endless series of Aha! experiences. This has certainly been my experience during ten to fifteen years of teaching myself to program in various languages. Once you have gotten started, computer programming can become an absolute joy. "There's so much to learn" actually becomes a source of excited anticipation rather than a burden. There is no limit to the potential for new insights and discoveries.

It has also been my experience that all this can be a burden for the learner. While there are obviously no statistics on the matter, I would guess that there are at least as many people struggling painfully with some form of computer education as there are people who are ecstatic about it.

Here's an important key in the difference between those two experiences of learning. For learning to be burdensome, there must be something to learn: some body of knowledge which the learner does not now know but must. The larger and the more complicated this body of knowledge, the more burdensome and loathsome the task of learning it.

In this context, a main function of teachers is to force learners to learn. In fact, the teachers' existence depends on the learners' unwillingness to learn on their own. This situation creates a clear and firm status relationship, with the teachers dominating over the learners and each in opposition to the other.

As an alternative, consider the situation in which a young child is given a hammer for the first time. While there is some body of knowledge comprising all the things that can be done with a hammer, none of that is relevant. Children in this situaton are not burdened, they are empowered. They can now make noises and dents they couldn't make before. The hammer is a source of delight rather than a burdensome new responsibility.

In comparison to other programming languages, Logo is particularly suited to the experience of discovery and joy rather than burden and pain. To begin, the basic body of knowledge is rather small. Indeed, as you've seen, one of the main strengths of Logo is that you create your own body of knowledge, your own set of techniques and commands. Even if a child only learned FD, RT, and REPEAT, this would allow the creation of many elaborate designs. Thus, it is not necessary to serve a long, dreary apprenticeship before being creative and innovative. Each new technique learned thereafter expands the child's total ability exponentially.

To be an effective Logo instructor, then, you need to be able to get out of the way and let students learn. Their learning must be their own. Mary Jo Moore described the task this way:[1]

---

1. Mary Jo Moore, "The Art of Teaching Logo," *Classroom Computer News,* April 1983, 28–29.

Logo lends itself to endless exploration and discovery. Ideally, each student follows a different timetable and makes different stops along the way . . . .

As teachers, our problem is knowing how to intercept students' discouragement when learning Logo—without intercepting their discovery.

The secret, then, is to know when to lend a hand and when to let the students work something out for themselves. Unfortunately, there is no handy guide to doing this, though just being conscious of the issue is a big part of getting the job done.

Ironically, the desire to produce Aha! experiences for your Logo students is generally counterproductive, as it will usually rob them of the thrill of discovery. In fact, if there is some*thing* you want to produce in their learning of Logo, that "thing" becomes part of some body of knowledge you know that they don't, something that keeps them inferior to you.

Teaching Logo effectively is something like telling a joke. It's great when you can tell a joke and people get it, but it's terrible when you try to explain it until they understand it. The joy of teaching and learning Logo comes when you can make a suggestion and have someone get it without being beaten into submission.

Styles of Learning

Moore's comments point to a related aspect of the teaching and learning of Logo: Students learn it in a variety of different ways, none of which is wrong and all of which can work.

Daniel Watt reported on an eighteen-month study of sixteen sixth-graders in the public schools of Brookline, Massachusetts, who were given instruction in Logo. Watt was struck by the different learning styles of the different students. In particular, Watt focused his attention on two students, Donald and Deborah.

Donald tended to plan his Logo designs mathematically, carrying out individual steps in a logical and systematic fashion. Deborah, on the other hand, was much more intuitive in her work. She planned little, taking whatever next step seemed appropriate in the realization of the picture she had in her mind.

Another observer of the Brookline study, Cynthia Solomon distinguished three common learning styles. First, the *planner* laid out the design for procedures in advance of writing them; Donald exemplified this approach. Solomon described the *macro-explorer* this way:[2]

> **This student likes to mess about with subprocedures or building blocks to arrive at a product, rather than starting out with a specific goal. In this case, the learner is intent on exploring the effect of the particular building block. Therefore, the result is open-ended.**

Third, Solomon found the *micro-explorers,* who were more cautious in examining the implications and ramifications of each new technique. The micro-explorer, for example, may test whether FD 50 FD 50 produces the same result as FD 100.

In the general computer literature as well as in discussions of Logo, writers sometimes speak of top-down versus bottom-up programming. The former approach is similar to that used by Solomon's planner: The big picture is created first, and then the details comprising it are worked out one by one. In bottom-up programming, on the other hand, the programmer begins with some simple elements and proceeds to develop something more complex out of them.

The point is not that one style is better than the other. Rather, Watt and Solomon have urged teachers to be prepared to deal with and support whatever individual styles students bring to the learning of Logo. In fact, Solomon encouraged children to learn and use all three approaches; in her own teaching, she has tried to plant seeds of all three.

---

2. Cynthia Solomon, "Introducing Logo to Children, *BYTE,* August 1982, 196–208.

Whether you are teaching one child or several classes, it's important that you realize there is no right or wrong way of learning Logo. Whatever your children do is probably right for them. By the same token, each child will operate at his or her own pace, and you can support children most by letting them choose the appropriate pace.

Concrete to Abstract

As discussed earlier in the book, both Piaget and Papert held the view that children learn most effectively when they progress from the concrete to the abstract. It was the gears of Papert's youth, for example, that let him grasp abstract concepts as his education progressed throughout life. Fundamentally, Logo is designed to support the grounding of abstract concepts in concrete objects and experiences. In introducing children to Logo, however, you can make it even more concrete.

It is an excellent idea to have children walk through Logo procedures physically before trying them at the computer. In introducing the BOX procedure, for example, you might proceed as follows:

1. Have one child walk out the outline of a box on the floor while another child makes notes on the moves the first one is making.
2. Have the second child convert his or her notes into Logo instructions such as, FD 10 RT 90.
3. Have the second child read the Logo instructions one at a time while the first child follows those instructions; check to see if the instructions produce the pattern desired.
4. Enter the instructions in the computer, try it out, and make whatever adjustments are appropriate.

As a variation on this method, Donna Bearden and Jim Muller[3] have suggested that you might have children fashion a turtle out of a walnut shell, decorating it however they choose. Then, they can move the turtle around a sheet of paper, simulating and anticipating the Logo turtle.

---

3. Donna Bearden and Jim Muller, "Turtle Graphics: On and Off the Screen," *Classroom Computer News*, April 1983, 33–34.

As still another variation, you might have the children create designs on the floor with rope or twine. (Tile floors are especially useful in this regard.) Then students can pace off the design, converting their actions into Logo instructions. The other possible variations on this theme are limited only by your imagination and theirs.

Simple to Complex

Another fundamental principle of both Logo and Piagetian learning theory is that children learn from the simple to the complex, using the simple things they have learned to construct more complex creations. As a corollary, any complex problem can be broken down into simpler components.

Recall the HOUSE created in Chapter 7. It's obviously too complex a problem for a young child learning Logo for the first time. But any child could learn to create a procedure to draw the frame of the house in short order. And, actually, the door isn't very difficult. In fact, with a little work, the windows. . . . The point is that each of the components of the house is pretty simple. In fact, the logic and techniques of putting the components together isn't all that difficult either. The secret lies in seeing the pieces in their simplicity rather than being intimidated by the whole.

This principle works effectively in both bottom-up and top-down programming. Looking from the bottom up, Logo's powers of REPEAT and recursion can easily turn the simplest of designs into something elaborate and complex. Who but an experienced Logo user would realize that this design is simply thirty-six boxes rotated 10 degrees from each other?

Rather than confronting children with complex designs, you would do well to teach them something absolutely simple—even boringly so. Then show them how slight adjustments can turn it into something awe-inspiring. Then step back and let them experiment with whatever variations their minds can concoct.

The simple-to-complex principle is equally important for top-down programming. As soon as your children begin to grasp the potentials of Logo, they will very likely start making plans that exceed their immediate grasp. This was my experience, for example, the first few times I began to teach my son to program. A charter member of the video game generation, Aaron always wanted his first effort to produce something to rival the most sophisticated of the arcade games—adding those modifications he had always felt would improve the arcade games. His efforts were doomed to frustration and failure.

Logo readily lends itself to the simplification of complex tasks and plans. If your students begin with an ambitiously complex vision, don't be too quick to dampen their plans. Have them begin by breaking the whole into components. Then have them begin designing the individual components. They are likely to produce more than you initially thought they could, and if they fail to make good on their original vision, they are almost certain to be sidetracked into something equally satisfying to them as they discover designs and directions neither they nor you anticipated.

I suggest for your consideration and use the following two axioms:

- ☐ No Logo design is so simple that it cannot be REPEATed and recursed into something complex beyond recognition.
- ☐ No design is so complex that it cannot be broken down into manageable components.

When your students or children discover these axioms for themselves, that discovery will probably have an impact on their lives that extends well beyond Logo.

Students Teaching Students

Those who have taught Logo in classroom settings have commonly found students spontaneously teaching each other. The excitement that Logo typically generates seems to produce a natural desire to share it. You should be on the alert, therefore, for ways of sharing the job of teaching Logo. You are likely to have many willing assistants.

Students also love to collaborate on Logo projects. Short of collaboration, you will find them swapping procedures with pride. All this is very much in the spirit of what Logo has to offer children and should be encouraged.

There Are No Mistakes in Logo

Earlier, I said there was no right or wrong learning style in Logo. I want to conclude this discussion with a more general point. It is possible to hold Logo as an error-free activity. That is, everything you do in Logo can be seen as a positive learning experience, as a necessary step in the direction of where you're going, whether you know where that is or not.

It is sometimes pointed out that the most sophisticated rockets and missiles are off course 99 percent of the time. The most advanced guidance systems operate on the basis of correcting errors. Too far to the left? Turn right. Now, too far to the right? Turn left. And so forth.

You would do well to encourage this view in your students as they learn Logo. They should be able to give the computer a command, note that it did not produce the result they intended, and take that information to indicate an adjustment is needed—nothing more. If you can save them from feeling wrong, invalidated, and inadequate in such situations, you will have contributed mightily to them. If you are really successful, they may even carry over some of that feeling into their other subjects.

As you can see, Logo can be a very special educational experience for your students, an experience that has an impact on their entire educational experience. Let's turn now to some of the practical, logistical considerations related to Logo.

The Logistics of Teaching Logo

This concluding section will look at some of the different ways you can organize and manage Logo instruction in the classroom. While I will not be presenting hard and fast rules in this regard—which would hardly be consistent with Logo itself—I will suggest some possibilities that might not have occurred to you. Ultimately, of course, you need to discover what works best for you and for your students. Ideally, you should make your students your partners in finding out what works best.

Managing Hardware

First, here is a review of the hardware involved in presenting Logo to students. This has already been discussed in Chapter 1, so this review will be from the management and logistical point of view.

Here's the minimum equipment you'll need to use Logo:

- ☐ Computer, such as an Apple IIe
- ☐ Disk drive, controller card, and cable
- ☐ Video monitor

If you have more than one computer for your students, it will be necessary for you to have one disk drive and one monitor for each of the computers.

Managing Riches

If you happen to have several computers available for your students—for example, if you are teaching a large class in computer use—you should arrange the computers around the perimeter of the room with students facing the walls, rather than arranging them in traditional classroom rows and files.

Arranged around the walls of the room, everybody will be able to look at their neighbors' screens and see what everyone else is doing, and you will be able to see everything. This makes it easier for you to monitor the entire class and encourages students to share their results with their friends.

Printing Hard Copy

In addition to this minimum configuration, it is really useful to add a printer so your students can print permanent copies of their Logo creations. These are the components required to print hard copies of Logo screen displays:

- ☐ A dot-matrix printer with a graphics capability. The Epson and Star-Gemini are popular brands used with the Apple.
- ☐ An interface controller card that fits inside the computer and sends instructions to the printer. The Grappler+ is a popular version used with the Apple.
- ☐ A cable connecting the controller card to the printer. This cable comes with the controller card.
- ☐ A supply of computer paper.
- ☐ A Logo procedure that instructs the computer to print whatever is on the graphics screen at the time.

Appendix C presents methods for printing out the text and graphics produced by Logo. At this point, let's focus on the logistics of printing in the classroom.

While it would be nice to have a separate printer for each computer, this is not necessary. There are two alternatives.

1. If you have a controller card for each computer, you should place the printer so that it is within reach of the several cables connected to the controller cards. This way, it is only necessary to unplug one computer from the printer and plug in another.
2. If you have only one controller card, then that computer will be the only one that prints hard copies of graphics displays. Your students will be able to create and save designs using any of the computers. When they are ready to print hard copies, they will move to the computer attached to the printer, put their disk in the disk drive, load the appropriate file, run the appropriate procedure, and print.

In either case, you will want to work out some system for coordinating the use of the printer. You might invite the students to suggest ways of handling this. In general, whenever you can turn responsibility over to them in a Logo environment, that's to the good.

Posters

Your students will be greatly assisted by large posters reminding them of the basic Logo commands and techniques. Placed on the walls facing the users, such posters—modeled after the reference card at the end of this book perhaps—will remind students of both the range of commands available as well as the format for using them.

This, too, is an excellent opportunity to involve students. Why not have them prepare posters as a special assignment? You could hold a contest and put the best posters on the wall.

By the same token, you should encourage students to make up posters about utility procedures they create. Suppose one student has created an excellent procedure for drawing leaves for trees. A poster showing the proper use of the procedure as well as a sample of the output could be a powerful acknowledgment for the student creating it and a useful tool for everyone else.

Floppy Disks

Your Logo package will come with one or two Logo system disks. Since these probably cannot be copied, you need to take special care of them. It may work for you to boot up the system in the morning, take away the system disk, and have the students use their own data disks thereafter.

It is very important for each student to have his or her own data disk. This will give students a place to save their own procedures without worrying about interfering with anyone else or having someone else erase their procedures. Each student should be responsible for storing his or her own disk, though you may want to provide a storage facility for them.

Managing Students

The key to managing students in learning Logo is to let them manage themselves. Logo works best when students are self-motivated and self-pacing. The less structure you put around Logo, the better. Moreover, it's important to realize that some conventional educational principles actually conflict with Logo. "Don't copy" is an example.

Past experience has shown students are eager to share what they learn about Logo. When they create a procedure that they are especially fond of, they want to show it to their friends. Moreover, as they learn of procedures their friends have created, they are eager to add those procedures to their own toolkits. Cynthia Solomon commented on this aspect of Logo:[4]

> **Sharing in this learning process is a self-empowering experience for all participants. A different way of looking at learning and teaching emerges, one based on the Piagetian idea that even very young children have theories. Thus, teaching and learning are not a matter of being wrong or right, but rather a process of debugging.**

The implication of this is that you would do well to let students work together. There are several ways you can take advantage of this. For example, you should be open to students working on team projects, and you might even assign it if you feel that's appropriate.

Similarly, you should be able to get some students to serve as tutors, assisting younger children and/or those just starting out. Logo seems to provide an opportunity for people to experience the real thrill of participating in someone else's Aha! moment.

Assignments and Problems

Problem solving is a powerful avenue for learning Logo. A common format is to present an outcome, such as a graphics design, and challenge students to write procedures to reproduce it. Bear three things in mind when you do this:

1. Don't make the graphics problems too difficult. As you've seen several times, a simple box can be rotated and replicated beyond recognition, so be careful not to let your cleverness become a frustration for your students.

4. Cynthia Solomon, "Introducing Logo to Children," *BYTE,* August 1982, 208.

2. There are usually several ways of creating a particular result in Logo, so don't demand that students achieve it using the "right" one.
3. The purpose of problem-solving exercises is to provide students with an opportunity to master Logo, not to solve specific problems. Thus, don't despair if a particular problem takes them off in an unexpected direction that expands their vision—be grateful.

Regarding content, this book offers numerous problems for your students. You will, of course, make up more. At the same time, don't overlook your students as a source of more problems to be solved. Why not have a contest to see who can create the best problem for others to solve? And be sure to carry over problems from one class to another and from one year to another.

Conclusion

This concludes our examination of Logo. I've enjoyed the opportunity to share it with you, and I hope it's been fun for you. I'm sure you'll have fun sharing it with your students.

Logo's potential for your students extends well beyond the possibility of creating computer designs. On the one hand, it is a way of opening up the vast potential of computers to your students. Once your students have mastered Logo, they will be ready to learn and use other computer languages.

More important, mastering Logo will empower your students in problem solving more generally. The abilities they develop in their study of Logo should carry over into their other subjects. Thus, your efforts represent a potent gift to your students.

Appendix A

A Logo Bibliography

If you find you want to learn more about Logo, you will have no trouble finding sources. In the past few years, Logo has become very popular among educators and has been the focus of numerous books and articles. While it would not be possible to list all the published sources on Logo, a number of them are supplied in this appendix. In addition to giving you specific references, the listings contained in this appendix will alert you to the names of individuals and journals that frequently address Logo.

As indicated earlier, there is one fundamental Logo reference that stands out from the rest: *Mindstorms* by Seymour Papert is the primary book about Logo, written by its chief creator. Papert has written of his work with Piaget as well as his purpose in creating Logo. *Mindstorms* is generally regarded as the official reference on the philosophy of Logo.

Each version of Logo, of course, comes with its own manuals, and you should learn to use them effectively. Some are primarily reference books; others contain tutorials for teaching you Logo.

Here are some of the Logo manuals you are likely to work with:

Davidson, Laurence J.
1982 *Apple Logo: Reference Manual*. New York: Logo Computer Systems, Inc.

Solomon, Cynthia
1982 *Apple Logo: Introduction to Programming through Turtle Graphics*. New York: Logo Computer Systems, Inc.

These two manuals come with the Apple Logo program. Solomon provides an introduction to Logo programming. Davidson's book is a more technical reference book. You will be able to read both of these with no trouble once you've completed the present book.

Grammer, Virginia Carter
1982 *The Terrapin Logo Language for the Apple II*. Cambridge, Mass.: Terrapin, Inc.

This is the official manual for Terrapin Logo for the Apple II.

Dr. Logo Language Reference Manual. Pacific Grove, Calif.: Digital Research.
1983

Meet Dr. Logo. Pacific Grove, Calif.: Digital Research.
1983

These present the IBM PC version of Logo.

The remainder of this appendix lists other books and articles you might like to read in learning more about Logo.

Computer Journals and Magazines

Most computer journals and magazines have articles on Logo from time to time, as you'll see in the listing of articles. In addition, some have regular columns on Logo. While these change from time to time, here are some you might look for.

Lawler, Robert
"Logo Ideas," *Creative Computing*

Martin, Kathleen, and Tim Riordon
"The Logo Center," *The Computing Teacher*

Muller, Jim
"Logo, the Voice of the Turtle," *Softalk*

Thornburg, David
"Friends of the Turtle," *Compute*

Books on Logo

Abelson, Harold

1982 *Apple Logo*. Peterborough, N.H.: *BYTE*.

1982 *Logo for the Apple II*. New York: McGraw-Hill.

Albrecht, Bob, and Ramon Zamora

1983 *Teach Yourself TI Logo*. New York: McGraw-Hill.

Bearden, Donna

1983 *One, Two, Three, My Computer and Me: A Logo Funbook for Kids*. Reston, Va.: Reston Publishing Co.

Bearden, Donna, Kathleen Martin, and Jim Muller

1983 *The Turtle's Sourcebook*. Reston, Va.: Reston Publishing Co.

Bitter, Gary G., and Nancy Ralph Watson

1983 *Apple Logo Primer.* Reston, Va.: Reston Publishing Co.

Burnett, J. Dale

1983 *Logo: An Introduction*. Morris Plains, N.J.: Creative Computing Press.

Goldenberg, E. Paul

1979 *Special Technology for Special Children*. Baltimore: University Park Press.

Papert, Seymour

1979 The Computer Age: A Twenty-Year View. Cambridge, Mass.: M.I.T. Press.

1980 *Mindstorms: Children, Computers, and Powerful Ideas*. New York: Basic Books.

Ross, Peter

1983 *Introducing Logo for the Apple II Computer, Texas Instruments 99/4A, and Tandy Color Computer.* Reading, Mass.: Addison-Wesley.

Thornburg, David

1983 Discovering Apple Logo. Reading, Mass.: Addison-Wesley.

Watt, Daniel

1983 *Learning with Logo*. New York: McGraw-Hill.

Articles on Logo

Abelson, Harold

1982 "A Beginner's Guide to Logo," *BYTE,* August.

Bamberger, Jeanne

1982 "Logo Music," *BYTE,* August.

Boecker, Heinz-Dieter, and Gerhard Fischer

1982 "Logo Project PROKOP," *BYTE,* August.

Carlson, Edward H.
1982 "The Three Faces of Apple LOGO," *Micro,* October.

Carter, Ricky
1983 "The Complete Guide to Logo," *Classroom Computer News,* April.

Ciarcia, Steve
1982 "High-Resolution Sprite-Oriented Color Graphics," *BYTE,* August.

Cron, Mary
1983 "Trouble in Logoland," *Teaching, Learning, Computing,* December.

diSessa, Andrea A., and Barbara Y. White
1982 "Learning Physics from a Dynaturtle," *BYTE,* August.

Goldenberg, E. Paul
1982 Logo—A Cultural Glossary," *BYTE,* August.

Gorman, Henry, Jr.
1982 "The Lamplighter Project," *BYTE,* August.

Grady, David
1983 "High-Tech Teaching," *Learning,* August.

Harvey, Brian
1982 "Why Logo?" *BYTE,* August.

Hechinger, Fred M.
1982 "About Education," *New York Times,* April 12.

Higginson, William
1982 "Leading Fish to Water," *BYTE,* August.

Jewson, Jan and Roy D. Pea
1982 "Logo Research at Bank Street College," *BYTE,* August.

Lawler, Robert W.
1982 "Designing Computer-Based Microworlds," *BYTE,* August.

Lemmons, Phil
1982 'Logo Update," *BYTE,* August.

Leron, Uri
1982 "The Group of the Turtle," *BYTE,* August.

Lough, Tom and Steve Tipps
1983 "Is There Logo after Turtle Graphics?" *Classroom Computer News,* April.

Markuson, Carolyn, Joyce Tobias, and Tom Lough
1983 Logo Fever," *INSTRUCTOR,* January.

Muller, James
1982 "The Friendly Languages," *Creative Computing,* October.
1982 "Young People's Logo Association," *BYTE,* August.

Nelson, Harold
1982 "Logo: Not Just for Kids," *Microcomputing,* March.

Papert, Seymour
1980 "New Cultures from New Technologies," *BYTE,* September.
1981 "Computers and Computer Cultures," *Creative Computing,* March.
1982 "Micros Becoming a Social Force," *Infoworld,* April 12.

Peterson, Marty
1983 "M.I.T. Logo: Educational Program for the Apple," *Infoworld,* January 31.

Rowe, Neil D.
1982 "More Poly's," *Creative Computing,* April.

Solomon, Cynthia
1982 "Introducing Logo to Children," *BYTE,* August.

Steffin, Sherwin
1983 "Kids and Computers, Part 1: Choosing the Right Software at the Right Time," *Softline,* September/October.

Watt, Daniel
1979 "A Comparison of the Problem Solving Styles of Two Students Learning; Logo: A Computer Language for Children," *Creative Computing,* December.
1982 "Logo in the Schools," *BYTE,* August.
1983 "Learning with Logo," *Classroom Computer News,* April.
1983 "Logo: What Makes It Exciting?" *Popular Computing,* August.

Watt, Molly
1982 "What Is Logo?" *Creative Computing,* October.

Weinreb, W.
1982 "Problem Solving with Logo," *BYTE,* November.

Weir, Sylvia
1981 "Logo and the Exceptional Child," *Kilobaud Microcomputing,* September.

Weir, Sylvia, and Daniel Watt
1982 "Logo: A Computer Environment for Learning-Disabled Students," *The Computing Teacher,* Volume 8, No. 5.

Williams, Gregg
1982 "Logo for the Apple II, the TI-99/4A, and the TRS-80 Color Computer," *BYTE,* August.

Appendix B

File Management

This appendix will help you become familiar with the way Logo files are organized in the computer and show you how to manage those files. As you'll see, Logo's structure is quite logical and straightforward. This discussion centers on files being created within the computer's memory and then stored on floppy disks. Let's begin by looking at floppy disks.

The Logic and Techniques of File Management

Preparing Disks for Use in Logo

You have already had some experience with disks if you've gotten this far in the book. The Logo system is contained on a disk that you need to use in booting the system. You may have even saved some files on the Logo disk.

Recall the booting process: There was a point at which the computer offered you the opportunity to replace the Logo disk with another one. As you get more and more involved in Logo, you will want to store your files on a separate disk—it would not be unusual for you to create several disks full of Logo creations.

If you buy some blank disks, you will discover that they cannot be used right away. They need to be **initialized** first; this means erasing any information contained on them and creating file formats that the Apple will be able to work with. Your Apple manual has instructions on the initializing of disks. It's a fairly simple process, so in case you can't find the instructions in your manual, here's a brief description of the process.

To begin, you must boot up your computer with some disk other than Logo. If you have a System Master disk, that would be perfect, but all you need to do is get to a point—outside of Logo—where the computer has presented you with a > or] prompt and a flashing cursor to the right of the prompt.

Remove the System Master disk, insert your blank disk in the disk drive, and enter the following four lines:

```
NEW
10 PRINT "HELLO"
20 END
INIT HELLO
```

After you've entered INIT HELLO, the disk drive should spring into action, making a sickly, grinding sort of sound. Don't worry—that's what it's supposed to do. It's now in the process of initializing the disk. The process will take the better part of a minute to complete. You'll know it's over once the disk drive stops and the prompt returns. Your disk is now ready for service in Logo. When you next boot up the Logo system and you are invited to insert your own file disk, this is the one to insert.

Warning: Never do this with a disk you *don't* want to initialize, since it will *erase* everything that might be on the disk. If you do this with your Logo disk, for example, you won't have Logo on it any more. As soon as you have some file disks to use for storing your Logo creations, you should put a write-protect sticker on your Logo program disk, covering up the notch as described in Chapter 1. That way you will be less likely to ruin your Logo disk accidentally.

Now here's a look at the structure of Logo files and how to manage them.

Workspace

When you first load the Logo system into your computer, a portion of the computer's random access memory (RAM), called the **workspace,** is set aside for your use. It is useful to think of the workspace as a blank sheet of paper for you to write on. Whenever you create a procedure, that procedure is written into your workspace. Whenever you finish editing a procedure by entering CTRL-C, the old version of the procedure is erased from the workspace and the new version is written in its place.

Whenever you instruct Logo to run a procedure, such as BOXES, it searches through the workspace for a procedure of that name. If it finds one, it performs the operations specified in that procedure.

Saving Procedures on Disk

Whenever you turn your computer off or otherwise exit from Logo, all the procedures contained in your workspace disappear. The easiest way for you to solve this problem is to copy the entire workspace into a file on the disk. As indicated at the close of Chapter 6, this is accomplished by the command:

```
SAVE "CHAP6
```

where CHAP6 is the name you've assigned to the file. You can assign almost any name you want. If you try to use an illegal name or some word that has already been reserved by Logo, the computer will tell you so, and you can simply try another file name.

Remember, you are assigning a file name to the *entire* workspace and saving it all, not just a particular procedure. If you attempt to use a file name that you have already used, you will be told: FILE ALREADY EXISTS. If you want to use that name—for instance, if you are updating the file—you first need to erase the name as follows:

```
ERASEFILE "CHAP6
```

Now you are able to enter SAVE "CHAP6 and have the current workspace saved under that name.

There are two problems with this procedure. First, it is inconvenient, requiring two commands to update a file. There's also some danger of accidental erasures of files. Don't be unduly nervous about this matter, but do be cautioned.

Once you are working with several Logo files, there is a danger that you may ERASEFILE and SAVE one file under the name of another. Say you have been working on CHAP6 a lot, updating the disk file frequently. You get in a habit of periodically entering ERASEFILE "CHAP6 and SAVE "CHAP6. Then you do some work on a file named FILE-B. By habit, you enter ERASEFILE "CHAP6 and SAVE "CHAP6. You now have a very big problem. You have just erased CHAP6 and replaced it with an updated copy of FILE-B. Any work you did on CHAP6 is lost.

Here's a way you can use Logo to make file management easier and avoid the danger just described at the same time. If you have labeled a particular file CHAP6, you can create the following procedure within that file:

```
TO UPDATE
ERASEFILE "CHAP6
SAVE "CHAP6
END
```

Now all you need to do is enter UPDATE, and the procedure will erase the old file and save the new version. In addition to making life easier in this regard, this method avoids the danger of accidental misnaming. You should create an UPDATE procedure for each file, being sure to use the correct file name in each case. Then you can have the confidence that entering UPDATE—no matter what file you are working on—will result in its being saved under the correct name.

Loading Files into Your Workspace

Procedures that have been saved as just described can be retrieved later. Perhaps you created a set of procedures and saved them under the name CHAP6, and then you turned off the computer and went about your business. The next time you came back to Logo, you could pick up where you left off by entering LOAD "CHAP6. Now, everything in the workspace you saved under that name will be copied off your disk and into the current workspace. It's possible, by the way, to LOAD more than one file into the workspace at a time. In fact, you can load two files into the workspace and save the combination under a third name. The only limit is the size of the RAM in your computer.

Getting Beyond the RAM Limit

Once you get deeply involved in Logo projects, you will eventually run into the problem of having too little RAM. For example, I tried to fit all the graphics for Chapter 7 in one workspace, along with a superprocedure that would print all of them in order without my having to do anything. Unfortunately, there wasn't room for the whole thing. I'm going to describe a way of solving this problem, even though you probably won't need the technique right away.

My main file was called CHAP7. It contained the various procedures for drawing designs and a superprocedure called FIGURES, which drew the designs and then printed them out on paper. When I ran out of space in CHAP7, I created an overflow file called CHAP7A. I also created a superprocedure in CHAP7A called FIGURES2, which did the same job in CHAP7A that FIGURES did in CHAP7. Finally, FIGURES closed with the following lines:

```
    .
    .
    .
ERALL
LOAD "CHAP7A
FIGURES2
END
```

As you can see, the instructions above erase everything in the workspace (ERALL), LOAD the file called CHAP7A, and run the new superprocedure, FIGURES2. To print all the figures, then, I LOADed CHAP7 and ran FIGURES. The procedure chugged along, drawing and printing the designs one by one. Then there was an interruption in the process as the disk drive sprang into action. Once CHAP7A had been LOADed, the process resumed, and the remaining figures were printed—without my having to do anything.

Creating Packages of Procedures

Sometimes, it makes sense to work with something less than your whole workspace. You may have created a set of procedures you use often in a variety of situations. Perhaps you want to use the housing procedures created in Chapter 7 over and over. You can establish them as a package as follows:

```
PACKAGE "HOUSING [FRAME WNDW DOOR ROOF CHIM]
```

HOUSING is the name assigned to the list of procedures to be brought together into a single package. Now you can save and load the package without saving the whole workspace. Here's an example of how you could save the package:

```
SAVE "HOUSING "HOUSING
```

HOUSING is now the name of a package in the file currently in the workspace and also the name of a new file on the disk.

Now you can load the package into the workspace and add it to various disk files with the command:

```
LOAD "HOUSING
```

The diagram of Logo storage structure provides a schematic review of the structure of Logo components. Notice that the disk can contain several files, with names such as CHAP9, INTRO, or CHAP6. The bottom portion of the figure details the contents of one such file: CHAP6. As you can see, the file contains several procedures (such as BOX, HOUSE, or FRAME. Notice that some of the procedures are organized in packages, while others are not.

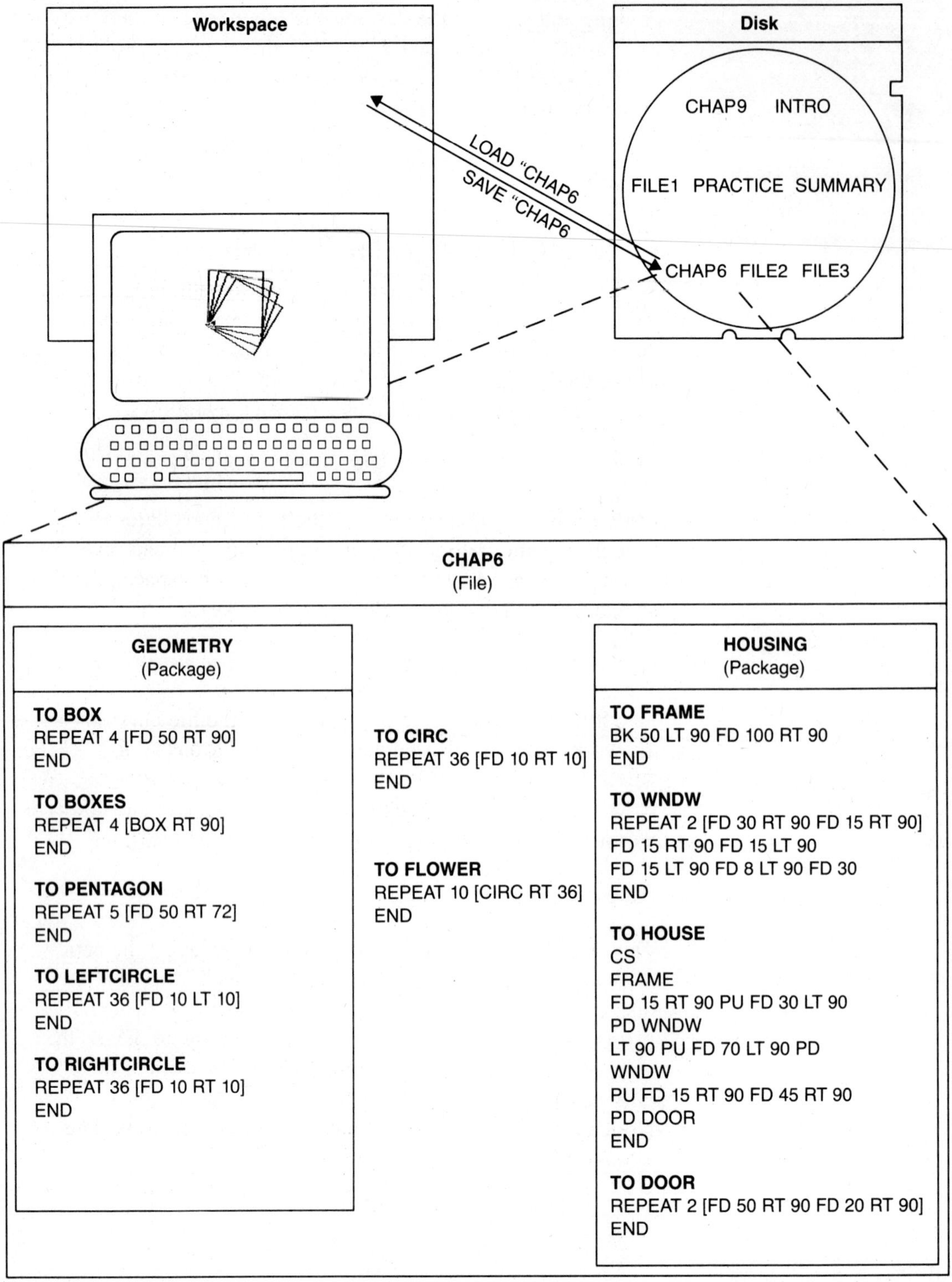

Logo storage structure

Files are copied from disk to workspace by the LOAD command. They are copied from workspace to disk by the SAVE command. It is important to realize that when you LOAD a file into your workspace from the disk, that file still remains on the disk. And when you SAVE a workspace to disk, the workspace is not affected.

This means that if you LOAD a file, make radical changes to some of your procedures, and then regret the changes, there is no need to worry. The disk file hasn't been affected by anything you've done to the workspace.

The only way you can affect a disk file is through the command ERASEFILE, as already introduced, or by using the UPDATE procedure discussed earlier. Suppose you've loaded CHAP6 into your workspace. You've made changes to the file—adding and editing procedures, for example. If you are sure that you want to replace the old version of CHAP6 with the new one, you do that in two stages.

First, ERASEFILE "CHAP6 erases the old file from the disk. This means that you no longer have a saved version of CHAP6. Second, SAVE "CHAP6 saves the current contents of your workspace under the name CHAP6. Notice that during the time between these two steps you do not have a saved copy of the file on your disk. Don't worry unduly, but you need to know that if you turn off the computer, if you exit Logo, or if the electricity goes off during this interval, you will have lost CHAP6:—both the new and the old versions.

As a simple precaution, you may want to save a copy of CHAP6 as CHAP6BACK or something similar, updating it periodically. You can even write a procedure to handle the updating automatically:

```
TO BACKUP
ERASEFILE "CHAP6BACK
SAVE "CHAP6BACK
END
```

Finding Out What You Have

As you create more and more procedures, packages, and files, you will soon be unable to remember everything you've done. This is no problem. There are several methods for finding out what you have.

CATALOG will get you a listing of all the files stored on your disk, in this format:

```
A 002 HELLO
T 006 PR5.LOGO
T 003 POLIES.LOGO
T 012 CHAP6.LOGO
T 008 HOUSING.LOGO
T 014 CHAP9.LOGO
```

The first file in this listing is a special one, essential to the disk working, but you won't have to do anything with it. The rest of the files shown are all Logo files, indicated by the suffix .LOGO. This suffix is added by the computer, and you *do not* use it in loading or saving files.

The numbers shown to the left of the file names indicate the approximate amount of space they take up on the disk. Space, in this case, is measured in thousands of **bytes,** where a byte equals a single character such as a letter or a digit. The letter T appearing in the leftmost column is a computer symbol for the type of file ("text"). The A appearing to the left of the first line indicates that HELLO is an Applesoft BASIC program.

Entering POTS gets you a list of the procedures in the current workspace, in the following form:

```
TO BOX
TO BOXES
TO FOLD :TIMES :THICK
TO SPI :DIST
TO RIGHTCIRCLE :SIZE
```

Notice that the listing for each procedure indicates whether the procedure expects inputs.

If you want to see the detailed listings of your procedures—similar to what you see when you EDIT a procedure—there are several ways of getting them.

- ☐ PO "HOUSE will produce a listing of the procedure named HOUSE.
- ☐ PO [ROOF CHIM] will produce a listing of the procedures CHIM and ROOF
- ☐ POPS "HOUSING will produce listings of all the procedures contained in the package HOUSING.
- ☐ POPS [HOUSING GEOMETRY] will produce a listing of all the procedures in both of the packages named.
- ☐ POPS will get you the listings of all the procedures in the current workspace.

Erasing Materials

You have already seen that the command ERASEFILE "CHAP6 will erase the entire file CHAP6 from the disk. Sometimes you will want to engage in less extensive surgery.

At times you may want to erase procedures you've created. There are a number of options for doing this. If you simply want to erase a specific procedure, say HOUSE, you can do that with the command:

```
ERASE "HOUSE
```

Now the procedure is no longer in your workspace. You have *not* erased the procedure from your disk, however. That won't happen until you save the workspace again—this time without the erased procedure.

There is an abbreviation for ERASE: ER. Also, you can erase more than one procedure at a time, as follows:

```
ER [HOUSE ROOF DOOR]
```

To repeat, the procedures have been erased from the workspace but not from your disk. Here are some other erasing options:

- ☐ ERPS "HOUSING erases all the procedures contained in the package HOUSING.
- ☐ ERPS [HOUSING GEOMETRY] erases the procedures of both packages.

Finally, for a full housecleaning of your workspace, the command ERALL erases everything in the current workspace.

Burying Procedures

Sometimes you may want to set aside some packages for special treatment. Perhaps you have created a package of basic geometric figures—called GEOMETRY and including BOX, TRIANGLE, LEFTCIRCLE, ARC, and so on—that you utilize in connection with the procedures of several files.

While you could store a package like this in each of your files, the resulting duplication would fill up your disk more than necessary. Logo provides a solution to this problem. Suppose you have a file, EUCLID, which utilizes several of the procedures you've packaged in GEOMETRY.

To work with EUCLID, then, you would load both EUCLID and GEOMETRY into your workspace with separate load commands:

```
LOAD "EUCLID
LOAD "GEOMETRY
```

At this point, if you ask for a listing of the procedures in your workspace (using POPS, POALL, and so on), you'll get everything. If GEOMETRY contains many long-established and unchanging procedures, those will tend to get in the way of your work with the procedures of EUCLID. Moreover, if you change EUCLID procedures and want to save the modified version, the new disk file will include GEOMETRY as well as EUCLID.

The command BURY "GEOMETRY has a significant effect on the situation just described. While you have full access to all the procedures of GEOMETRY, they will be ignored by the commands ERALL, ERPS, POPS, POTS, and SAVE. This means you can call for a listing of procedures without getting those from GEOMETRY. When you save a revised version of EUCLID, it will not contain the GEOMETRY procedures.

The command UNBURY "GEOMETRY does what you think it does: It undoes the work of BURY. Now the procedures contained in GEOMETRY will be treated like all the others in the workspace.

Other Commands

Logo offers a variety of other commands relevant to file maintenance. Some of those found in Apple Logo will be briefly mentioned here. If you are using another version of Logo, you may not have these commands, and you may have other commands that are not discussed here. You should study your Logo manual to learn what's available for you.

- ☐ PPS will tell you, among other things, which packages your procedures fall in.
- ☐ PR NODES will give you an idea of the amount of space remaining in the workspace, reported in **nodes.** A node equals five bytes.
- ☐ RECYCLE will cause Logo to undertake a cleaning-up procedure, which may leave you more space in your workspace.

Moving Files from Disk to Disk

Suppose you've already created a number of procedures and have stored them on the original Logo system disk. Now you want to move them to a separate file disk. Here's what you do.

Boot the Logo system. When you are invited to insert your file diskette, leave the Logo disk in the drive (if that's where you've stored your files). Now load any file you want to transfer to another disk, such as LOAD "CHAP6.

As soon as you have gotten your ? prompt back, signaling that the file has been loaded, take out the disk you just loaded from and replace it with your new disk. Now enter SAVE "CHAP6, or whatever file name is appropriate. You can use any name you want at this point; it needn't be the same one you used on the old disk. When the disk goes on this time, it will be saving the file on your new disk.

This means you can move files around however you choose. You can load up a workspace with procedures and packages from several files on several disks and then store the composite workspace as a new file on a new disk.

Some Common Bugs

Getting OUT OF SPACE. This is a common problem as you create more and more procedures in a workspace. You can monitor how closely you are coming to filling the workspace with the PR NODES command. If you have more materials than will fit into one workspace, then save one workspace worth on disk and ERALL the workspace to start on another file.

This problem will often arise when you try to edit a procedure—after you enter CTRL-C. In such cases, the procedure will not be revised. That is, any changes you've made have been lost.

Getting FILE ALREADY EXISTS. You'll get this message any time you attempt to save your workspace using a name that has already been used as a file name. If you are merely updating that file, you must ERASEFILE first and then SAVE. As suggested earlier, you can avoid this problem by writing the UPDATE procedure.

Erasing undefined procedures. If you attempt to erase a procedure that doesn't actually exist, the computer will let you know that. If you enter ER "PROC11, and assuming you have no PROC11 in the workspace, the computer will say PROC11 IS UNDEFINED.

Erasing nonexisting files. You'll get a similar response if you attempt to erase a file that doesn't exist. Say you enter ERASEFILE "FILE83 but you don't have a file of that name. The computer will respond FILE NOT FOUND.

Forgetting the quotation mark before names. Undoubtedly, more than once during your first twenty file operations you will try to SAVE or LOAD a file like this: SAVE CHAP6, omitting the quote mark that must precede a procedure name in such cases. When you do this, the computer will merely explain:

```
CHAP6 DIDN'T OUTPUT TO SAVE
```

The same will happen if you try to ER HOUSE.

Teaching Objectives

The materials of this appendix go well beyond what you will usually want to teach your students. Here's what most of your students should accomplish in regard to disk management.

- ☐ Students will be able to SAVE the contents of the computer workspace into a disk file.
- ☐ Students will be able to erase disk files.
- ☐ Students will be able to use CATALOG to learn the contents of a disk.
- ☐ Students will be able to LOAD a disk file into the computer's workspace.
- ☐ Students will be able to use POTS to list the procedures in the workspace.
- ☐ Students will be able to use ER to erase procedures.
- ☐ Each student will have his or her own disk.

Teaching Techniques and Materials

Concrete Learning

The materials of this appendix can fairly readily be made concrete. You can have students write their procedures on index cards, so the cards represent the procedures. Packages can be represented by stapling a set of procedures together. A small box can represent a file; put procedures in it. You can use a table to represent a floppy disk; put the boxes (files) on the desk (disk). Finally, have a student's desk represent the workspace.

For each box (file), also write the file name on a sheet of paper and place it under the box. This serves as a reminder that when you load a disk file into the workspace it still remains on the disk as well. Have students practice loading files into the workspace, have them write new procedures in the workspace, and add them to the disk files. Have students say the appropriate Logo commands as they experiment with the file structure.

Here's another way to demonstrate file operations concretely if you have ready access to a photocopy machine. Place a sheet of paper on a student's desk. This represents a workspace. Have the student write several procedures on the paper. After the sheet contains several procedures, make a copy of the sheet and place the copy on another desk—representing the disk—pointing out that the command SAVE "CHAP6 (or some other file name) accomplishes that operation in Logo. Write some more procedures on the original sheet. Now introduce the command "ERASEFILE "CHAP6 and throw away the copy currently existing in memory. Make a new copy of the sheet in the workspace, containing the added procedures. With the command SAVE "CHAP6 put the new copy on the disk-desk.

Once students grasp the ideas of SAVE and ERASEFILE, throw away the sheet on the workspace-desk. Equate this with turning off the computer. (Later, you can do this to illustrate ERALL.) Now indicate that you want to work on your Logo procedures some more, and introduce students to the LOAD "CHAP6 command. To illustrate, make a photocopy of the sheet on the disk-desk and put the copy in the workspace. Now make changes to the workspace sheet, SAVE it, and so on.

When they actually work with the computer, be sure to show students where the different parts of the file structure exist physically. The workspace exists inside the computer. You might even open up the computer and point to the RAM chips. Files, in turn, are located on the disk. It will be useful for students to have these concrete anchors for the concepts of workspace and file.

Mind-size Bites

File management, as you've seen in this appendix, includes a great many details. Be careful not to overwhelm your students by giving them too much at once. (I apologize if I've done that with you.) Fortunately, the materials fit into mind-size bites.

You can begin with the relationships among procedure, workspace, file, and disk. Students will already know what procedures are. Since they have worked with more than one procedure at a time, they will be able to grasp that those several procedures exist somewhere. Introduce them to the concept of the workspace. Then you can teach them the equivalence between workspace and file—that they are copies of each other—using some of the techniques for concrete learning discussed earlier, perhaps.

Next you can have students see that there can be several files on the same disk. Finally, show them how to move procedures from one file to another.

Simple to Complex

Begin by teaching students the fundamentals of file management—those things they need to know just to get by. SAVE, LOAD, and ERASEFILE will let them handle their most pressing need for permanence. You can simplify matters further by writing an UPDATE procedure for them to use in place of ERASEFILE and SAVE. Once they have mastered the fundamentals, let them see some of the additional options available to them.

Student Exercises

Pencil and Paper Exercises

1. Write the Logo commands that will achieve each of the following:
    a. Make a disk copy of a set of procedures currently in the workspace. (Use the name FILE1.)

b. Copy a disk file named FILE1 into the workspace.
c. Get a list of all the procedures in the workspace.
d. Erase a procedure named MOON from the workspace.
e. Get a list of all the files contained on a disk.
f. Update the disk record of the file (named FILE1) currently in the workspace (2 commands).

2. Write out the names of ten fictitious procedures in two lists of five each. Each list represents a disk file. Give each file a name. Now, write out the steps involved in creating a third file that will contain the first two procedures from each of the original files.
3. Write a procedure that will allow you to update disk files in a single command (replacing ERASEFILE and SAVE).

At the Computer

1. Get a list of all the files contained on your disk.
2. Move two disk files into your workspace.
3. Get a list of the procedures contained in the workspace.
4. LOAD a file into the workspace. ERASE a procedure. Now see if you can get the ERASEd procedure back.

Lesson Plan Elements

- ☐ SAVE
- ☐ ERASEFILE
- ☐ CATALOG
- ☐ LOAD
- ☐ POTS
- ☐ ER
- ☐ Creating a disk for each student

Review of Logo Commands

NAME	EXAMPLE	FUNCTION
SAVE	SAVE "CHAP6	Makes disk copy of the workspace.
ERASEFILE	ERASEFILE "CHAP6	Erases a file from the disk.
LOAD	LOAD "CHAP6	Copies disk file into workspace.
PACKAGE	PACKAGE "SUBSET [PROC1 PROC2 PROC3 PROC4]	Gathers several procedures under a single name.
CATALOG	CATALOG	Lists the files contained on the disk.
POTS	POTS	Lists the procedures contained in the workspace.
PO	PO "PROC1	Lists the instructions that make up the procedure specified.
	PO [PROC1 PROC2 PROC3]	Lists the instructions that make up the procedures specified.
POPS	POPS "PACK1	Lists the instructions that make up all the procedures contained in the package specified.
	POPS	Lists the instructions that make up all the procedures in the workspace.
ERPS	ERPS "PACK1	Erases all the procedures in the package specified.
	ERPS [PACK1 PACK2]	Erases all the procedures in packages specified.
BURY	BURY "PACK1	While the procedures contained in the buried package can still be used as normal, they are unaffected by global commands, such as POTS or ERALL.
UNBURY	UNBURY "PACK1	Cancels the effects of the previous BURY.
PPS	PPS	Identifies the packages that the procedures in a workspace are included in.
NODES	PR NODES	Tells you the amount of space remaining in the workspace, measured in five-byte NODES.
RECYCLE	RECYCLE	Tidies up loose ends in the workspace to increase the usable space remaining.

Appendix C

Printing Logo Graphics

A Powerful Idea

The ability to print your Logo designs on paper (**hard copy**) adds a new dimension to your teaching of Logo. You will be able to display students' work; they will be able to take their work home to their parents, show it to their friends, and so on. In addition, you'll be able to prepare teaching materials to hand out to students. For example, most of the designs presented in this book were created with Logo, printed by computer, and simply reprinted in the book.

How to Do It

The ability to print copies of Logo work is based on both hardware (equipment) and software (program) requirements.

Printer

The first thing required for the printing of Logo work is, reasonably enough, a **printer.** Not just any computer printer will work, however. As you may already know, there are two main types of computer printers currently in use. First, **daisy-wheel** printers are essentially modifications of the IBM Selectric typewriter technology, with fixed characters carried on a wheel that spins and strikes the paper through an inked ribbon. If an A is to be printed, the wheel spins to a position with the A facing the paper and strikes. These are sometimes called letter-quality printers, although that is more of a value judgment than a technical designation.

The other major type of computer printer is based on a **dot-matrix** design. Instead of fixed characters on a spinning wheel, the typing element for this kind of printer can be thought of as a small block with a grid of holes in it, illustrated here in Logo, of course. Each of the dots in this matrix represents a hole with a pin in it. The pattern is what would be printed if all the pins were extended so they would strike the paper through the inked ribbon.*

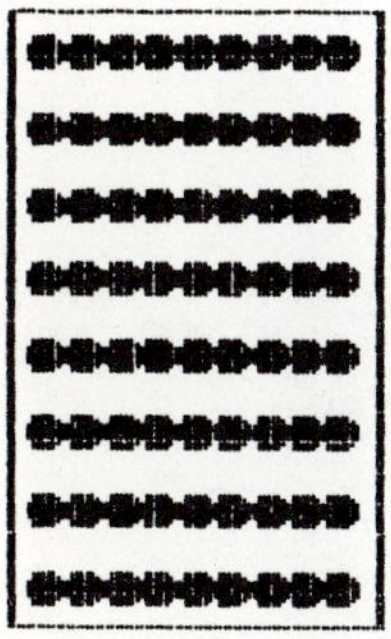

Letters and other characters are printed when the computer tells the printer to extend only some of the pins. Here are some examples. (This is the same system that your video display uses, incidentally.)

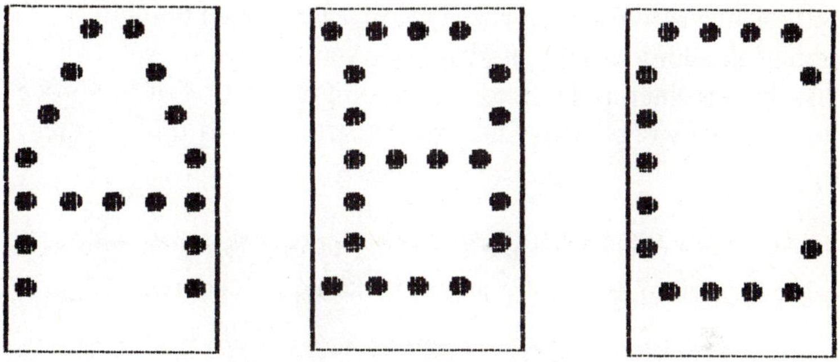

You will need a dot-matrix printer to print graphics. Not all dot-matrix printers have a graphics capability, however; check to make sure yours does.

Two very popular printers currently are the Epson and the Star-Gemini. The comments in the remainder of this appendix are appropriate to those two printers and may also work with other printers. In any event, the principles are the same.

---

*Actually, the print head consists of one column of pins that create a grid by striking several times in succession.

Interface Card

Just as the disk drive has an **interface card** that communicates between the drive and the computer, there is also an interface card that translates between the computer and the printer. Not all interface cards will cause the printing of Logo designs, so if you are buying equipment you should make sure it has that capability.

The Grappler + interface card is a popular one for the Apple and Epson (or Star-Gemini) and has the capability of printing Logo graphics. The card comes with a cable that connects the card to the printer.

.PRINTER 1 and .PRINTER 0

Once a proper printer has been properly attached to your computer, you can enter this command:

```
.PRINTER 1
```

From now on, any instructions you type into the computer, as well as any of its written answers, will be printed on your printer in addition to being displayed on the screen. You can test this by entering POTS to see if you get a listing of the procedures in the workspace. Entering .PRINTER 0 turns this feature off.

This in itself doesn't get the computer to print your designs, however. To do that, you must write some procedures.

Some Printing Procedures

Here is a procedure that will cause the graphics display on your screen to be printed on the printer. It is a procedure that works with an Apple, a Grappler + interface, and an Epson or Star-Gemini printer. Other configurations may need somewhat different procedures.

```
TO PRINTSMALL
.PRINTER 1
```

```
(TYPE CHAR 9 "G CHAR 13)
.PRINTER 0
END
```

As you continue you will learn all the parts of this procedure. For the time being, however, try using this procedure without knowing why or how it does what it does.

Once you've entered this procedure, you can get hard copy results this way:

1. Create a design on the video screen.
2. Enter PRINTSMALL.

The printer will probably pause for a moment; then it will start printing the design. You find it's pretty slow, but it's worth it.

Here's an example of a design printed using PRINTSMALL.

You'll also notice that the procedure has switched colors. Whereas the video display is white on black, the printout is black on white. If you want to have the printer print white on black, this procedure will achieve that for you.

```
TO PRINTREVERSE
.PRINTER 1
(TYPE CHAR 9 "GI CHAR 13)
.PRINTER 0
END
```

Notice that the difference between the two procedures is found in the middle line, between CHAR 9 and CHAR 13. The G in both procedures stands for graphics. The I in the second procedure stands for inverse.

Here's the previous design printed with PRINTREVERSE.

You can also get oversized printouts. The following procedure will rotate the design 90 degrees on the paper and double its size.

```
TO PRINTBIG
.PRINTER 1
(TYPE CHAR 9 "GRD CHAR 13)
.PRINTER 0
END
```

In this latest modification, the R *rotates* the design and D *doubles* the size of the hard copy display. Here's what the result looks like.

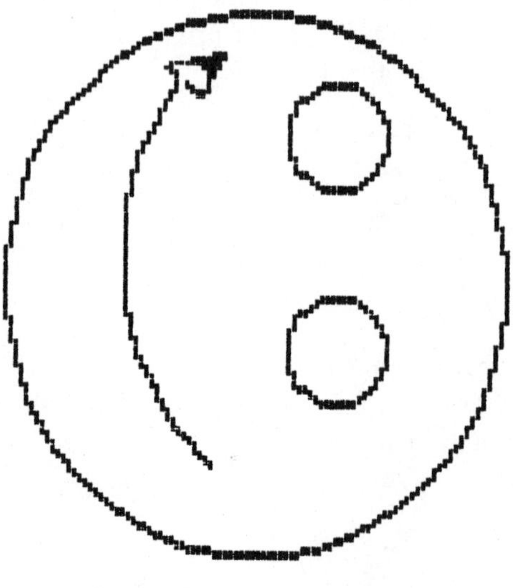

As you can see, you have several options for printing hard copy displays of your Logo designs.

SCRUNCH

If you are at the computer now, draw a circle and then print it out. Here's the way I drew the circle shown.

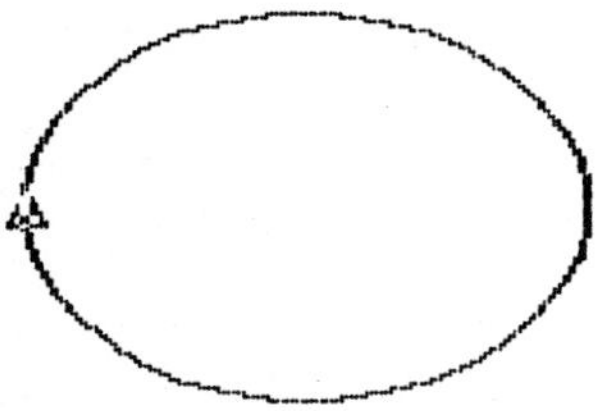

```
REPEAT 36 [FD 10 RT 10]
```

Notice how the circle is a little squashed down. On the screen, however, it looked perfectly round. Depending on your hardware configuration, you may find that the pictures on the screen don't correspond perfectly to the printed versions. There is a solution to this problem, however. Logo has a feature called SCRUNCH that lets you modify the proportions of your designs.

To begin, enter PR SCRUNCH. This asks the computer to PRINT the current value of SCRUNCH. The first time you ask, the computer will probably answer .8. You can change the value of SCRUNCH as follows:

```
SETSCRUNCH 1.2
```

If you don't like the circles you've been printing, you should experiment with different values of SCRUNCH. I find that 1.2 works best for my system. When I SETSCRUNCH 1.2, the designs on my video monitor look tall and thin—and they look perfect when they are printed out. Here's how my circle looks on paper when I SETSCRUNCH 1.2.

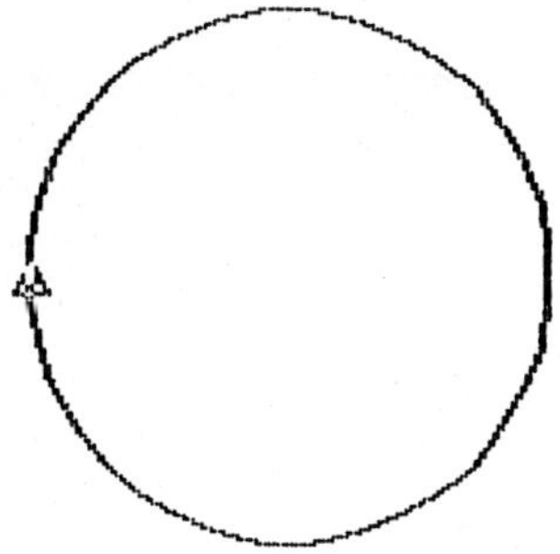

Some Common Bugs

Nothing happens. If you create a Logo design, enter the name of a print procedure, and nothing happens, check the following:

- ☐ Is the printer connected properly?
- ☐ Is the printer turned on?
- ☐ Does the printer have a graphics capability?
- ☐ Does your printer interface card support the printing of graphics?

System prints words but not graphics. While I can't definitively diagnose all the problems you might have, I want to let you know of at least one situation that produces this situation. Modems and other control cards in the computer may interfere with your printing of graphics. You can check this by removing everything except the disk control card and the printer control card and try it again. *Warning:* Don't do anything inside your computer until you've turned off the power.

The bottom-line solution to problems with regards to printing is to involve the people from whom you purchased the equipment. If you are buying the printer and/or interface card, make sure they know you need to have it print Logo graphics. Then insist that they get it working for you.

Review of Logo Commands

NAME	EXAMPLE	FUNCTION
.PRINTER 1		Turns on the printer.
.PRINTER 0		Turns off the printer.
SCRUNCH	PR SCRUNCH	Gets the computer to tell you the current ratio of vertical to horizontal scales.
SETSCRUNCH	SETSCRUNCH 1.2	Sets the ratio of vertical to horizontal scales.

Appendix D

Advanced Mathematics

Chapter 9 presented some of Logo's mathematical capabilities. Beyond the fundamental arithmetic operations of addition, subtraction, multiplication, and division, you saw how to extract square roots and select random numbers. This appendix will present some of Logo's other mathematical capabilities.

Realize that this appendix won't explain mathematics per se. For example, I'm not going to explain what a cosine is, but I'll tell you how to get cosines from Logo in case you want some.

Sines and Cosines

Logo calculates sines and cosines with ease. Here's all there is to it:

```
?PR SIN 90
1
?PR COS 45
.707107
```

Here's an example of a procedure using SIN and the result that procedure would produce:

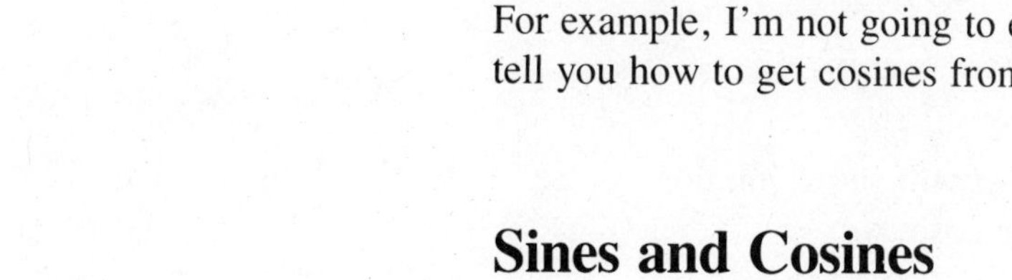

DOSIN 10

```
TO DOSIN :N
SETH :N FD 10 * SIN :N
DOSIN :N + 5
END
```

Notice what a similar procedure using COS produces:

```
TO DOCOS :N
SETH :N FD 10 * COS :N
DOCOS :N + 5
END
```

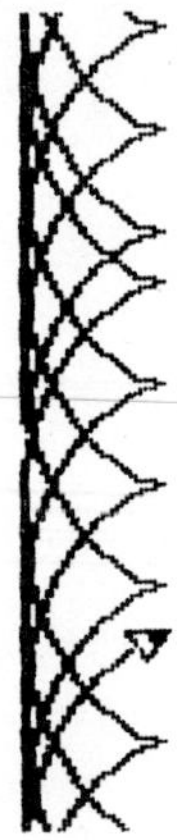

DOCOS 10

ARCTAN

Arc tangents are acquired with equal ease, as the following examples illustrate:

```
?PR ARCTAN 2
63.4348
?PR ARCTAN 444
89.8710
```

Your *Apple Logo Reference Manual* will show you how to use ARCTAN to obtain arc sines and arc cosines.

Exponents

While Logo doesn't have a primitive operator to handle exponentiation, you can create a simple procedure to do the job:

```
TO EXP :N :P
MAKE "N1 :N
REPEAT (:P - 1) [MAKE "N :N * :N1]
OUTPUT :N
END
```

```
?PR EXP 3 2
9
?PR EXP 5 3
125
?PR EXP 2 6
64
```

INT and ROUND

These are two useful commands. INT truncates complex numbers: It drops any decimal portions of a number. For example:

```
?PR INT(3.345)
3
?PR INT(65.999)
65
```

ROUND, on the other hand, rounds a complex number to the nearest integer:

```
?PR ROUND 3.1
3
?PR ROUND 3.9
4
```

PRODUCT, QUOTIENT, and REMAINDER

PRODUCT is equal to the * operator. Here are some examples:

```
?PRODUCT 3 4
12
?PRODUCT 5 5
25
```

QUOTIENT divides two numbers and truncates the result, as follows:

```
?QUOTIENT 12 2
6
?QUOTIENT 13 2
6
```

REMAINDER calculates the remainder left from divisions like those illustrated in terms of QUOTIENT.

```
?REMAINDER 12 2
0
?REMAINDER 13 2
1
```

These are some of the additional mathematical operators available in Logo. You should refer to your Logo manuals for more materials on this. More important, you should look at ways you can build procedures to extend on those operators. For example, SQRT (SQRT :N) yields the fourth root of :N. If you are interested in mathematical calculations, you will find Logo a powerful tool to assist you.

Appendix E

Apple Logo Tool Kit

In addition to the Apple Logo system, Apple Computer also has an *Apple Logo Tool Kit,* a set of two disks containing extensions of the basic Logo package. One of the disks contains sample procedures, mostly prepared by children. The other disk contains sophisticated procedures that allow the Logo user a variety of advanced capabilities. This appendix will briefly review some of those advanced capabilities.

HIRES.TEXT

This set of procedures allows you to print text on the graphics screen, adding elegance to your creations. Shown is one example of how you might use this capability.

This file allows you to give speech to your cartoon characters, label parts of a design, and so on. Unfortunately, the system itself uses up a good deal of the computer's available memory, so you can't create very complex designs.

PICTURES

This file lets you store your designs on a disk and retrieve them later. Note that you store the *designs,* not the procedures that created them. To use this system, you will create a separate disk for the stored designs.

TEACH and ZOOM

These two files are similar to Junior Logo, as presented in Chapter 15 of this book. In addition to letting users create designs through single-key commands, these systems record the commands entered so the designs can be recreated, step by step, later. This record/replay facility was designed as a way of letting teachers review the steps their students go through in creating designs, noting any particular problems the students are having.

TEXTPRO

This is a elementary text-processing system, designed to give young users an experience of writing on the computer. As the manual states, the system "simplifies the task of loading, saving, and printing files." The editing commands, however, are the same ones used for editing procedures, which are fairly clumsy in comparison with other text-processing systems.

To support children in using the system, TEXTPRO comes with two sample letters that illustrate the various formatting techniques available in the system.

MUSIC and Other Sounds

Probably the gem of the *Apple Logo Tool Kit* is its music capability. That's right, music. Logo lets you compose and play simple songs on the Apple. Once you LOAD "MUSIC, which takes awhile, the computer will play "Twinkle, Twinkle, Little Star" to demonstrate its ability.

At this point, you can write procedures specifying notes and durations. As with graphics procedures, you can attempt to create a tune, try it, correct it, try it again, and so on. There are two options that make it simpler, however.

ALPHAPLAY transforms your Apple keyboard into a musical instrument. Pressing keys results in notes, arranged in alphabetical order. C-C-J-J-L-L-J, for example, produces the beginnings of "Twinkle, Twinkle, Little Star."

COMPOSE is more serious stuff. This transforms your keyboard into a sort of organ. Now pressing the comma produces middle C, L is C-sharp, the period is D, with the rest of the keys assigned notes in accordance with their physical placement on the keyboard. A diagram in the manual relates the computer keyboard to the organ keyboard.

Once the computer is in the COMPOSE mode, you can begin composing songs in earnest, recording them for future replaying. You can begin by picking out the first few notes you want. Once you have them the way you want them, press CTRL-T, play them again, and they are recorded. Pressing CTRL-T again stops the recording so you can hunt and peck some more. Another file, EFFECTS, is similar to MUSIC but contains some special sound effects. Still another file, SWEEPS, produces a sliding sound that lets you create, among other things, the sound of a burglar alarm.

Miscellaneous Utilities

In addition to the files described, the *Apple Logo Tool Kit* contains a number of useful utilities for mathematical computations, printing, file management, communicating with robots, and so forth.

Appendix F

Terrapin/Krell Logo, Dr. Logo (IBM PC), and TRS-80 Color Logo

This book has presented one particular version of Logo, *Apple Logo*. There are several other versions of Logo, however, and some are even designed for the Apple. This appendix says a little about some of the other versions of Logo, in the event that you may be using one. Even if you learn Logo in a college course using Apple Logo, you may later get to teach it in a school that has Terrapin Logo.

This appendix will draw your attention to some of the more significant differences between Apple Logo and the other versions discussed. This way, you should be able to make the adjustment if necessary. As you'll see, Logo is essentially Logo, and the differences that distinguish the various versions are often relatively minor.

Terrapin/Krell Logo

Two companies, Terrapin Inc. and Krell Software Corporation, are licensed to sell the same version of Logo, developed by the Massachusetts Institute of Technology. Terrapin and Krell Logo are distinguished only by the additional materials that accompany the main program. The Terrapin Logo package is discussed here, but any comments on how its commands differ from Apple Logo apply to Krell Logo as well.

On the whole, this popular version of Logo is very similar to Apple Logo. It operates on an Apple II and is booted the same way as Apple Logo.

Here is a translation table that will show you some of the differences in commands and where different words in the two languages accomplish the same things.

APPLE LOGO	TERRAPIN LOGO
CS	DRAW
CLEAN	CS
TEXTSCREEN	ND or NODRAW
SETBG	BG
SETPC	PC
PENREVERSE	PC 6
CTRL-L	CTRL-F (FULLSCREEN)
LOAD	READ
ERALL	ERASE ALL or ER ALL
POS	XCOR, YCOR
SETCURSOR	CURSOR
INT	INTEGER
FENCE	NOWRAP
SETPOS	SETXY
READLIST	REQUEST or RQ

READCHAR	READCHARACTER or RC
TYPE	PRINT1
SETSCRUNCH	.ASPECT
RECYCLE	.GCOLL
PR NODES	.NODES
.PRINTER	OUTDEV

There are some other minor differences between the two versions of Logo. To EDIT a procedure, you do not use a quotation mark before the name of the procedure in Terrapin Logo. In most situations, however, you use quotation marks with names just as in Apple Logo.

The format for IF statements also differs slightly. For example, you might write a recursive procedure in which a counter, :NUM, is reduced to 0. When it reaches 0, you want the procedure to STOP. Here's how that would be accomplished in the two versions of Logo.

- ☐ Apple Logo: IF :NUM = 0 [STOP]
- ☐ Terrapin: IF :NUM = 0 THEN STOP

Here's a small yet potent difference. You'll recall that to do mathematical calculations in Apple Logo, you need to use PR (as in PR 4 + 5) or else the computer will respond with an error message, such as I DON'T KNOW WHAT TO DO WITH 9. You may recall it was suggested that you simply let the computer protest, since you got the answer you wanted, saving yourself a couple of keystrokes without hurting the computer. In Terrapin Logo, if you type 4 + 5 the computer responds RESULT: 9.

This is a potent difference because the mere change of wording in the computer's response—substituting RESULT: for I DON'T KNOW WHAT TO DO WITH—shifts the apparent meaning of the computer's communication. In Apple Logo, it suggests you have made a mistake; in Terrapin Logo, it merely gives you what you asked for. This simple shift of wording will inevitably affect the way students interact with the computer.

There are other minor differences. Whereas you LOAD files from the disk in Apple Logo, you READ them in Terrapin Logo. As in Apple Logo, the new file is added to whatever is already in the workspace.

Utilities Disk

Terrapin Logo comes with a utilities disk that contains many features similar to those contained in the *Apple Logo Tool Kit* (see Appendix E). One file contains a MUSIC system similar to Apple Logo's, though it seems to lack the equivalent of COMPOSE. The utilities disk also makes it possible for you to save pictures directly, rather than the procedures that produce them.

SHAPE.EDIT on the utilities disk allows you to create a new shape for the turtle. In fact, you can create several shapes for it, write procedures to change the shapes, and move the different shapes around the screen in a rough approximation of animation.

Printing

The Terrapin manual provides guidelines for printing Logo results on paper. For the Grappler+ interface card discussed in Appendix C, the manual suggests this procedure:

```
TO HC
 OUTDEV 1
 (PRINT1 CHAR 9 "G CHAR 13)
 OUTDEV 0
END
```

The manual offers this procedure for use with the Silentype printer:

```
TO HC
 OUTDEV 1
 PRINT1 CHAR 17
 OUTDEV 0
END
```

As suggested at the outset, Terrapin Logo and Apple Logo are very similar to one another. But here is a somewhat different version of Logo.

Dr. Logo for the IBM PC

Dr. Logo was created for use with the IBM PC computer. While the logic and the commands are essentially the same as in Apple Logo, there are some fundamental differences.

To begin, Dr. Logo's graphics can only be displayed on a color monitor. If you have a monochromatic monitor (such as black and white), you can do Logo calculations and text processing, you can even move the turtle around, but you will not be able to see the turtle unless you have a color monitor.

Second, Dr. Logo offers a much wider range of colors than the systems examined thus far. Although you can only specify pencolors 1–3, the colors they represent depend on the background color in effect at the time, and you can specify lots of background colors.

Third, the IBM PC offers more available memory to Logo than is possible with Apple Logo or Terrapin Logo. This means that you can create more procedures and more complex ones in a single workspace.

Finally, you should use lower-case letters when working with Dr. Logo.

Here is a list of some of the differences between Apple Logo and Dr. Logo commands:

DR. LOGO	APPLE LOGO
copyon	.PRINTER 1
copyoff	.PRINTER 0
erf	ERASEFILE
getfs	CATALOG

On the whole, Dr. Logo is more powerful than Apple Logo, with several commands that are not available in Apple Logo. Here are some of the special Dr. Logo commands:

COMMAND	FUNCTION
bye	Reboots Logo.
changef	Changes the name of a disk file.
copyf	Makes a copy of a disk file.
edall	Loads all the procedures and variables into the editor buffer.
edns	Loads all the variables into the editor buffer.
edps	Loads all the procedures into the editor buffer.
printscreen	Prints (on paper) everything shown on the graphics screen.
setsplit	Specifies the number of lines to be assigned to text in a splitscreen condition.

TRS-80 Color Logo

Logo is also available for Radio Shack's TRS-80 Color Computer—on disk, cassette, or ROM (read only memory) cartridge. While the basic logic and the commands of Logo are the same as in Apple Logo, there are several system differences. Here are a few of them.

TRS-80 Logo is organized in four modes. When you begin a Logo session you are in the BREAK mode, and you can return to it at any time by pressing the BREAK key on the keyboard. This is the mode in which you read and save files. Typing an E while in the BREAK mode takes you into the EDIT mode, where procedures are created and changed. While procedures look like those created in Apple Logo, entering the EDIT mode brings all the existing procedures into the workspace, so you can move around, editing several of the procedures before leaving EDIT. Typing R while in the BREAK mode takes you to the RUN mode where, appropriately enough, you can run procedures. Finally, typing @ while in the RUN mode takes you to the DOODLE mode. In the latter, you will have access to single-keystroke Logo similar to Junior Logo, which was presented in Chapter 15.

One of the most unusual features of TRS-80 Logo is the possibility of creating multiple turtles (up to 255), which appear to operate on the screen simultaneously. New turtles are created by a HATCH command. If you are working with TRS-80 Logo, refer to your manual for further instructions.

Here are some additional differences between TRS-80 Logo and Apple Logo.

Turning the Turtle

When turning the turtle on the screen (for example, RT 23), you will find that the turtle's display only points in increments of 45 degrees. Thus, if the turtle is facing straight up and you enter RT 17, the turtle won't move. If you enter the same command again—totaling 34 degrees to the right—the turtle will shift its position to point 45 degrees to the right. While the turtle will move in whatever directions you specify, the turtle's display only points to the nearest increment of 45 degrees. Thus, if you type FD 50 after the two commands just described, the turtle will move fifty steps in a direction 34 degrees from straight up, but the turtle itself would still be facing 45 degrees to the right.

SETX and SETY

As in Apple Logo, it is possible to move the turtle around the screen by SETX and SETY commands. (As noted later, the turtle doesn't draw a line when moving around in this fashion.) If you use these commands, however, you need to know that the screen locations are numbered differently in TRS-80 Logo. The diagram below shows the way the TRS-80 screen is numbered.

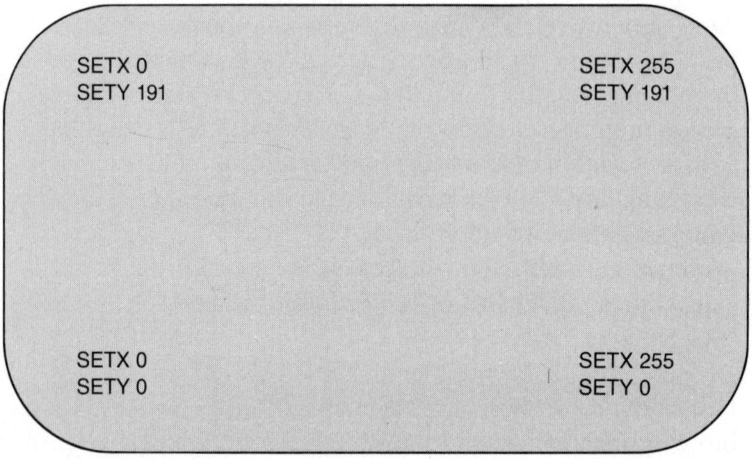

COLORSET

COLORSET 0 and COLORSET 1 call up different sets of colors. The numbers specified with PC and BG produce different colors, depending on which COLORSET condition is in effect.

Recursion

TRS-80 Color Logo allows recursive procedures, just as Apple Logo does. In the case of the TRS-80, however, recursion will fill up the workspace and eventually result in:

MY MEMORY IS TOO FULL

REPEAT

The commands to be REPEATed are enclosed in parentheses instead of brackets.

MAKE

When creating names and assigning values to them with the MAKE command, use a colon instead of a quotation mark. Here are two illustrations.

- ☐ Apple: MAKE "NUM 10
  TRS-80: MAKE :NUM 10
- ☐ Apple: MAKE "NUM :NUM + 5
  TRS-80: MAKE :NUM :NUM + 5

Notice that the colon is used in referencing names when they are used later, just as in Apple Logo—for example, PRINT :NUM.

Command Differences

Here are some of the minor differences in the commands that comprise TRS-80 and Apple Logo.

TRS-80 LOGO	APPLE LOGO
CLEAR	CS, CLEARSCREEN
HOME	PU HOME PD
SETX	PU SETX PD
SETY	PU SETY PD
BG	SETBG
PC	SETPC

Answers:

Exploring Further, Student Exercises, Logo Challenges

CHAPTER 2

Exploring Further

1. a. CS FD 30 RT 90 FD 60 RT 90 FD 30 RT 90 FD 60 HT

   (Remember: You can enter these commands separately or all at once, as you choose.)

   b. CS FD 70 RT 72 FD 70 RT 72 FD 70 RT 72 FD 70 RT 72 FD 70 HT
2. CS FD 5 RT 90 FD 10 RT 90 FD 15 RT 90 FD 20 RT 90 FD 25 RT 90 FD 30 RT 90 FD 35
3. a. CS LT 30 FD 50 BK 100 FD 50 RT 60 FD 50 BK 100 HT

   b. CS FD 30 RT 90 FD 10 LT 90 FD 5 LT 90 FD 25 LT 90 FD 5 LT 90 FD 10 RT 90 FD 60 RT 90 FD10 LT 90 FD 5 LT 90 FD 25 LT 90 FD 5 LT 90 FD 10 RT 90 FD 30 HT

   c. CS RT 60 FD 10 LT 60 BK 60 RT 90 FD 10 BK 20 HT
4. a. CS RT 80 FD 60 LT 160 FD 50 RT 160 FD 40 LT 160 FD 30 RT 160 FD 20 HT

   b. CS FD 40 RT 120 FD 20 RT 120 FD 40 LT 120 FD 20 HT

   c. CS RT 30 BK 30 LT 82 FD 90 RT 170 FD 70 LT 70 FD 60 LT 20 BK 50 HT

Student Exercises

Pencil and Paper Exercises

1. No answers provided. Use Logo to check your answers.
2. a. I

   b. N

   c. T

   d. F

   e. X
3. 1
4. a. No

   b. Yes

   c. Yes

   d. Yes

At the Computer

1. No answer provided.
2. a. CS LT 90 FD 50 RT 90 FD 50 RT 90 FD 50 HT

   b. CS FD 20 LT 45 FD 20 RT 90 FD 20 LT 45 FD 20 HT

   c. CS FD 50 RT 90 FD 20 LT 135 FD 30 LT 90 FD 30 LT 135 FD 20 HT

   d. CS FD 50 LT 30 BK 30 RT 60 FD 30 LT 30 BK 50 HT

   e. CS RT 45 FD 50 RT 90 FD 5 RT 90 FD 100 RT 90 FD 5 RT 90 FD 50 HT

A Logo Challenge

CS RT 18 FD 70 RT 144 FD 70 RT 144 FD 70 RT 144 FD 70 RT 144 FD 70 HT

CHAPTER 3

Exploring Further

1. SETBG 1 SETBG 2 SETBG 3 SETBG 4 SETBG 5
2. a. FD 50 PE BK 50 PD

   b. FD 50 PENREVERSE BK 50 PD

c. FD 50 SETPC 0 BK 50 SETPC 1
(Notice I've returned things to normal in each case, either with PD or SETPC 1.)
3. No answer provided.
4. No answer provided.

Student Exercises

Pencil and Paper Exercises

1. No answer provided.
2. No answer provided.
3. No answer provided.
4. a. PD takes no input. Just enter PD.
   b. Misspelled. Correct form is PENERASE.
   c. FD must be separated from input. Enter FD 100 and FD 50.

At the Computer

1. No answer provided.
2. No answer provided.
3. No answer provided.

A Logo Challenge

Enter this sequence 360 times:
FD 1 RT 1

CHAPTER 4

Exploring Further

1. REPEAT 18 [FD 10 RT 10]
   REPEAT 9 [FD 10 LT 10]
   REPEAT 15 [FD 5 RT 3]
2. The background flashes between black and white.
3. A star.
4. No answer provided.

Student Exercises

Pencil and Paper Exercises

1. For example, REPEAT 3 [FD 30 RT 120]
2. A box. The "extra" REPEATs just retrace the original box.
3. REPEAT 3 [BK 30 LT 90]
4. a. The number of times to REPEAT must be specified.
   b. REPEAT is misspelled.
   c. Brackets, not parentheses, must be used.
   d. Nothing wrong, although it doesn't do much.

At the Computer

1. For example, REPEAT 600 [RT 10]
2. For example, REPEAT 800 [FD 1]
3. REPEAT 30 [FD 5 PU FD 5 PD RT 12]
4. REPEAT 17 [FD 5 RT 360/17]
5. CTRL-G

A Logo Challenge

REPEAT 36 [FD 20 RT 170 FD 20 LT 160]

CHAPTER 5

Exploring Further

1. a. REPEAT 4 [REPEAT 3 [FD 30 RT 120] RT 90] HT
   b. REPEAT 36 [REPEAT 3 [FD 30 RT 120] RT 10] HT
   c. REPEAT 10 [REPEAT 5 [FD 30 RT 72] RT 36] HT
2. REPEAT 6 [REPEAT 6 [FD 30 RT 60] RT 60] HT
3. REPEAT 4 [REPEAT 5 [PD FD 20 RT 90] PU FD 30] PD HT

Student Exercises

Pencil and Paper Exercises

1. REPEAT 2 [REPEAT 3 [FD 30 RT 120] LT 120]
2. REPEAT 3 [REPEAT 3 [FD 30 RT 120] RT 60]
3. REPEAT 3 [REPEAT 4 [FD 30 RT 90] RT 45]
4. No answer provided.
5. a. The number of times for the first REPEAT must be specified.

b. Missing [after REPEAT 4 and missing] after RT 30.

6. a. (z)
   b. (x)
   c. (y)

At the Computer

1. REPEAT 3 [REPEAT 4 [FD 20 RT 90] PU FD 25 PD]
2. REPEAT 3 [REPEAT 4 [FD 20 RT 90] PU FD 45 RT 45 PD]
3. REPEAT 6 [REPEAT 3 [FD 20 RT 120] LT 60]
   REPEAT 6 [REPEAT 3 [FD 20 RT 120] RT 60]
4. REPEAT 6 [REPEAT 4 [FD 20 RT 90] RT 60]
5. REPEAT 12 [REPEAT 3 [FD 20 RT 120] FD 20 LT 30]

A Logo Challenge

REPEAT 9 [REPEAT 36 [FD 5 RT 10] RT 80]

CHAPTER 6

Exploring Further

1. TO SEVENSIDE
   REPEAT 7 [FD 50 RT 360/7]
   END
2. No answer provided.
3. TO FIG2
   REPEAT 360 [FD 50 BK 50 RT 1]
   END
4. TO FIG3
   REPEAT 90 [FD 30 BK 30 RT 2 FD 60 BK 60 RT 2]
   END

Student Exercises

Pencil and Paper Exercises

1. TO BOX
   REPEAT 4 [FD 50 RT 90]
   END
2. TO TRIANGLE
   REPEAT 3 [FD 50 RT 120]
   END
3. END is needed as the last line.
4. First line should be TO STAR.
5. Without PENDOWN or PD in second line, turtle won't draw the design.
6. TO, END
7. REPEAT 4

At the Computer

1. REPEAT 36 [FD 10 LT 10]
2. REPEAT 2 [FD 50 LT 90 FD 100 LT 90]
3. REPEAT 5 [FD 50 LT 72]
4. REPEAT 3 [REPEAT 18 [FD 3 RT 10] REPEAT 18 [FD 3 LT 10]]
5. No answer provided.

A Logo Challenge

TO CHALL6
REPEAT 36 [FD 10 RT 10]
PU RT 135 FD 45 LT 117 PD
REPEAT 5 [FD 34 PU FD 22 PD FD 34 RT 144]
END

CHAPTER 7

Exploring Further

No answers provided.

Student Exercises

Pencil and Paper Exercises

No answers provided.

At the Computer

1. No answer provided.
2. No answer provided.
3. REPEAT 10 in FIVES.
4. RT 36 in DESIGN.

A Logo Challenge

```
TO SIX
REPEAT 6 [FD 10 RT 60]
END

TO ILLUSION
REPEAT 6 [SIX RT 60]
END

TO CHALL7
REPEAT 6 [ILLUSION FD 40 RT 60]
END
```

CHAPTER 8

Exploring Further

No answers provided.

Student Exercises

Pencil and Paper Exercises

1. HELLO must be preceded by quotation mark.
2. Brackets are needed for more than one word.
3. TYPE CHAR 32
4. REPEAT 39 [TYPE "OBOY!]
5. No answer provided.
6. No answer provided.

At the Computer

1. No answer provided.
2. No answer provided.
3. PR "HELLO, PR "HOW PR "ARE PR "YOU?
4. ```
   TO GREET
   TYPE "H
   TYPE "E
   TYPE "L
   TYPE "L
   TYPE "O
   END
   ```
5. No answer provided.

A Logo Challenge

```
TO CHALL8
PR [ROSES ARE RED,]
REPEAT 2 [TYPE CHAR 32]
PR [VIOLETS ARE BLUE.]
PR [LOGO IS DYNAMITE,]
REPEAT 2 [TYPE CHAR 32]
PR [AND SO ARE YOU.]
END
```

CHAPTER 9

Exploring Further

1. No answer provided.
2. Here's one example:
   ```
   TO ARC
   FD 50 RT 90
   FD (50 * 3.1416) / 36
   REPEAT 10 [RT 10 FD (100 * 3.1416) / 36]
   RT 10 FD (50 * 3.1416) / 36
   END
   ```
3. No answer provided.

Student Exercises

Pencil and Paper Exercises

1. 5.5
2. 16
3. 45
4. PR (4 + 5 + 6 + 7) / 4 = 5.5

At the Computer

1. a. 24
   b. 4
   c. 5
2. PR SQRT(5 * 6 − 7 + 2)
3. PR (8 + 6) / 2
4. REPEAT 10 [PRINT 1 + RANDOM 100]
   ```

A Logo Challenge

```
TO CHALL9
TYPE [3 × 1 =] TYPE CHAR 32 PR 3 * 1
TYPE [3 × 2 =] TYPE CHAR 32 PR 3 * 2
TYPE [3 × 3 =] TYPE CHAR 32 PR 3 * 3
TYPE [3 × 4 =] TYPE CHAR 32 PR 3 * 4
TYPE [3 × 5 =] TYPE CHAR 32 PR 3 * 5
TYPE [3 × 6 =] TYPE CHAR 32 PR 3 * 6
TYPE [3 × 7 =] TYPE CHAR 32 PR 3 * 7
TYPE [3 × 8 =] TYPE CHAR 32 PR 3 * 8
TYPE [3 × 9 =] TYPE CHAR 32 PR 3 * 9
TYPE [3 × 10 =] TYPE CHAR 32 PR 3 * 10
TYPE [3 × 11 =] TYPE CHAR 32 PR 3 * 11
TYPE [3 × 12 =] TYPE CHAR 32 PR 3 * 12
END
```

CHAPTER 10

Exploring Further

1. MAKE "RAND RANDOM 100 (or any other number)
2. TO ROLL
   MAKE "D1 1 + RANDOM 6
   MAKE "D2 1 + RANDOM 6
   MAKE "TOT :D1 + :D2
   TYPE [YOU HAVE ROLLED A]
   TYPE CHAR 32 TYPE :D1
   TYPE CHAR 32 TYPE [AND A]
   TYPE CHAR 32 TYPE :D2
   TYPE CHAR 32 TYPE [FOR A TOTAL OF]
   TYPE CHAR 32 PR :TOT
   END
   (Remember: RANDOM 6 selects a number at random from 0 through 5, so adding 1 changes the range to 1 through 6.)
3. TO NAMELIST
   MAKE "NAMES [SAM MARY PAT]
   MAKE "I 1
   REPEAT 3 [PR ITEM :I :NAMES MAKE "I :I + 1]
   END
4. TO DOUBLE
   MAKE "NUM 1
   REPEAT 7 [PR :NUM MAKE "NUM :NUM * 2]
   END
5. TO SQUARERAND
   REPEAT 5 [MAKE "R (1 + RANDOM 5) PR :R * :R]
   END

Student Exercises

Pencil and Paper Exercises

1. a. MAKE "NUM 10
   b. MAKE "NAMES [SAM MARY JANE]
   c. PR :NAMES
2. a. PR :X + :Y
   b. MAKE "NAMES [JOE PAT JAN]
   c. MAKE "X 23
3. For example, MAKE "NAME [EARL BABBIE]
   PR LAST :NAME
4. a. RED
   b. PURPLE
   c. GREEN
   d. BLUEYELLOW
5. 8

At the Computer

1. For example, MAKE "HOUSE [ROOF DOOR WALL WINDOW FLOOR]
2. TO LISTHOUSE
   PR ITEM 1 :HOUSE
   PR ITEM 2 :HOUSE
   PR ITEM 3 :HOUSE
   PR ITEM 4 :HOUSE
   PR ITEM 5 :HOUSE
   END
3. TO LISTHOUSE
   MAKE "N 1
   REPEAT 5 [PR ITEM :N :HOUSE MAKE "N :N + 1]
   END
4. PONS
5. ERN "HOUSE
   PONS

A Logo Challenge

```
TO CHALL10
MAKE "N 3
MAKE "X [ONE TWO THREE]
REPEAT 3 [TYPE ITEM :N :X TYPE CHAR 32 MAKE
   "N :N - 1]
END
```

CHAPTER 11

Exploring Further

1. No answer provided.
2. ```
   TO STAR :SIZE :TURN
   RT :TURN
   REPEAT 5 [FD :SIZE RT 144]
   END
   ```
3. ```
   TO CIRCLE :SIZE :STEPS
   REPEAT :STEPS [FD (4 * :SIZE) / :STEPS RT 360 /
      :STEPS]
   END
   ```

Student Exercises

Pencil and Paper Exercises

1. ```
   TO BOX :SIZE
   REPEAT 4 [FD :SIZE RT 90]
   END
   ```
2. ```
   TO POLY :SIDES
   REPEAT :SIDES [ FD 50 RT 360 / :SIDES]
   END
   ```
3. REPEAT 5 [FD :SIZE RT 144]
4. ```
   TO LEFF :ANGLE
   RT 360 - :ANGLE
   END
   ```
5. No answer provided.

At the Computer

1. ```
   TO CIRCLE :SIZE
   REPEAT 36 [FD :SIZE RT 10]
   END
   ```
2. ```
   TO STAIRS :SIZE
   REPEAT 5 [FD :SIZE RT 90 FD :SIZE LT 90]
   END
   ```
3. :Y is missing from title line.
4. Should be RT :Y in line 2.

A Logo Challenge

```
TO DESIGN :SIDES :SIZE :ANGLES
REPEAT :SIDES [FD :SIZE RT :ANGLES]
END
```

CHAPTER 12

Exploring Further

1. ```
   TO CUBE :N
   OUTPUT :N * :N * :N
   END
   ```
2. ```
   TO CUBE.TABLE
   MAKE "N 1
   PR [TABLE OF CUBES]
   PR [ ] PR [ ]
   REPEAT 10 [TYPE :N TYPE CHAR 32 TYPE
      [CUBED IS] TYPE CHAR 32 PR CUBE :N
      MAKE "N :N + 1]
   END
   ```
3. ```
   TO TURN :NAME
   PR (SE (WORD LAST :NAME ",) FIRST :NAME)
   END
   ```

Student Exercises

Pencil and Paper Exercises

1. a. 12
   b. 66
   c. 25
   d. 51
2. a. 12.75
   b. 82.5
   c. 26
   d. 50
3. X and Y must be preceded by colons.
4. I DON'T KNOW WHAT TO DO WITH 7 (You should have said PR CALC 3 4 5.)

At the Computer

1. ```
   TO CALC :X :Y
   OUTPUT :X + :Y
   END
   ```
2. ```
   TO CALC :X :Y
   OUTPUT :Y / :X
   END
   ```
3. ```
   TO CALC :X :Y
   OUTPUT :X - :Y
   END
   ```
4. ```
   TO CALC :X :Y
   OUTPUT :X * :Y
   END
   ```
5. ```
   TO DOIT :NAME
   OUTPUT FIRST :NAME
   END
   ```

A Logo Challenge

```
TO POWER :N :P
MAKE "NP 1
REPEAT :P [MAKE "NP :NP * :N]
OUTPUT :NP
END
```

CHAPTER 13

Exploring Further

1. No answer provided.
2. ```
   TO SQUARE
   PR [ENTER A NUMBER]
   MAKE "NUM FIRST READLIST
   TYPE :NUM TYPE CHAR 32 TYPE [SQUARED
     IS] TYPE CHAR 32
   PR :NUM * :NUM
   END
   ```
3. ```
   TO NAMES
   PR [ENTER YOUR NAME]
   MAKE "N READLIST
   PR FIRST :N
   PR LAST :N
   END
   ```
4. No answer provided.

Student Exercises

Pencil and Paper Exercises

1. a. Should be: READLIST
   b. Should be: "NAME
   c. Should be: IF :ANS = "YES [STOP]
2. It will draw a box.
3. READLIST should be used instead of READCHAR. The computer will act after the Y is entered and will *not* draw the box.
4. Fourth line should read: IF :ANS = "Y [REPEAT 4 [FD 50 RT 90]]

At the Computer

1. ```
   TO INTERSTAR
   PR [WHAT SIZE STAR WOULD YOU LIKE?]
   MAKE "SIZE READLIST
   REPEAT 5 [FD FIRST :SIZE RT 144]
   END
   ```
2. ```
   TO DIVIDE
   PR [ENTER TWO NUMBERS]
   MAKE "NUMS READLIST
   PR (FIRST :NUMS) / (LAST :NUMS)
   END
   ```
3. ```
   TO NAMES
   PR [ENTER YOUR FULL NAME]
   MAKE "NAME READLIST
   REPEAT 100 [PR LAST :NAME]
   END
   ```
4. ```
   TO NAMES
   PR [ENTER YOUR FULL NAME]
   MAKE "NAME READLIST
   IF :NAME = [FORGET IT] [STOP]
   REPEAT 100 [PR LAST :NAME]
   END
   ```

A Logo Challenge

```
TO DESIGNS
PR [HOW MANY SIDES DO YOU WANT?]
MAKE "SIDES FIRST READLIST
PR [HOW LONG DO YOU WANT THEM?]
MAKE "LENGTH FIRST READLIST
PR [WHAT ANGLE DO YOU WANT?]
MAKE "ANGLE FIRST READLIST
REPEAT :SIDES [FD :LENGTH RT :ANGLE]
END
```
```

CHAPTER 14

Exploring Further

1. For example:
```
TO TRIANGLE
RT 10 FD 50 RT 120
TRIANGLE
END
```
2.
```
TO SPI.T :L
FD :L
RT 120
SPI.T :L + 5
END
```
3.
```
TO XES :L
REPEAT :L [TYPE "X] PR [ ]
XES :L + 1
END
```
4. Folding the paper sixty-seven times will result in its being one light year thick. You can determine how long a light year is as follows: PR 286000 * 60 * 60 * 24 * 365. Or you could work it out step by step like this:

MAKE "SEC 286000	(miles light travels in a second)
MAKE "MIN :SEC * 60	(miles light travels in a minute)
MAKE "HR :MIN * 60	(miles light travels in an hour
MAKE "DAY :HR * 24	(miles light travels in a day)
MAKE "YR :DAY 365	(miles light travels in a year)

5. It will cause the turtle to move randomly around the screen. Eventually, the whole display will be white.

Student Exercises

Pencil and Paper Exercises

1. Nothing.
2. The computer will print a list of numbers, each twice the size of the one preceding it:

```
 2
 4
 8
16
```

and so forth.

3.
```
TO STAR
FD 100 RT 144
STAR
END
```
4.
```
TO STAR :LEN
FD :LEN RT 144
STAR :LEN
END
```

At the Computer

1.
```
TO TRIANGLE
FD 100 RT 120
TRIANGLE
END
```
2.
```
TO STAR :LEN
FD :LEN RT 144
STAR :LEN * 1.1
END
```
3.
```
TO PENTSPI :N
FD :N RT 72
PENTSPI :N * 1.1
END
```
4.
```
TO RAYS
FD 100 BK 100 RT 10
RAYS
END
```
5.
```
TO RAYS2 :L
FD :L BK :L RT 7
RAYS2 :L + 2
END
```

A Logo Challenge

```
TO DESIGN :L :S :R
IF :L > 100 [STOP]
FD :L RT (360 / :S)
DESIGN :L * :R :S :R
END
```

CHAPTER 15

Exploring Further

1. IF :RK = "R [REPEAT 3 [FD 50 RT 120]]
2. No answer provided.
3. No answer provided.

Student Exercises

No answers provided.

A Logo Challenge

```
TO JRLOGO2
CS
FULLSCREEN
SETSCRUNCH 1.2
JRL 1
END

TO JRL2
MAKE "RK READCHAR
IF :RK = "L [FD 25]
IF :RK = "K [PE BK 25 PD]
IF :RK = ", [RT 90 JRL3]
IF :RK = "O [LT 90 JRL1]
JRL2
END

TO JRL3
MAKE "RK READCHAR
IF :RK = ", [FD 25]
IF :RK = "O [PE BK 25 PD]
IF :RK = "K [RT 90 JRL4]
IF :RK = "L [LT 90, JRL 2]
JRL3
END

TO JRL4
MAKE "RK READCHAR
IF :RK = "K [FD 25]
IF :RK = "L [PE BK 25 PD]
IF :RK = "O [RT 90 JRL1]
IF :RK = ", [LT 90 JRL3]
JRL4
END

TO JRL 1
MAKE "RK READCHAR
IF :RK = "O [FD 25]
IF :RK = ", [PE BK 25 PD]
IF :RK = "L [RT 90 JRL2]
IF :RK = "K [LT 90 JRL4]
JRL 1
END
```

CHAPTER 16

Exploring Further

1. For 7:00, CS SETH 360 * (7/12) FD 50
   For 7:15, CS SETH 360 * (7.25/12) FD 50
2. ```
   TO MINUTE :M
   RT 360 * (:M/60) FD 45
   END

   TO HOUR :H :M
   RT 360 * ((:H + (:M/60)) / 12) FD 30
   END

   TO CLOCK :H :M
   CS HT
   PE LT 90 FD 50 RT 90 PD
   REPEAT 36 [FD 10 RT 10]
   PU HOME PD
   HOUR :H :M
   PU HOME PD
   MINUTE :M
   END
   ```
3. ```
   TO RANDOMBURST
   REPEAT 20 [MAKE 'L RANDOM 100 MAKE "A
      RANDOM 360 SETH :A FD :L BK :L]
   END
   ```

Student Exercises

Pencil and Paper Exercises

No answers provided.

At the Computer

1. ```
   TO SETBOX
   PU SETPOS [−50 −50] PD
   SETY 50
   SETX 50
   SETY −50
   SETX −50
   PU HOME PD
   END
   ```
2. ```
   TO CROSS
   SETPOS [−100 −100]
   SETPOS [100 100]
   SETPOS [0 0]
   SETPOS [−100 100]
   SETPOS [100 −100]
   END
   ```
3. ```
   TO DESIGN
   SETPOS [−50 50]
   SETX 50
   HOME
   SETY −50
   END
   ```
4. ```
   TO STARS
   CS PU SETPOS [−100 50] PD
   MAKE "X −100
   REPEAT 4 [STAR MAKE "X :X + 50 PU SETX
      :X PD]
   PU SETPOS [−100 −50] PD
   MAKE "X −100
   REPEAT 4 [STAR MAKE "X :X + 50 PU SETX
      :X PD]
   END

   TO STAR
   REPEAT 5 [FD 50 RT 144]
   END
   ```

A Logo Challenge

```
TO MINUTE :M
RT 360 * (:M / 60) FD 45
END

TO HOUR :H :M
RT 360 * ((:H + :M / 60) / 12) FD 30
END

TO CLOCK :H :M
HOUR :H :M
PU HOME PD
MINUTE :M
PU HOME
WAIT 3600
PE HOUR :H :M
PU HOME
PE MINUTE :M
PU HOME PD
CLOCK :H :M + 1
END
```

CHAPTER 17

Exploring Further

1. ```
   TO PROC1 :AL
   PR :AL
   IF BUTFIRST BUTLAST :AL = " [STOP]
   PROC1 BUTFIRST BUTLAST :AL
   END
   ```
2. ```
   TO PROC2 :N :AL
   REPEAT :N [TYPE CHAR 32]
   PR :AL
   IF BUTFIRST BUTLAST :AL = " [STOP]
   PROC2 :N + 1 BUTFIRST BUTLAST :AL
   END
   ```
3. ```
   TO PICK :L
   PR ITEM (1 + (COUNT :L) / 2) :L
   END
   ```
4. No answer provided.

Student Exercises

Pencil and Paper Exercises

1. TWO
2. RED YELLOW GREEN BLUE PINK
3. HAPPY NEW YEAR
4. THING
5. For example,
   ```
   MAKE "F1 "EA
   MAKE "F2 "RL
   MAKE "L1 "BAB
   MAKE "L2 "BIE
   PR (SE (WORD :F1 :F2)(WORD :L1 :L2))
   ```
   ```

At the Computer

1. ```
TO PICK :A
PR LAST :A
END
```
2. ```
TO PICK :A
PR LAST BUTLAST :A
END
```
3. No answer provided.
4. No answer provided.
5. ```
TO ALPHIE :AL
PR :AL
IF BUTFIRST :AL = " [STOP]
ALPHIE BUTFIRST :AL
END
```
6. ```
ALPHIE2 :AL
PR :AL
IF BUTLAST :AL = " [STOP]
ALPHIE2 BUTLAST :AL
END
```

A Logo Challenge

```
TO NAMING :N
PR ( SE "ENTER ( WORD "NAME :N ) "OR "'END' )
MAKE "NAME READLIST
IF :NAME = [END] [STOP]
MAKE ( WORD "NAME :N ) :NAME
NAMING :N + 1
END
```

CHAPTER 18

Exploring Further

1. No answer provided.
2. ```
TO X
CLEARTEXT
SETCURSOR [20 12] PR "X
SETCURSOR [19 11] PR "X
SETCURSOR [21 11] PR "X
SETCURSOR [19 13] PR "X
SETCURSOR [21 13] PR "X
SETCURSOR [18 10] PR "X
SETCURSOR [22 10] PR "X
SETCURSOR [18 14] PR "X
SETCURSOR [22 14] PR "X
END
```
3. ```
TO CONVERT
PR [ENTER SOME WORD]
MAKE "TX FIRST READLIST
PR [WHICH OF THESE DO YOU WANT?]
TYPE CHAR 32 PR [1. INVERT TO BLACK ON
   WHITE]
TYPE CHAR 32 PR [2. FLASHING]
MAKE "ANS READCHAR
IF :ANS = "1 [INVERT :TX]
IF :ANS = "2 [FLASH :TX]
END
```
   Note: INVERT and FLASH are presented in the main body of the chapter.
4. No answer provided.

Student Exercises

Pencil and Paper Exercises

1. For example, 69 65 82 76
2. FANTASTIC
3. No answer provided.
4. No answer provided.
5. For example:
```
TO L
SETCURSOR [10 10] PR "L
SETCURSOR [10 11] PR "L
SETCURSOR [10 12] PR "L
SETCURSOR [10 13] PR "L
SETCURSOR [10 14] PR "L
SETCURSOR [10 15] PR "L
SETCURSOR [11 15] PR "L
SETCURSOR [12 15] PR "L
SETCURSOR [13 15] PR "L
END
```

At the Computer

1.

27 = [	37 = %	47 = /
28 = `	38 = &	48 = 0
29 =]	39 = '	49 = 1
30 = ∧	40 = (	50 = 2
31 = _	41 =)	51 = 3
32 = (space)	42 = *	52 = 4
33 = !	43 = +	53 = 5
34 = "	44 = ,	54 = 6
35 = #	45 = −	55 = 7
36 = $	46 = .	56 = 8

```
57 = 9        60 = <     63 = ?
58 = :        61 = =     64 = @
59 = ;        62 = >
```

2.
```
TO CODE :X
IF :X = " [PR [ ] STOP]
TYPE ASCII FIRST :X TYPE CHAR 32
CODE BUTFIRST :X
END
```

3.
```
TO DECODE :X
IF :X = [ ] [PR [ ] STOP]
TYPE CHAR FIRST :X
DECODE BUTFIRST :X
END
```

4.
```
TO FILL
MAKE "H 0
REPEAT 39 [SETCURSOR (SE :H :0) TYPE "X
   MAKE "H :H + 1]
END
```

5.
```
TO FILL
MAKE "V 0
REPEAT 23 [MAKE "H 0 REPEAT 39 [SETCUR-
   SOR (SE :H :V) TYPE "X MAKE "H :H + 1]
   MAKE "V :V + 1]
END
```

CHAPTER 19

Exploring Further

1.
```
TO INFLATION
MAKE "OLDWAGE 5
MAKE "OLDPRICE .65
PR [BREAD NOW COSTS 65 CENTS A LOAF]
PR [ENTER THE NEW COST OF BREAD,]
PR [IN CENTS:]
MAKE "P FIRST READLIST
LABOR :P / 100
END
```

2. Add to INFLATION:
```
MAKE "CYCLE 0
```
Add to LABOR:
```
MAKE "CYCLE :CYCLE + 1
PR (SE [CYCLE NUMBER] :CYCLE)
```

3. No answer provided.

A Logo Challenge

```
TO INFLATION
MAKE "OLDWAGE 5
MAKE "OLDPRICE .65
LABOR .75
END

TO LABOR :NEWPRICE
MAKE "INC :NEWPRICE / :OLDPRICE
MAKE "PERCENT (100 * (:INC - 1))
PR [THIS IS LABOR SPEAKING]
PR [SINCE PRICES HAVE INCREASED BY]
SP 3 (PR SE :PERCENT "PERCENT)
PR [IT WILL BE NECESSARY TO CHANGE]
SP 3 PR [OUR WAGES BY THAT PERCENT]
MAKE "NEWWAGE (:INC * :OLDWAGE)
(PR SE [THE NEW WAGE IS] :NEWWAGE)
MAKE "OLDPRICE :NEWPRICE
PR [ ]
MANAGEMENT :NEWWAGE
END

TO MANAGEMENT :NEWWAGE
MAKE "INC :NEWWAGE / :OLDWAGE
MAKE "PERCENT (100 * (:INC - 1))
PR [THIS IS MANAGEMENT SPEAKING]
PR [SINCE WAGES HAVE INCREASED BY]
SP 3 [PR SE :PERCENT "PERCENT)
PR [IT WILL BE NECESSARY TO RAISE
THE PRICE]
SP 3 PR [OF BREAD BY THAT PERCENT]
MAKE "NEWPRICE (:INC * :OLDPRICE)
(PR SE [THE NEW PRICE IS] :NEWPRICE)
MAKE "OLDWAGE :NEWWAGE
PR [ ]
MAKE "INC RESOURCE
MAKE "INC (100 + :INC) / 100
MAKE "NEWPRICE (:INC * :NEWPRICE)
(PR SE [THAT CHANGES THE PRICE TO]
:NEWPRICE)
PR [ ]
WAIT 900
LABOR :NEWPRICE
END
```

```
TO RESOURCE
PR [HAS THE COST OF SUPPLIES INCREASED]
PR [OR DECREASED? ENTER PERCENT
    CHANGE:]
PR [( E.G., 20, −10 )]
OUTPUT FIRST READLIST
END

TO SP :N
REPEAT :N [TYPE CHAR 32]
END
```

APPENDIX B

Pencil and Paper Exercises

1. a. SAVE "FILE1
   b. LOAD "FILE1
   c. POTS
   d. ER "MOON
   e. CATALOG
   f. ERASEFILE "FILE1 SAVE "FILE1
2. For example:

```
FILE1        FILE2
  PROC1        PROC6
  PROC2        PROC7
  PROC3        PROC8
  PROC4        PROC9
  PROC5        PROC10
LOAD "FILE1
LOAD "FILE2
ER [PROC3 PROC4 PROC5 PROC8 PROC9
  PROC10]
SAVE "FILE3
```

3. For example:

```
TO UPDATE
ERASEFILE "CHAP6
SAVE "CHAP6
END
```

At the Computer

1. No answer provided.
2. No answer provided.
3. No answer provided.
4. Simply LOAD the file again from the disk.

Index

Notes

Notes

Notes

Notes

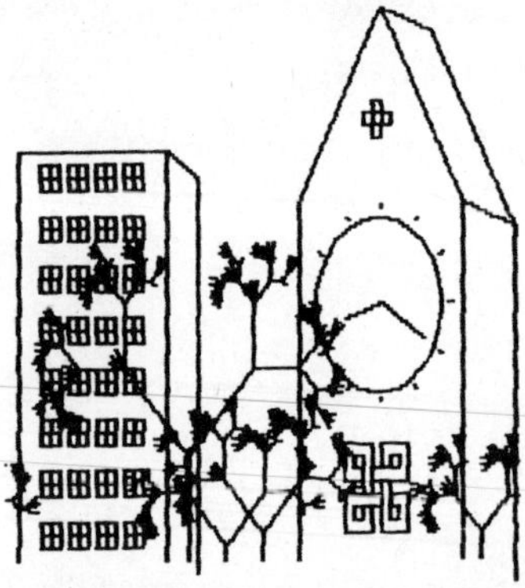

The CAMPUS procedure on the disk creates this campus scene—with a clock that actually keeps time!

Another Powerful Idea from Wadsworth!

The design above is just one of the many Logo creations contained on the PROCEDURES DISK FOR APPLE LOGO FOR TEACHERS, by Earl Babbie.

Convenient, timesaving, error-free, the disk contains procedures for creating the designs presented in these sections of each chapter in the book:

- Illustrations
- Exploring Further
- Student Exercises
- Logo Challenges

While the book contains detailed instructions for creating all these designs, this disk saves you the trouble of having to enter the instructions and assures you of error-free operations. The disk is compatible with Apple II, Apple IIe, and Apple II Plus computers.

TO ORDER, detach and mail to:

WADSWORTH, INC.
Order Department
7625 Empire Drive
Florence, KY 41042

LOGO84

Please send me _____ copies of the PROCEDURES DISK FOR APPLE LOGO FOR TEACHERS, by Earl Babbie (ISBN 0-534-03393-8) at $15.95 each, plus postage and handling charges.

SAVE! Send your payment with this coupon and we'll pay postage and handling charges. (CA, KY, MA, MI, NJ, NY, NC, WA residents include appropriate sales tax.) Payment will be refunded if we are unable to complete your order within 60 days.

☐ Payment is enclosed
  ☐ check
  ☐ money order
☐ Bill me
☐ Charge my credit card:
  ☐ Visa
  ☐ Mastercard

Card # ____________

Expiration Date ____________

Signature ____________

Please provide address on credit card account if it differs from mailing address.

Please ship order to: (print clearly to insure prompt delivery)

Name/Title ____________

Institution ____________

Street Address ____________

City ________ State ________ Zip ________

All disks shipped within 30 days.
Price and availability subject to change without notice.

Frequently Used Logo Commands

NAME	EXAMPLE	FUNCTION
ASCII	PR ASCII("A)	Learns the ASCII code number for the character specified. In this case, the computer will return the number 65.
BACK BK	BK 90	Moves turtle backward.
BUTFIRST	PR BUTFIRST :ALPHA	Selects all items in a list *except* the first one.
BUTLAST	PR BUTLAST :ALPHA	Selects all items in a list *except* the last one.
CATALOG	CATALOG	Lists the files contained on the disk.
CHAR	PR CHAR 65	Specifies a character by using its ASCII code number. This example will cause the computer to print A.
CHAR 32	TYPE CHAR 32	Inserts a space between alphabetical data.
CLEARSCREEN	CS	Erases the screen and sends the turtle HOME.
CO	CO	Causes the computer to resume operations following a PAUSE.
COUNT	PR COUNT :ALPHA	Counts the number of items in a list. Thus if :ALPHA were [RED BLUE GREEN], the answer to this instruction would be 3.
CTRL-C	CTRL-C	Terminates the edit mode.
CTRL-G	CTRL-G	Interrupts Logo in the middle of whatever it is doing at the time.
CURSOR	PR CURSOR	Asks the computer to report the current location of the cursor on the text screen, in the form of horizontal and vertical locations.
DOT	DOT[50 50]	Tells the computer to put a dot at the location specified; the turtle does not move.
EDIT	EDIT "BOX	Initiates the edit mode, so changes to the procedure named BOX can be made.
END	END	Signals the completion of a procedure definition.
ER	ER "PROC ER [PROC1 PROC2]	Erases the specified procedures from the workspace.
ERASEFILE	ERASEFILE "CHAP6	Erases a file from the disk.
ERN	ERN "M ERN[ABC]	Erases the specified variables from the workspace.
FIRST	PR FIRST :M	Specifies the FIRST item in a list.
FORWARD FD	FD 50	Moves turtle forward.
FULLSCREEN CTRL-L	FULLSCREEN	Dedicates the entire screen to graphics.
HEADING	PR HEADING	Asks the computer to report the turtle's current heading.
HIDETURTLE HT	HT	Causes turtle to disappear.
HOME	HOME	Moves turtle to the center of screen without changing its heading.
IF	IF :X = "R [RT 90]	IF the condition specified is satisfied, then the instructions contained in the brackets are executed. IF the condition is not met, then the whole statement is simply ignored.
ITEM	PR ITEM 2 :M	Specifies a particular item in a list (in this case, the second item).

NAME	EXAMPLE	FUNCTION
LAST	PR LAST :M	Specifies the LAST item in a list.
LEFT LT	LT 60	Turns turtle to left.
LOAD	LOAD "CHAP6	Copies disk file into workspace.
MAKE	MAKE "NUM 5	Declares a variable name and assigns one or more values to it.
OUTPUT	OUTPUT :X / :Y	As a command within a procedure, OUTPUT causes the computer to exit the procedure, carrying the specified value with it. It is necessary to specify what is to be done with the value: PRinting it, for example.
PENDOWN PD	PD	Lowers pen so it leaves a trail.
PENERASE PE	PE	Instead of drawing lines, turtle erases lines it crosses.
PENREVERSE	PENREVERSE	Turtle changes whatever it passes over: black to white, white to black.
PENUP PU	PU	Lifts pen so it doesn't leave a trail.
POS	PR POS	Asks the computer to report the turtle's location on the screen, expressed in terms of its *x* and *y* coordinates.
POTS	POTS	Lists the procedures contained in the workspace.
PRINT PR	PR 23	Prints alphabetical and numerical data and moves to the next line.
RANDOM	RANDOM 10	Selecting random numbers, in this case among the numbers 0 through 9.
READCHAR	MAKE "X READCHAR	Computer waits for a character to be entered at the keyboard and then assigns that value to the name indicated. In the case of the present example, whatever key is hit will be assigned to the name :X.
READLIST	MAKE "X READLIST	Computer waits for one or more characters followed by a carriage return. In this case, whatever is entered is assigned to the name :X.
REPEAT	REPEAT 4 [FD 50 RT 90]	Causes Logo to repeat the operations contained in the brackets as many times as are specified.
RIGHT RT	RT 45	Turns turtle to right.
SAVE	SAVE "CHAP6	Makes disk copy of the workspace.
SE	(SE :X :Y)	Instructs the computer to consider the variables specified as a set.
SETBG	SETBG 0	Sets color for the background of Logo designs.
SETCURSOR	SETCURSOR [10 10]	Moves the cursor to the location specified, with the numbers in brackets indicating first the horizontal and then the vertical locations.
SETH	SETH 90	Changes turtle's direction to the heading specified (in degrees).
SETPC	SETPC 1	Sets color for the pen.
SETPOS	SETPOS [50 50]	Moves the turtle to the location specified.
SHOWTURTLE ST	ST	Displays the turtle.
SPLITSCREEN CTRL-S	SPLITSCREEN	Causes most of the video screen to be dedicated to graphics, with the bottom four lines used for text.
SQRT	SQRT(4)	Finds the square root.